Wineries &
Vineyards
of New Zealand 2005

Wineries & Vineyards
of New Zealand 2005

OPEN TO VISIT

Compiled by Barbara Dyer

Hodder Moa Beckett

A catalogue record for this book is available from the National Library of New Zealand.

ISBN 1-86971-000-2

Published in 2004 by Hodder Moa Beckett Publishers Ltd
[a member of the Hodder Headline Group]
4 Whetu Place, Mairangi Bay
Auckland, New Zealand

Designed and produced by Grace Design
Printed by Everbest Printing Ltd, China

Contents

A special thank you to all the people from wineries and vineyards throughout New Zealand who made this book possible and also to my friends and family who provided support and encouragement. Thanks go to Hodder Moa Beckett Publishers for giving me the opportunity to put this book together and especially to the editorial and production team who have made the manuscript into a reality.

In the process of creating *Wineries &Vineyards of New Zealand* I have been privileged to travel to all the wine regions throughout New Zealand where I have been reminded of what a fabulous country New Zealand really is, with its magnificent landscape and friendly, helpful people.

Barbara Dyer
September 2004

Introduction

New Zealand has long been famed for its stunning, unspoiled landscape. Equal to the international acclaim for its beauty is that for its fine wines. Climate, geography and human skill have combined to produce highly distinctive, premium quality wines, which are 'the riches of a clean, green land'.

International acclaim

New Zealand Sauvignon Blanc is rated throughout the world as the definitive benchmark style for this varietal. The growing recognition for New Zealand Chardonnay, Pinot Noir, Méthode Traditionelle sparkling wines, Riesling, Cabernet Sauvignon and Merlot blends is helping to further cement New Zealand's position as a producer of world class wines.

Diverse styles

New Zealand is a country of contrasts with dense, native forest, snow-capped mountains and spectacular coastline. With wine growing regions spanning the latitudes of 36 to 45 degrees and covering the length of 1000 miles (1600km), grapes are grown in a vast range of climates and soil types, producing a diverse array of styles. The northern hemisphere equivalent would run from Bordeaux (between the latitudes of 44 and 46 degrees) down to southern Spain.

Temperate maritime climate

New Zealand's temperate, maritime climate has a strong influence on the country's predominantly coastal vineyards. The vines are warmed by strong, clear sunlight during the day and cooled at night by sea breezes. The long, slow ripening period helps to retain the vibrant varietal flavours that make New Zealand wine so distinctive.

Food friendly wines

New Zealand cuisine draws inspiration from the traditional kitchens of France and Italy, as well as the exotic dishes of Asia and the Pacific Rim. Wine styles have evolved to complement this extensive menu. There are bright and zesty wines such as Sauvignon Blanc and Riesling for fresh and subtly spiced dishes, while complex, mellow Chardonnay, Cabernet Sauvignon/Merlot blends and Pinot Noir offer a timeless marriage with the classical dishes of Europe.

Ensuring the future

New Zealand's small population, distant location and agricultural economy have earned the country a 'clean, green' image. Visitors often describe it as 'an unspoiled paradise'. New Zealand's winemakers are determined to keep it this way. Innovative practices in the vineyard and winery, which deliver quality in a sustainable and environmental manner, ensure that New Zealand meets a growing world demand for wines that have been produced in a 'clean and green' fashion.

For further information on the NZ wine industry,
go to **www.nzwine.com** the industry body's official website.

Wine Regions of New Zealand

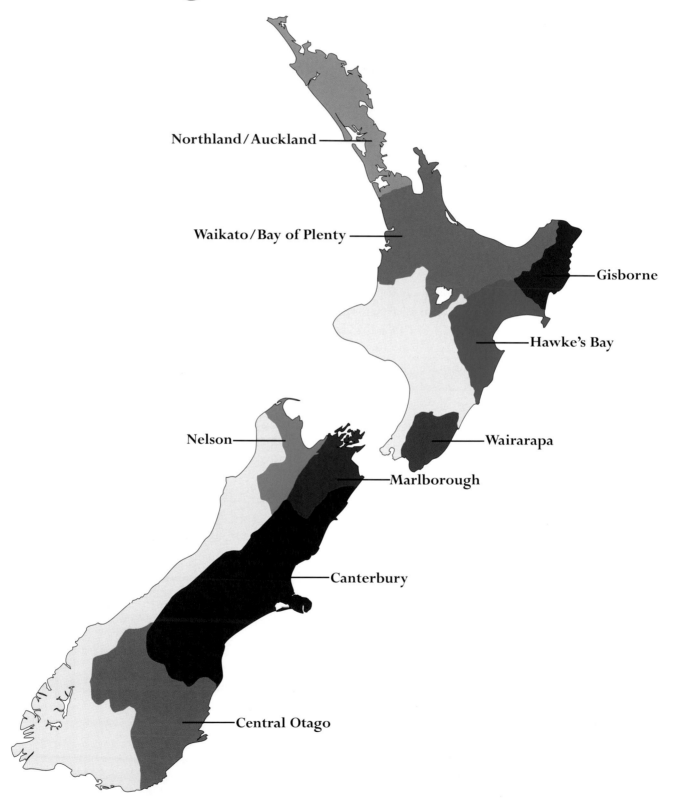

Northland/Auckland

Waikato/Bay of Plenty

Gisborne

Hawke's Bay

Wairarapa

Nelson

Marlborough

Canterbury

Central Otago

Wine Varietals

New Zealand offers a vast portfolio of wines. Over 25 different grape varieties are planted in commercial quantity in New Zealand, although the classic varieties of Chardonnay, Sauvignon Blanc, Pinot Noir, Cabernet Sauvignon, Merlot and Riesling account for the lion's share.

Varieties that respond to warmer growing conditions, such as Cabernet Sauvignon and Merlot, are more popular in the North Island. Varieties which favour cooler conditions such as Sauvignon Blanc, Riesling and Pinot Noir are more widely planted in the cooler South Island regions and in some North Island sites such as Martinborough.

Sauvignon Blanc

New Zealand Sauvignon Blanc is acclaimed throughout the world as the definitive benchmark style for the varietal. Its exuberant, pungent flavours have dazzled wine critics everywhere.

Sauvignon Blanc can produce lush, fleshy wine with nectarine and peach flavours in Hawke's Bay or more pungent and zestier wine with gooseberry, passionfruit and capsicum flavours when it is made from Marlborough grown grapes.

Chardonnay

New Zealand Chardonnay is all about quality and diversity. The varied regional conditions combined with a winemaker's skill and innovation mean that Chardonnay in New Zealand comprises a myriad of ever evolving styles, capable of appealing to a wider range of palates.

Gisborne Chardonnay is often soft and beguiling with pineapple and peach flavours, while Chardonnay grown in Canterbury is more likely to be crisper with strong citrus/grapefruit and white peach characters.

Aromatics

With a climate ideal for the production of Aromatic wines, praise is now resounding for the increasing number of vibrant, world-class and regionally distinctive examples of New Zealand Riesling, Gewürztraminer and Pinot Gris.

Sparkling Wine

A temperate climate, combined with the planting of the classical champagne varieties Chardonnay, Pinot Noir and Pinot Meunier, plus the use of the latest winemaking technology have enabled New Zealand to produce outstanding sparkling wine, now acclaimed throughout the world. Local winemakers have adapted traditional winemaking methods, but they produce wine styles unique to New Zealand with subtle fruit flavours that express the character of an array of vineyard sites

Pinot Noir

New Zealand is now acknowledged as one of the few countries to have successfully come to grips with this fickle, but supremely aristocratic grape variety. The temperate climate and long sunshine hours have combined with winemaker passion and skill to produce world class highly sought after Pinot Noir.

Martinborough Pinot Noir is typically intense and rich with ripe plum flavours while Central Otago Pinot Noir tends to be finer and more aromatic, with the distinctive flavour of black cherries.

Cabernet Sauvignon and Merlot

The aristocratic stable mates, Cabernet Sauvignon and Merlot are star performers, particularly in New Zealand's warmer northern region. New Zealand Cabernet Sauvignon boasts structure and elegance, whilst a richness and warmth exude from New Zealand Merlot. In partnership, Cabernet Sauvignon and Merlot can be vibrant or richly mellow, powerful or subtly elegant.

Auckland

AUCKLAND, in the north of the North Island, is New Zealand's eighth largest wine region, producing around three per cent of the national crop. In this warm, humid region the vineyards are scattered over a large area and produce chiefly warm, ripe reds and ripe, rounded Chardonnays. Auckland's soils are mainly shallow clays over hard silty clay subsoils or sandy loams. Many of New Zealand's largest wine companies have their headquarters and production facilities in **Auckland**, processing grapes grown around the country. West of Auckland is the Henderson Valley, the region's traditional winemaking area, while newer vineyards are clustered in the north-west around the townships of **Kumeu**, **Huapai** and **Waimauku**. Outlying sub-regions include Matakana and Mahurangi, north of Auckland around the townships of **Warkworth** and **Matakana**, which has an enviable reputation for Cabernet Sauvignon and has undergone a very rapid expansion in both red and white wine production. The Hauraki Gulf island of Waiheke is known for high-quality red wines based on Cabernet Sauvignon, Merlot and Cabernet Franc. There are also vineyards in South Auckland and more recently in rolling farmland further south around **Clevedon**.

For more information on the Auckland region visit www.aucklandtourism.co.nz, www.matakanawine.com or www.waihekewine.co.nz or contact the Auckland Visitor Information Centre: Sky City Atrium, corner Federal and Victoria Streets, Auckland, (09) 979 2333, info@aucklandnz.com

Matua Valley Wines

Matakana Estate

HISTORY

Auckland has held a key place in New Zealand's wine history, with many well-known families in the wine industry, especially those of Croatian (Dalmatian), Yugoslav and Lebanese descent, having pioneered winemaking in West Auckland in the late 19th century and early 1900s. The product of Lebanese immigrant Assid Corban's winery at Henderson became the first nationally distributed local brand. Winemakers produced mainly substitute ports and sherries until table wines became more popular in the 1960s. From this time, however, as the grape-growing industry moved to cheaper, drier regions further south in New Zealand, the region's importance began to decline. In recent years, the successes of Auckland-grown wines have helped inject new vigour into the region.

SOILS

Around Auckland soils are mainly free-draining shallow clays over silty clay subsoils or sandy loams. Drainage can be a problem with heavier clay soils. Waiheke Island's soils generally comprise free-draining weathered sedimentary rock.

CLIMATE

Auckland's climate is challenging, with plentiful rain and high humidity creating problems with fungal diseases. Vineyard management and exposure to breezes, such as on Waiheke, help combat this problem. Winters are mild and the region's warmth and sunshine favours red-wine production.

GRAPE VARIETIES AND WINE STYLES

Major varieties include Chardonnay, Merlot and Cabernet Sauvignon with lesser amounts of Cabernet Franc, Pinot Gris, Pinotage and Syrah. Ripe, rounded, tropical fruit-flavoured Chardonnays are a key style. Reds include soft, plummy Merlots and Cabernet Sauvignons with concentrated fruit flavours. Cabernet Franc is generally blended. Pinot Gris is made with either ripe stone-fruit characters or in dry, quince-flavoured wines. The region's rich, soft Pinotage is well respected as are its full-flavoured Syrahs.

SUB-REGIONS

Matakana and Mahurangi, north of Auckland, produce ripe, robust Cabernet Sauvignon, Merlot and excellent, intensely flavoured Chardonnays on free-draining soils.

Kumeu/Huapai/Waimauku, in the north-west, produces excellent wines across a range of varieties and styles from locally grown grapes as well as those from further afield.

West Auckland, in the Henderson Valley, produces little from locally grown fruit but a lot from outside of the region.

South Auckland and Clevedon are newer areas, with north-facing hillsides in Clevedon being home to specialist vineyards producing chiefly red wines, including Merlot, Cabernet Sauvignon, Malbec and Syrah.

Waiheke, in the Hauraki Gulf, has since the 1980s produced intensely concentrated Cabernet Sauvignon wines, ripely flavoured Merlots and rich, full-bodied Chardonnays.

Events

- **Devonport Wine and Food Festival.** The region's largest annual wine and food festival. Held in Devonport, Auckland, in February. www.devonportwinefestival.co.nz
- **Waiheke Island Wine Festival.** A celebration of the island's vinous offerings. Held in February. www.waihekewine.co.nz
- **Kumeu Food & Wine Festival.** Showcases West Auckland winerys and local food. Held in February. (09) 410 8537

Hyperion Wines

Stonyridge Vinyard

Vin Alto

Twilight Vineyards

13

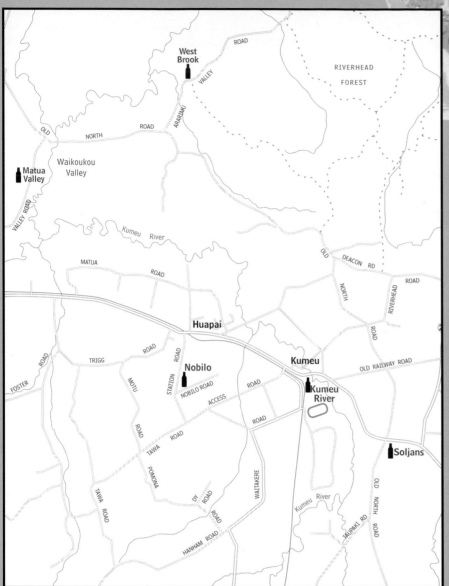

West Brook

RIVERHEAD FOREST

Matua Valley

OLD NORTH ROAD

Waikoukou Valley

VALLEY ROAD

ARADIMU ROAD

VALLEY

ROAD

Kumeu River

MATUA ROAD

DEACON RD

OLD

NORTH ROAD

RIVERHEAD ROAD

ROAD

Huapai

FOSTER ROAD

TRIGG ROAD

MOTU ROAD

STATION ROAD

NOBILO ROAD

Nobilo

ACCESS ROAD

ROAD

Kumeu

OLD RAILWAY ROAD

Kumeu River

TAWA ROAD

POMONA

DY ROAD

WAITAKERE ROAD

ROAD

Soljans

OLD NORTH ROAD

TAWA ROAD

HANHAM ROAD

Kumeu River

TAUPAKI RD

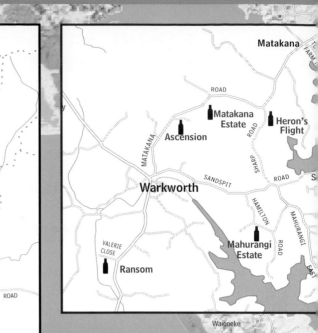

Matakana

ROAD

Matakana Estate

Heron's Flight

Ascension

MATAKANA

SHARP ROAD

SANDSPIT

ROAD

Warkworth

HAMILTON ROAD

MAHURANGI ROAD

EAST

VALERIE CLOSE

Ransom

Mahurangi Estate

Waioneke

She Bea

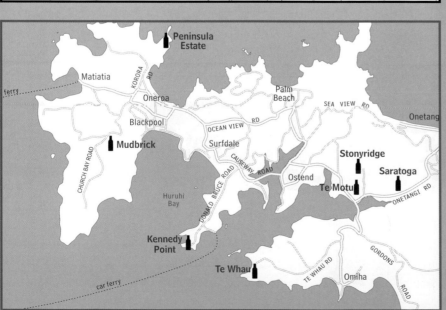

Peninsula Estate

Matiatia

KORORA RD

Oneroa

Palm Beach

SEA VIEW RD

Onetang

ferry

Blackpool

OCEAN VIEW RD

Mudbrick

Surfdale

CHURCH BAY ROAD

CAUSEWAY ROAD

DONALD BRUCE ROAD

Ostend

Stonyridge

Saratoga

Te Motu

ONETANGI RD

Huruhi Bay

Kennedy Point

Te Whau

TE WHAU RD

GORDONS ROAD

Omiha

car ferry

Ascension Vineyard & Café

Ascension's striking Spanish Mission-style winery and restaurant presents a stunning entrance to the rolling, vine-draped hills of Matakana. Darryl Soljan is a fifth-generation winemaker who along with his wife Bridget planted their steep north-facing vineyard in 1996. They now craft small batches of very individual wines from both traditional and unusual grape varieties. The award-winning restaurant and cellar door has fantastic views of the surrounding vineyard and countryside. Ascension's team of chefs combine fresh local produce with Mediterranean-influenced flavours to create a truly memorable dining experience. Events ranging from special dinners to outdoor concerts are regular features, and there are often art exhibitions in the gallery.

WINES
'The Zealot' Pinotage, 'The Rosarium' Rosé, 'The Druid' Chardonnay, 'The Apogee' Viognier, 'The Rogue' (an exotic white wine), 'The Twelve Apostles' Merlot, 'The Ascent' Reserve Merlot Cabernet Malbec, 'The Ascent' Reserve Chardonnay, 'Epiphany' Matakana Pressings (Bordeaux blend), Méthode Traditionnelle NV

RECENT AWARDS
Small production means Ascension have insufficient quantities to meet show requirements. They believe the customer is the best judge, which is why many of the wines sell out soon after release.

480 Matakana Rd, Matakana
Tel: (09) 422 9601
Fax: (09) 442 9602
Email: ascension@xtra.co.nz.
Website: www.ascensionvineyard.co.nz

DIRECTIONS
Turn off SH1 at the traffic lights just north of Warkworth. Turn left and follow Matakana Rd. Ascension is 4km on the right.

OPENING HOURS Cellar Door & tastings: summer Mon–Fri, 10am–5pm; Sat & Sun, 9am–5pm; winter: Mon–Fri, 11am–4pm; Sat & Sun, 9am–5pm.

WINERY SALES Cellar door, retail, mail order, Internet

PRICE RANGE $19–$60

TASTING & TOURS
Tasting fee: $8 to sample the range. Winery tours with Darryl Soljan by arrangement; min. 12 people. Fee: $15 pp, diners: $8 pp.

RESTAURANT Open daily. Restaurant: brunch & lunch as per cellar door; dinner: public holidays and daily from Boxing Day until Auckland Anniversary Weekend.

OWNERS
Darryl & Bridget Soljan

WINEMAKER
Darryl Soljan

DATE ESTABLISHED 2000

Heron's Flight Vineyard & Café

On a sun-drenched slope overlooking the Matakana River valley and the Sandspit Estuary, this 4.5-hectare vineyard was originally planted with traditional French varietals, but these have now been replaced with Italian red grapes: Sangiovese (Tuscany's greatest red grape and their premium wine) and Dolcetto (from Piedmont). Since its French beginnings, Heron's Flight has evolved into a Tuscan-style farm where the vines intermingle with fig, mulberry and olive trees. At the heart of the vineyard is the café where you can relax with a glass of wine or a coffee, fabulous food (made from local produce) and enjoy the stunning views from the courtyard.

AWARDS
Heron's Flight's philosophy is that wine is best assessed in the company of friends and food – and for this reason choose not to enter competitions.

OTHER PRODUCTS
'Flights of Fancy' products, including Sangiovese verjus, aged Cabernet wine vinegar, Ratafia (quince fruit liqueur), home-made preserves, olive oil

49 Sharp Rd, Matakana
Tel: (09) 422 7915
Fax: (09) 422 9654
Email: contact@heronsflight.co.nz
Website: www.heronsflight.co.nz

DIRECTIONS Turn off SH1 at the traffic lights just north of Warkworth. Turn left and follow Matakana Rd for 6km. Turn right into Sharp Rd; the vineyard is 500m on the left.

OPENING HOURS
7 days, 10am–5pm

WINERY SALES Cellar door, retail, mail order, Internet

PRICE RANGE $24–$50

TASTING & TOURS
Tasting fee: $5 pp. Tutored

tastings can be arranged for groups. Tours by appointment, min 5 people.

CAFÉ
7 days: seasonal menu features freshly prepared soups, salads, platters, breads and salsas, and home-made desserts.

PICNIC AREA Gourmet food to go for picnickers. The self-guided vineyard walk has interesting picnic spots by the stream and waterfall.

OWNERS
David Hoskins & Mary Evans

WINEMAKER
David Hoskins

DATE ESTABLISHED 1987

Hyperion Wines

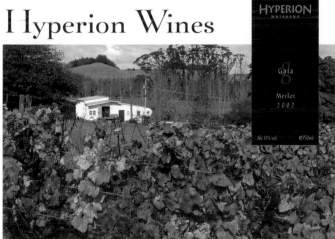

Hyperion Wines comprises two small vineyards located in the heart of the Matakana winegrowing region. The vineyards and wine label are named after the mythological Greek sun-god Hyperion. The winery, the oldest in the district, is a characterful converted cowshed surrounded by rustic farm buildings, set in a quietly idyllic pastoral location with vistas to vineyard and surrounding hills. Hyperion's speciality is in Bordeaux varieties, with Merlot performing particularly well on the warm clay slopes plus classic Cabernet Sauvignon. Winery visitors are welcomed to the tiny tasting room with its interesting quotations and photographs where they can talk to the winemaker/proprietors.

WINES
Hyperion's family tree provides sub-names to distinguish between the various wines: Pinot Gris *'Phoebe'*, Guardian of the Moon; Chardonnay *'Helios'*, a later sun-god; Pinot Noir *'Eos'*, Goddess of the Dawn; Cabernet Sauvignon *'the Titan'*, Hyperion personified; Merlot *'Gaia'* the Earth, Hyperion's mother; Cabernet/Merlot *'Kronos'*, a god of agriculture.

RECENT AWARDS
Hyperion 'the Titan' Cabernet Sauvignon 02 – Silver Medal: Romeo Bragato Wine Awards 03, 4 stars Michael Cooper *Winestate* magazine Nov/Dec 03; Hyperion 'Gaia' Merlot 02 – 86/100 & 4 stars NZ Reds Tasting: *Cuisine* magazine (Nov 03)

188 Tongue Farm Rd, Matakana
Tel: (09) 422 9375
Email: info@hyperion-wines.co.nz
Website: www.hyperion-wines.co.nz

DIRECTIONS Just past Matakana village travelling east, turn first right off Leigh Rd into Tongue Farm Rd and travel 1.5km to the end.

OPENING HOURS
Weekends & holidays: summer, 10am–6pm; winter, 10am–5pm. Open 7 days 27 December–6 February (Waitangi Day). Other times by appointment.

WINERY SALES Cellar door, retail, mail order, Internet

PRICE RANGE $20–$90

TASTING & TOURS
Tasting is free of charge. Tours for groups by arrangement; small charge per person.

OTHER FACILITIES
No café but Morris & James Café is on the same road.

OWNERS
John & Jill Crone

WINEMAKER John Crone

DATE ESTABLISHED 1994

Mahurangi Estate Winery

Mahurangi Estate was established with a vision of becoming one of New Zealand's favoured wine producers and a great destination to visit. They own two vineyards in separate regions of New Zealand — Matakana and the Gimblett Gravels in Hawke's Bay. Mahurangi also produce a range of premium wines from carefully chosen fruit from vineyards throughout the country.

The contemporarily designed winery has sweeping rural views over the vineyards and surrounding countryside. Visitors can enjoy platter-style lunches and seasonal blackboard specials while sampling their range of wines, or just relax with a picnic and soak up the atmosphere. Artworks by a variety of local artists and sculptors are exhibited in the winery.

WINES
Mahurangi Estate Chardonnay, Rosé, Malbec/Cabernet Sauvignon/Merlot, Syrah, Hawke's Bay Chardonnay, Marlborough Sauvignon Blanc, Marlborough Riesling, Gimblett Gravels Cabernet Sauvignon/Merlot

MAHURANGI
ESTATE

Hamilton Rd, Warkworth
Tel: (09) 425 0306
Fax: (09) 435 0307
Email: enquiries@mahurangi.co.nz
Website: www.mahurangi.co.nz

DIRECTIONS
Turn off SH1 at the traffic lights at the north of Warkworth. Turn right and follow Sandspit Rd for 3 km. Turn right into Hamilton Rd and follow for 1.6km.

OPENING HOURS
Mon–Fri: summer, 10am–5pm; winter, 11am–4pm. Weekends & public holidays: all year, 10am–5pm. Closed Good Friday & Christmas Day.

WINERY SALES Cellar door, retail, mail order, Internet

PRICE RANGE $17–$25

TASTING & TOURS
Tasting is free of charge. Tours by arrangement.

RESTAURANT
Reservations: (09) 425 0306

PICNIC AREA Overlooking the Mahurangi Harbour and Kawau Bay is an attractive area to enjoy a picnic with a glass of Mahurangi Estate wine.

OTHER FACILITIES
Available for a limited number of weddings and private functions.

OWNERS
Group of 120 private shareholders.

WINEMAKER
Under contract in Hawke's Bay.

DATE ESTABLISHED 1996

Matakana Estate

Ransom Wines

From Auckland, Ransom Wines is the first vineyard you reach on the Matakana wine trail. Family owned and operated, their 8-hectare vineyard is planted in Pinot Gris, Chardonnay, Cabernet Sauvignon, Merlot, Cabernet Franc and Malbec vines. The very stylish winery building is an impressive example of contemporary New Zealand architecture. Designed so that visitors can view the winemaking process, the airy glass and timber gallery opens out onto a courtyard with expansive views over the vineyards to the bush-clad Mahurangi hills. At the wine bar visitors can taste the full flight of available wines accompanied by delicious platters of local speciality foods.

Matakana Estate was established for the sole purpose of crafting distinctly individual, high-quality wines — wines that capture the natural characteristics of each grape variety and reflect the unique Matakana terroir. Visiting Matakana Estate is an intriguing experience for anyone with an appreciation for fine wine. Here, you can enjoy a wine-tasting experience that allows you to discover Matakana Estate wines and the winemaking approach in a relaxing and reflective environment. Visitors are encouraged to sit back and relax with a tray of tasting samples and a booklet of tasting notes whilst overlooking the stunning vista of vines stretching out into the valley in neatly ordered rows below them.

MATAKANA ESTATE

WINES

Sémillon, Pinot Gris, Chardonnay, Cabernet Merlot Malbec Franc, Syrah

RECENT AWARDS

Matakana Estate Pinot Gris was listed in *The Wine List 2004: The Top 250 Wines of the Year* (UK's No. 1 wine guide)

WINES

Clos de Valerie Pinot Gris, Gumfield Chardonnay, Barrique Chardonnay, Vin Gris (a cabernets-based Rosé), Mahurangi Cabernet, Franc, Merlot; Dark Summit Cabernet, Franc, Merlot, Grand Mère Noble Chardonnay.

RANSOM

Clos de Valerie
Pinot Gris

2003

12.5%vol   750ml

Matakana Rd, Matakana
Tel: (09) 425 0494
Fax: (09) 425 0595
Email: cellar@matakana-estate.co.nz

DIRECTIONS
Turn off SH1 at the traffic lights just north of Warkworth. Turn left and follow Matakana Rd for 3km. Entrance is at the far end of the vineyard.

OPENING HOURS
Mon–Sun, 10am–5pm

WINERY SALES Cellar door, mail order, restaurants, selected fine wine stores

PRICE RANGE $22–35

TASTING
Tasting fee: $5, refundable on purchase.

OWNERS
Kevin Fitzgerald & Pat Vegar–Fitzgerald, Peter & Jean Vegar, Paul Vegar

WINEMAKERS
Kevin Fitzgerald & Ben Dugdale

DATE ESTABLISHED 1996

46 Valerie Close, Warkworth
Tel: (09) 425 8862
Fax: (09) 425 8862
Email: ransom.wines@xtra.co.nz

DIRECTIONS
Turn off SH1 just 3km south of Warkworth. The winery is 500m off the main road.

OPENING HOURS
Summer: 7 days, 10am–5pm;
Winter: Tues–Sun, 10am–5pm

WINERY SALES
Cellar door, retail, selected restaurants, mail order, Internet

PRICE RANGE $17–$35

TASTING & TOURS
Tasting trays are available. Tours by arrangement.

FOOD OPTIONS
Lunch platters; wine & cheese matching a speciality.

OTHER FACILITIES
Available for private functions.

OWNERS
Marion & Robin Ransom

WINEMAKER
Robin Ransom

DATE ESTABLISHED 1993

Kennedy Point Vineyard

Kennedy Point Vineyard and winery, situated on the southwest side of Waiheke Island, focuses on growing and producing premium Cabernet Sauvignon and Syrah wines that reflect the terroir of their 2.5-acre home vineyard. Tucked among the pohutukawa trees overlooking Kennedy Bay, this is the perfect setting to enjoy wine-tasting. You can sit on the winery decks in the sunshine, with the cool breeze and a sea view, or at the tables in the vineyards and olive grove. Light lunch platters are available to enjoy with a full tasting or a glass of their fine wines.

WINES
Kennedy Point Cabernet Sauvignon, Syrah, Merlot, Marlborough Sauvignon Blanc

ACCOMMODATION
The self-contained vineyard guesthouse provides spectacular views of the Hauraki Gulf and sunsets over Rangitoto Island. You can explore the 13 acres of vineyard, olive groves, pasture and surrounding waterfront areas. Beautifully furnished, each suite is fully equipped for comfort and includes breakfast provisions: 1 x 1 bedroom suite, 1 x 2 bedroom suites or the complete house (sleeps 6) are available from $200–$325 per night.

44 Donald Bruce Rd, Surfdale
Tel: (09) 372 5600
Fax: (09) 372 6205
Email: info@kennedypointvineyard.com
Website:www.kennedypointvineyard.com

DIRECTIONS From the Subritzky car ferry, Kennedy Point Vineyard is the first driveway on the right. From Matiatia, turn right at the roundabout after Surfdale to Donald Bruce Road.

OPENING HOURS January: Wed–Sun, 12pm–4pm; February–May: weekends & public holidays, 12pm–4pm; rest of year by appointment.

WINERY SALES Cellar door, retail, mail order, Internet

PRICE RANGE $18–$45

TASTING & TOURS Tasting fee: $3 pp, refundable on purchase of any two bottles of wine. Tours by appointment. Fee: $6.

FOOD OPTIONS An assortment of light lunch platters, with wine match suggestions, are available during summer.

PICNIC AREA Among the olive groves and vines.

OTHER PRODUCTS Estate grown and bottled, Kennedy Point Olive Oil

OWNERS Susan McCarthy and Neal Kunimura

WINEMAKER Herb Friedli

DATE ESTABLISHED 1996

Mudbrick Vineyard & Restaurant

Mudbrick Vineyard and Restaurant is nestled into the hillside at Church Bay, overlooking the sparkling waters of the Hauraki Gulf and beyond to Auckland City, providing spectacular day and evening views. Mudbrick has much to offer the wandering visitor: choose to forage amongst the potager gardens, enjoy pétanque, or walk to the trig station for a 360-degree view. For those who like to discover special finds, the cellar shop is a real treat, with a delightful ambiance and thoroughly absorbing produce and products on display, not to mention an impressive range of tasting wines. Then of course there is that spectacular view from the terrace for lunch. A wonderful day out on Waiheke Island, with something for everyone to enjoy.

WINES
Mudbrick Chardonnay, Cabernet Sauvignon Franc, Reserve Merlot Cabernets Malbec, Shepherds Point Waiheke Island Chardonnay, Cabernet Sauvignon Merlot

RECENT AWARDS
Mudbrick wines regularly receive 4- and 5-star ratings from magazines including *Winestate* and *Cuisine*.

Church Bay Rd, Oneroa
Tel: (09) 372 9050
Fax: (09) 372 9051
Email: mudbrick@ihug.co.nz
Website: www.mudbrick.co.nz

DIRECTIONS From Ocean View Rd turn into Mako St then right into Church Bay Rd.

OPENING HOURS
Cellar Shop: 7 days, 11am–4pm. Restaurant: 7 days, lunch 12pm–3pm, dinner from 6pm. Closed Christmas Day.

WINERY SALES Cellar door, retail, mail order, Internet

PRICE RANGE $18–$35

TASTING & TOURS
Tasting fee: $5, includes a tasting of 6–8 wines. Tours by appointment. Fee: $8, includes guided vineyard tour and tasting.

RESTAURANT Reservations advisable: (09) 372 9050.

OTHER PRODUCTS Waiheke olives and other locally made gourmet food items and gifts, plus a range of wine-related items.

OTHER ACTIVITIES Pétanque

OTHER FACILITIES Available for weddings, celebrations and corporate functions.

OWNERS Robyn & Nick Jones

WINEMAKER Martin Pickering

DATE ESTABLISHED 1992

Peninsula Estate Wines

L ocated high on a northern point of Waiheke Island, Peninsula Estate has to be one of the most picturesque vineyards in New Zealand. Visitors can savour the panoramic views of Oneroa Bay, the Hauraki Gulf and Coromandel while enjoying superb wines.

Peninsula Estate has a simple philosophy — to make world-class premium red wine that can be cellared confidently for many years and be enjoyed with good food. The vineyard, planted in 1986 with Cabernets Sauvignon and Franc, Merlot, Malbec and a little Chardonnay, has expanded to 12 acres and now includes Syrah, Viognier and Petit Verdot. All wines are 100 per cent estate-grown and bottled at the on-site winery to ensure total control of the quality and style.

WINES

Hauraki (Cabernets/Merlot/ Malbec), Zeno (Syrah),

Oneroa Bay (Cabernets/Syrah/ Merlot, Rosé, Chardonnay)

52A Korora Rd, Oneroa
Tel: (09) 372 7866
Fax: (09) 372 7840
Email: wines@peninsulaestate.co.nz
Website: www.peninsulaestate.com

DIRECTIONS
From Matiatia turn left into Korora Rd just before entering Oneroa village. Follow the road for 500m and Peninsula Estate is on the right.

OPENING HOURS
Tasting & sales: Nov–Easter, 11am–3.30pm

WINERY SALES Cellar door, retail, mail order, Internet

PRICE RANGE $15–$45

TASTING & TOURS
A small tasting fee applies, refundable on purchase. Tours by appointment.

OWNERS
Geoff & Rose Creighton

WINEMAKER
Christopher Lush

DATE ESTABLISHED 1985

Saratoga Estate Winery

S arotaoga Estate is named after Saratoga, a wine community in the heart of California's wine country, where the owners have strong links. This boutique winery plans to develop exclusive wine styles through the combination of Californian and European influences melded with Waiheke Island's unique growing conditions. The winery, surrounded by 10 acres of vines planted in Cabernet Sauvignon, Merlot, Malbec, Cabernet Franc, Syrah, Sangiovese and Chardonnay, produces a range of premium wines. Visitors can sample these at the cellar door or over an extended lunch in the Waiheke sunshine with a glass of one of their renowned Bordeaux-style reds or rosé.

WINES
Sarotoga Estate Rosé, Chardonnay, Sauvignon Blanc, Cabernet Sauvignon, Cabernet Sauvignon/Merlot, Veritas Reserve, Bell Tower (Cabernet Merlot), Molly's Paddock Merlot

OTHER PRODUCTS
Grappa (a clear spirit, made with grape skins with a 45% alcohol level).

72 Onetangi Rd, Onetangi
Tel: (09) 372 6450
Fax: (09) 302 0576
Email: wine@saratogaestate.com
Website: www.sarotogaestate.com

DIRECTIONS
Follow Ostend Rd (the main road) into Onetangi Rd towards Onetangi Beach. Saratoga is on the left, across from the golf club.

OPENING HOURS Summer: fine days and by appointment.

WINERY SALES Cellar door, retail, mail order, Internet

PRICE RANGE $10–$40

TASTING & TOURS
Tasting fee: $2 per wine, refundable on purchase.

FOOD OPTIONS
Sarotoga Estate offers light snacks and refreshments when the cellar door is open.

OTHER FACILITIES
Available for private functions, conferences or weddings.

OWNERS
David & Pamela McCabe

WINEMAKERS
Rachael Dutton & Rob Gore

DATE ESTABLISHED 1997

Stonyridge Vineyard

Stonyridge Vineyard was conceived and is operated with the sole intention of making the greatest Bordeaux-style red wine in the world. Named 'Larose' as a tribute to the rose — the most aromatic, colourful, intense and beautiful of all flowers — this involves meticulous organic viticulture and traditional winemaking techniques. On a sunny north-facing slope, the main vineyard provides a stunning backdrop to the rose-coloured winery and restaurant where you can relax with fine food and wine, overlooking a valley of shimmering olive trees and rows of vines.

WINES

Stonyridge Larose (Cabernet Sauvignon, Merlot, Cabernet Franc, Malbec, Petit Verdot blend); Airfield (created if the vintage doesn't reach the Larose standard); Row 10 Chardonnay, Syrah, Grenache, Mourvèdre, Malbec; Verandah Selection (wines from around New Zealand, under the Stonyridge brand, sold at the café)

RECENT AWARDS

'For its arresting power, complexity and richness, and sheer vintage-to-vintage brilliance, Stonyridge Larose must be ranked as New Zealand's greatest claret-style red': Michael Cooper, *Wine Atlas of New Zealand*; 'One of the top 20 cabernets in the world': Rodger Voss, *The World Guide to Cabernet*, London.

80 Onetangi Rd, Ostend
Tel: (09) 372 8822
Fax: (09) 372 8766
Email: enquiries@stonyridge.co.nz
Website: www.stonyridge.co.nz

DIRECTIONS

Follow Ostend Rd (the main road) into Onetangi Rd towards Onetangi Beach. Stonyridge is on the left and well signposted.

OPENING HOURS

Labour Weekend–Easter: 7 days, 11.30–5pm; Easter–Labour Weekend: weekends only, 11.30am–5pm

WINERY SALES

Cellar door, retail, mail order

PRICE RANGE $25–$125

TASTING & TOURS

Tours and tastings available (35–45 mins), Sat & Sun, 11.30am. Fee: $10 pp, includes tour of vineyard, olive grove, cellar and two tastings. All wines available by the glass in the café.

CAFÉ

Open for lunches; reservations advisable: (09) 372 8822.

OTHER FACILITIES Available

for weddings and private functions.

OWNER Stephen White

WINEMAKER

Martin Mackenzie

DATE ESTABLISHED 1982

Kennedy Point Vineyard

Stonyridge Vineyard

Kumeu River Wines

76 Onetangi Rd, Onetangi
Tel: (09) 372 6846 (vineyard)
Fax: (09) 372 6846
Email: terry@winezeal.co.nz
Website: www.te-motu.com

DIRECTIONS
Follow Ostend Rd (the main road) into
Onetangi Rd towards Onetangi Beach.
Te Motu shares lower driveway with
Stonyridge, but turn right at bridge for
Te Motu.

OPENING HOURS
Summer: 7 days, winter: Thurs–Sun

RESTAURANT
Summer: lunches daily (closed Wed);
dinner Fri & Sat evenings from 7pm.
Winter: lunch Thurs–Sun

WINERY SALES
Cellar door, retail, mail order, Internet

PRICE RANGE $35–$250

TASTING & TOURS
Vertical tasting by arrangement. Tours
by appointment.

RESTAURANT
The Shed. Reservations recommended:
(09) 372 6884.

OTHER FACILITIES
A separate area under 'The Big Top' is
available for private functions.

OWNERS
Waiheke Vineyards Limited

WINEMAKERS
John & Paul Dunleavy

DATE ESTABLISHED 1988

Te Motu Vineyard

Te Motu Vineyard lies in the Onetangi Valley, sheltered from the north by the ridge which
guards Onetangi Beach and from the west by the rocky outcrop known as Stonyridge. The
name comes from the original Maori name for Waiheke — Te
Motu-Arai-Roa: 'island of long shelter' — and its expression in
a Celtic typeface was chosen by the owners, the Dunleavy
family, as a way to acknowledge pride in both their Irish and
New Zealand heritage. From the outset the Te Motu vision has
been to specialise in premium red wines blended from the
classic Bordeaux varieties — Cabernet Sauvignon, Merlot,
Cabernet Franc and Malbec — and in the Onetangi Valley the
Dunleavy family have found the perfect terroir to match their
vision.

At Te Motu's restaurant, The Shed, there is leisurely dining
outdoors or under cool verandahs in a picturesque vineyard
setting. You can taste the wine and enjoy fabulous cuisine
designed to complement the flavours of the many vintages of Te
Motu and Dunleavy wines, and a great selection of other styles
from around
New Zealand.

te motu
('the island)

**1999
Cabernet/Merlot
Waiheke Island**
Te Motu Vineyard
Onetangi Valley, Waiheke Island.

Alc Vol 12.5%   PRODUCE OF NEW ZEALAND   750 ml

WINES
Dunleavy Cabernet/Merlot & Te Motu
Cabernet/Merlot
Each constituent variety is aged separately in
barrels and tasted after a year to determine
which shall be drawn off for the second
wine, Dunleavy Cabernet/Merlot. The rest
is left to mature for another 6–9 months
before being bottled as Te Motu.

RECENT AWARDS
Te Motu does not enter competitions but
has been highly rated in wine publications in
the UK, USA and France.

David White

218 Te Whau Drive
Tel: (09) 372 7191
Fax: (09) 372 7189
Email: tony@tewhau.com
Website: www.tewhau.com

DIRECTIONS
Turn off Ostend Rd (the main road) at the Quarry and follow the signs to Te Whau Vineyard.

OPENING HOURS
Lunch, wine tastings and cellar-door sales: Labour Weekend–Easter: 7 days, 11am–5pm (closed Tues); Easter–Labour Weekend: Sat & Sun, 11am–4.30pm; dinner: Fri & Sat evenings from 6.30pm

WINERY SALES
Cellar door, retail, mail order, Internet

PRICE RANGE $39.50–$68.50

TASTING & TOURS
Tasting fee: $3. Tours by appointment only. Fee: $10 pp, includes tasting; minimum of 10 people.

RESTAURANT
Te Whau Vineyard Café. Reservations recommended: (09) 372 7191.

OTHER FACILITIES & ACTIVITIES
Degustation dinners featuring wine and food matching are held in the winter. Contact café for details. Available for private and corporate functions.

OWNERS
Tony & Moira Forsyth

WINEMAKER
Herb Friedli

DATE ESTABLISHED 1993

Te Whau Vineyard

Te Whau Vineyard is located at the end of the Te Whau Peninsula on Waiheke Island. Tucked into the hill above the vineyard slopes and the sea is the winery and café, with spectacular 360-degree views of the Hauraki Gulf and Auckland Isthmus. Te Whau produces two award-winning wines: a single-vineyard Chardonnay and their flagship wine, a Bordeaux-style red called 'The Point' that has received widespread critical acclaim. The steep north-facing slopes where the vines are grown are managed on an environmentally sustainable basis and all vineyard work is done by hand. Their winemaking philosophy is simple — strict fruit selection, gentle handling in the gravity-fed winery, maturation in French oak in the underground temperature-controlled cellar and bottling without fining or filtration.

The restaurant is heaven for wine lovers. The menu focuses on fresh unfussy food to complement the wines served. Awarded nationally and internationally, the extensive wine list includes classic local and international vintages. The restaurant also has a wine bar/tasting room and features contemporary New Zealand artwork which sets off its stunning architecture.

WINES
Te Whau Chardonnay, The Point (a blend of Cabernet Sauvignon, Cabernet Franc, Merlot and Malbec)

RECENT AWARDS
Te Whau Vineyard Café — Award of Excellence 2002: *Wine Spectator* magazine ('One of the Best Restaurants in the World for Wine Lovers'); The Point — 5 stars: Michael Cooper (for every vintage made)

TE WHAU
VINEYARD
WAIHEKE ISLAND

2000
THE POINT

CABERNET SAUVIGNON
MERLOT
CABERNET FRANC
MALBEC

14%VOL   750ML

PRODUCE OF NEW ZEALAND

DAVID WHITE

Babich Wines

Family owned and operated Babich wines was founded over 80 years ago by Josip Babich and today is one of New Zealand's leading wineries. The company has vineyards in the prime grape-growing regions of Marlborough, Hawke's Bay and Henderson, which is the original vineyard and home to the winery. Surrounded by rolling countryside, the Babich winery has one of the loveliest vineyard views in Auckland. Visitors are welcome to relax and enjoy the views from the outdoor deck or enjoy a game of pétanque in the picnic area. The cellar shop stocks all the present vintage wines as well as speciality wines only available from the shop.

WINES
All wines produced are marketed under the Babich brand. This incorporates the Babich Value Varietals, Babich Premium Varietals, 'Winemakers Reserve', 'Irongate', and 'The Patriarch' ranges. Varieties include: Chardonnay, Sauvignon Blanc, Pinot Gris, Riesling, Viognier, Gewürztraminer, Merlot, Syrah, Pinotage, Cabernet Sauvignon, Pinot Noir and blends.

RECENT AWARDS
Babich wines have always been well awarded and highly acclaimed both internationally and in New Zealand.

Babich Rd, Henderson
Tel: (09) 833 7859
Fax: (09) 833 9929
Email: info@babichwines.co.nz
Website: www.babichwines.co.nz

DIRECTIONS
Take the Lincoln Rd turn-off from the Northwestern Motorway. Turn right into Universal Drive, left into Swanson Rd, right into Metcalf Rd, left into Simpson Rd and then left into Babich Rd.

OPENING HOURS 7 days: Mon–Fri, 9am–5pm; Sat, 10am–5pm; Sun, 11am–5pm

WINERY SALES Cellar door, retail, mail/phone/fax orders

PRICE RANGE $10–$70

WINE TASTING
Tasting is free of charge. Large groups by appointment (tasting fee may apply).

FOOD OPTIONS
Cheeseboards, deli and snack foods are available to accompany tasting and for picnics.

PICNIC AREA
Located in the gardens with tables and a pétanque court.

OTHER PRODUCTS Wine accessories, clothing, wine gift packs, wine books and magazines

OWNERS Joe & Peter Babich

WINEMAKER
Adam Hazeldine

DATE ESTABLISHED 1916

AUCKLAND
West

Kumeu River Wines

Kumeu River Wines was established in 1944 when Mick and Katé Brajkovich and their son Mate settled in Kumeu. Mate died in 1992 and Kumeu River is now run by his wife Melba and their four children. Michael is the winemaker and has the distinction of being New Zealand's first Master of Wine; Milan, an engineer, is in charge of the vines; Marijana is the part-time accountant and Paul is marketing & export manager. Melba is managing director and is also often seen running the cellar-door shop. All of Kumeu River's grapes come from its surrounding vineyards where they have access to 39 hectares of vines and produce a range of wines that have built a huge reputation worldwide.

WINES
Kumeu River (premium range): Mate's Vineyard Chardonnay, Chardonnay, Pinot Gris, Melba (red blend), Merlot, Pinot Noir KR Village: Chardonnay, Pinot Noir, Merlot, Rosé

RECENT AWARDS
The Chardonnays from Kumeu River are particularly renowned internationally. Kumeu River Chardonnay — placed in *Wine Spectator*'s Top 100 wines of the world on six occasions. Kumeu River Chardonnay & Mate's Vineyard Chardonnay – rated as Super Classics by Michael Cooper, *Buyer's Guide to NZ Wines 2004*

550 SH16, Kumeu
Tel: (09) 412 8415
Fax: (09) 412 7122
Email: enquiries@kumeuriver.co.nz
Website: www.kumeuriver.co.nz

DIRECTIONS On SH16, just before Kumeu village.

OPENING HOURS Mon–Fri, 9am–5.30pm; Sat, 11am–5pm

WINERY SALES Cellar door, retail, mail order, Internet

PRICE RANGE $12.50–$47

TASTING & TOURS Tasting is free of charge, but a fee applies for groups of $10 pp which includes a tutored tasting and a tour. Tours need to be booked in advance and normally require a minimum of 10 people.

OWNERS
The Brajkovich family

WINEMAKER
Michael Brajkovich MW

DATE ESTABLISHED 1944

Matua Valley Wines

Matua Valley Wines is set in beautiful rolling hill country with the approach to the winery through the vines of the home vineyard. The cellar door lies in a park-like setting with trees providing shady picnic spots on the lawn. At the cellar door you can enjoy Matua's award-winning wines from around the country and a selection of gourmet treats to accompany your wine. For visitors wanting a more elegant lunch the fully licensed Hunting Lodge restaurant is just across the lawn. There are also the adjacent vineyard cottages for people who want to escape to the area for the weekend.

WINES
Labels: Ararimu Series, Innovator Series, Estate Series, Matheson Series, Shingle Peak, Regional Series, Settler Series
Wine Styles: Riesling, Sauvignon Blanc, Gewürztraminer, Pinot Gris, Chardonnay, Pinot Noir, Cabernet Sauvignon Syrah, Merlot, Botrytis Riesling, Late Harvest Riesling

RECENT AWARDS
Ararimu Chardonnay 2001 – Gold: International Wine Challenge 2003; Shingle Peak Botrytis Riesling, Judd Chardonnay 2003, Paretai Sauvignon Blanc 2003 – Gold: Air NZ Wine Awards 2003

Waikoukou Valley Rd, Waimauku
Tel: (09) 411 8301
Fax: (09) 411 7982
Email: sales@matua.co.nz
Website: www.matua.co.nz

DIRECTIONS
Turn into Waikoukou Valley Rd at Waimauku, follow for 2.5 km; Matua Valley is on the left.

OPENING HOURS 7 days: Mon–Fri, 9am–5pm; Sat, 10am–6pm; Sun, 11am–4.30pm

WINERY SALES
Cellar door, retail, mail order

PRICE RANGE $10.95–$39.95

TASTING Tasting is free of charge; groups of 10 or more are charged $5 pp. Groups need to book in advance.

RESTAURANT The Hunting Lodge. Open Wed–Sun. Reservations: (09) 411 8259.

OTHER FOOD OPTIONS
Cheeses, patés, salamis, olives and chutneys available.

PICNIC AREA In the gardens with barbecue facilities.

ACCOMMODATION Vineyard Cottages and Conference Centre. Bookings: (09) 411 8248.

OTHER FACILITIES Pétanque, croquet, children's play area

OWNERS
Beringer Blass Wine Estates

WINEMAKERS
Corey Hall & Joanne Gear

DATE ESTABLISHED 1978

Nobilo Wine Group – Huapai Winery

Rich in history, and with friendly and accommodating staff, Nobilo offers a comprehensive range of high-quality local and international wines — notably the award-winning Nobilo, Selaks and Drylands

portfolios. The history of the company in New Zealand stretches back to the early 1940s when the Croatian Nobilo family landed in New Zealand. They settled in Huapai and started planting vines in 1943. The company has since established and built up a thriving and respected wine business, and is now the second largest wine company in New Zealand. Nobilo strives to 'over-deliver' on quality an objective which was acknowledged at the prestigious 2003 International Wine & Spirit Competition in London when Nobilo Wine Group was awarded New Zealand Wine Producer of the Year.

WINES
Labels: White Cloud, Fernleaf, Fall Harvest, Station Road, House of Nobilo, Nobilo Icon, Selaks Premium Selection, Selaks Founders Reserve, Drylands
Wine styles: Sauvignon Blanc, Chardonnay, Riesling, Pinot Gris, Pinot Noir, Syrah, Merlot, Cabernet Sauvignon, Sparkling, Dessert Wines

RECENT AWARDS
Highest Awarded Winery Trophy: IWSC Chardonnay Challenge 2003; Nobilo Icon Chardonnay 2001 – Chardonnay of the Year Trophy: *Winestate* magazine Wine of the Year Awards 2003; House of Nobilo Poverty Bay Chardonnay 2002 – Best Buy of the Year: Michael Cooper's *Buyer's Guide to New Zealand Wines 2004*

45 Station Road, Huapai
Tel: (09) 412 6666
Fax: (09) 412 7124
Email: nobilo@nobilo.co.nz
Website: www.nobilo.co.nz

DIRECTIONS Follow the Helensville signs from Auckland City then turn left into Station Rd just past Kumeu village.

OPENING HOURS 7 days: Mon–Fri, 9am–5pm; weekends & holidays, 10am–5pm

WINERY SALES
Cellar door and mail order

PRICE RANGE $8–$100

TASTING
Tasting is free of charge.

OTHER PRODUCTS
Comprehensive range of imported wines from Australia, as well as South Africa and Italy

OWNERS
Constellation Brands Inc.

WINEMAKER
Chief winemaker: Darryl Woolley

DATE ESTABLISHED 1943

Soljans Estate

Frank Soljan, father of current owner Tony Soljan, established Soljans Wines in 1937 in Lincoln Road, Henderson. In 2002 Tony rebuilt Soljans Estate Winery in rural Kumeu. The surrounding vineyard is planted with Pinotage, Merlot and Cabernet Franc, but like most Auckland wineries, Soljans draws most of its grapes from New Zealand's major winegrowing regions. At Soljans' cellar door you can participate in winery tours and wine-tasting while browsing the vast selection of wine and wine-related products for sale. The restaurant, open for breakfast and lunch, has a Mediterranean-style menu with a New Zealand twist and each dish is matched with one of Soljans' award-winning wines.

WINES
Soljans Estate: Marlborough Sauvignon Blanc, Riesling, Gewürztraminer, Chardonnay, Rosé, Merlot Cabernet, Pinotage, Dessert Gewürztraminer.
Soljans Reserve: Chardonnay Merlot, Founders Port.
Premium Reserve: Tribute (Merlot/ Malbec).

Soljans Sparkling: Legacy Méthode Traditionnelle, Fusion Muscat.

RECENT AWARDS
Soljans most recent cache of 11 medals was awarded over the two most recent wine shows, the NZ Wine Society Royal Easter Show and the Air NZ Wine Awards.

366 State Highway 16, Kumeu
Tel: (09) 412 5858
Fax: (09) 412 5859
Email: cellar@soljans.co.nz
Website: www.soljans.co.nz

DIRECTIONS
At the end of the Northwestern Motorway, turn left onto SH16: Soljans is 4km on the left.

OPENING HOURS
Cellar door: 7 days, 9am–5.30pm. Café: Sept–May, Mon–Fri, 10am–4pm; Sat & Sun, 9am–4pm; Jun–Aug, Mon–Fri, 11am–3.30pm; Sat & Sun, 9am–4pm

WINERY SALES Cellar door, retail, mail order, Internet

PRICE RANGE $13.50–$35

TASTING & TOURS
Tasting is free of charge for groups of 10 and under; otherwise $5 pp. Daily tours: 11.30am & 2.30pm. Fee: $12 pp including souvenir wine glass.

CAFÉ
Reservations: (09) 412 2680.

OTHER FACILITIES Pétanque courts, children's playhouse. Available for functions.

EVENTS & ACTIVITIES
Soljans' Annual Harvest Celebration, Berba is held each year over Easter.

OWNERS Tony & Colleen Soljan

WINEMAKER Mark Compton

DATE ESTABLISHED 1937

West Brook Winery

Located in the beautiful Ararimu Valley, the West Brook vineyard and winery complex includes a winery, cellar door and superb visitor facilities. These include a designated tasting gallery overlooking the inner winery, the vineyards and rolling country vistas. Outside, landscaped terraced seating areas, shaded by trees, lead down to a brook to provide a tranquil country setting for picnics. Wines are made from grapes sourced from their own eight-hectare Waimauku estate and from leading vineyards in the Hawke's Bay and Marlborough regions. Produced under two labels: the West Brook Selection is true to varietal character and for early drinking; and the Blue Ridge Selection, the Vintage Reserve range is made only in small quantities when conditions are ideal.

WINES
The West Brook Selection:
Marlborough Sauvignon Blanc, Marlborough Riesling, Barrique Fermented Chardonnay, Barrique Aged Merlot Cabernet Franc.
Blue Ridge Selection:
Marlborough Sauvignon Blanc, Chardonnay, Late Harvest Riesling, Cabernet, Merlot.

AWARDS
West Brook has amassed Gold, Silver and Bronze medals in competitions worldwide and awarded top ratings by wine writers. They have also won trophies for their Chardonnay and Riesling.

215 Ararimu Valley Rd
Waimauku
Tel: (09) 411 9924
Fax: (09) 411 9925
Email: info@westbrook.co.nz
Website: www.westbrook.co.nz

DIRECTIONS From SH16 (towards Kumeu) turn right into Old North Rd and drive 7km through the forest, turn right into Ararimu Valley Rd. West Brook is 2km down on the left.

OPENING HOURS All year: Mon–Sat, 10am–5pm; Sun, 11am–5pm

WINERY SALES
Cellar door, retail, mail order

PRICE RANGE $17.95–$30.95

TASTING Tasting is free of

charge for groups of less than 8; otherwise a tasting fee applies (bookings required).

FOOD OPTIONS A range of snacks is available for picnics.

PICNIC AREA In the landscaped terraced seating areas, shaded by trees, or by the brook; tables provided.

EVENTS/ACTIVITIES
Food, wine and music festival held on Easter Sunday & Labour Weekend Sunday and Monday.

OWNERS
Anthony & Sue Ivicevich

WINEMAKERS Anthony Ivicevich & James Rowan

DATE ESTABLISHED 1935

Twilight Vineyards

Bruce and Joy Peart own and operate their boutique Twilight Vineyards in the picturesque Clevedon Valley, south of Auckland City. Even though the vineyard is located in Twilight Rd the name was chosen to mean: 'The first light of day, promising much, and the last light in the evening with (the afterglow of the sun) – a great time to reflect on the day and to enjoy fine wine.'

The first plantings were made in 1995 and now Twilight Vineyards consists of an eight-hectare Clevedon property and six and a half hectares in Gisborne's Ormond Valley. A new cellar door and tasting room opens in the spring of 2004 at the Clevedon vineyard where visitors are welcome to picnic in the beautiful rural surroundings and enjoy the fine Twilight wines.

WINES
Twilight Nouveau Red (blend), Merlot/Cabernet Sauvignon, Pinot Gris, Chardonnay, Reserve Chardonnay, Chenin Blanc, Diamond and Pearls (Sparkling Muscat)

RECENT AWARDS
2002 Reserve Chardonnay Bronze: Air NZ Wine Awards 2003, Bronze: NZ Wine Society Royal Easter Wine Show 2004; 2002 Twilight Chardonnay & Twilight Diamonds and Pearls – Best Buy Nov 03: *Tizwine*

105 Twilight Rd, Clevedon
Tel: (09) 292 9502
Fax: (09) 292 9502
Email: info@twilightvineyards.com
Website: www.twilightvineyards.com

DIRECTIONS Twilight Rd branches from the main road in Clevedon Village. The vineyard is 1km along on the left.

OPENING HOURS
Summer: Thurs Sun, 11am–4pm; Winter: holiday weekends only, 11am–4pm. Groups by appointment all year.

WINERY SALES Cellar door, retail, mail order, Internet

PRICE RANGE $14.95–$24.95

TASTING & TOURS
Tasting: a small fee applies. Tours and groups by appointment.

PICNIC AREA By the cellar door with extensive rural views over the Clevedon valley.

OTHER PRODUCTS Local artwork, preserves, sunhats, monogrammed tasting glasses and flutes

OWNER Bruce Peart

WINEMAKER Made under contract in Hawke's Bay.

DATE ESTABLISHED 1996

Vin Alto

Vin Alto is New Zealand's first vineyard and winery dedicated to the production of traditional Italian-style wines and boasts one of the largest selections of cloned Italian grape varieties in New Zealand. Here you will discover a little slice of Northern Italy - hills, views, Italian-style wines, olive groves, pine forest and deer farm all set in a peaceful rustic environment. A fascinating place to visit, you step back in wine history in Enzo's wine museum and see his extensive collection of centuries-old wine glass antiques and corkscrews. You will also find traditional Italian hospitality as you sample handmade wines and liqueurs, and learn something of their unique wine- and liqueur-making style.

WINES
From early times the Bettio family has made wine in northern Italy using specialised winemaking methods and grape varieties. These methods are still in use today at Vin Alto and include: Retico (the old Roman name for wine made from dried grapes) — Amarone-style; Ritorno — Ripasso-style Sangiovese; Celaio — Super Tuscan-style Sangiovese; Di Sotto — Cabernets Merlot & Sangiovese; Pinot Grigio; Chardonnay

OTHER PRODUCTS
Liqueurs, handmade using old Italian recipes: Limoncello, Cassis, Liqueur di Café

424 Creightons Rd, Clevedon
Tel: (09) 292 8845
Fax: (09) 292 8867
Email: vinalto@xtra.co.nz
Website: www.vinalto.com

DIRECTIONS
Heading towards Clevedon from the Southern Motorway, Vin Alto is 3km along Creighton Rd which runs off the Papakura-Clevedon Rd.

OPENING HOURS
Sat & Sun, 11am 4pm

WINERY SALES
Cellar door, retail, Internet

PRICE RANGE $20–$100

TASTING & TOURS A small fee applies. Tours by appointment.

FOOD OPTIONS
Traditional Italian antipasto dishes and piatini (small dishes made from Italian family recipes), to complement the wines.

OTHER FACILITIES & ACTIVITIES
Wine museum; special food & wine matching dinners by arrangement.

OWNERS
Enzo & Margaret Bettio

WINEMAKERS
Enzo & Margaret Bettio

DATE ESTABLISHED 1994

5 Kirkbride Road, Mangere
Phone: (09) 255 0660
Email: enquiries@villamaria.co.nz
Website www.villamaria.co.nz
New premises: 118 Montgomerie Road,
Mangere (in the latter half of 2004)

DIRECTIONS
Kirkbride Road site
Follow SH20 (as if you are going to
Auckland Airport). Turn right at the
lights into Kirkbride Road and follow
for approximately 1.5km until you
arrive at Villa Maria.
Montgomerie Road site
(latter half of 2004)
Follow SH20 towards Auckland
Airport. Turn right at the lights into
Montgomerie Road until you arrive
at Villa Maria.

OPENING HOURS
Mon–Fri, 9am–6pm, Sat & Sun,
9am–5pm

WINERY SALES
Cellar door, retail and mail order

PRICE RANGE Over $10

TASTING & TOURS
Wine tasting is free of charge. Tours by
appointment. Fee: $5.

OWNER George Fistonich

WINEMAKERS
Alastair Maling, MW, Group Winemaker
Corey Ryan, Senior Winemaker

DATE ESTABLISHED 1961

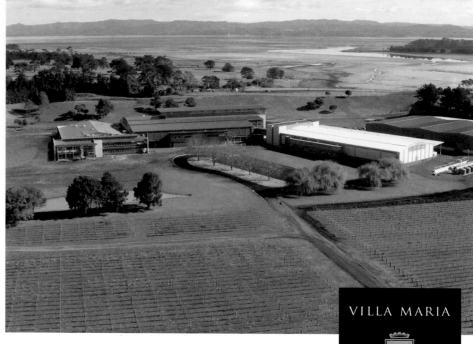

Villa Maria Auckland

Villa Maria is New Zealand's largest privately owned winery and produces New Zealand's most awarded wines. Founded in 1961 by owner and Managing Director George Fistonich, its cellar shop and head office are based on the original site at Kirkbride Road. Originally the Fistonich family property, this site has expanded over the last 40 years as Villa Maria has grown, and with a view to the next 40 years the winery will be relocating in 2004. In the interim, the original site is open for tastings and cellar-door sales.

The new Montgomerie Road site is located in an extinct volcano crater where a vineyard frames the entranceway to a state-of-the art winery, production line, warehouse and administration block. Stage two of development will ensure that visitors not only get to taste some of New Zealand's finest wines, but also get a glimpse into the art of winemaking.

* At the time of publication a relocation date was unconfirmed, please contact the cellar shop prior to your visit.

WINES
Villa Maria produces four distinctive ranges of wine.
Private Bin: A popular selection of varietal wines, well structured and displaying true varietal characteristics.
Cellar Selection: An emphasis on fruit quality and minimal handling results in intensely flavoured, elegant, food-friendly wines.
Reserve: Produced from the best vineyards in New Zealand's top winegrowing areas to ensure they exhibit the finest regional characteristics possible. Wines must be of exceptional quality to justify the 'Reserve' marque.
Single Vineyard: The creation of a Single Vineyard range has been a long-term vision of the Villa Maria winemaking and viticulture team. These wines are sourced from vineyards of exceptional quality and only when vintage conditions allow the sites to fully express their individual characteristics.

WINE STYLES ACROSS THE RANGES
Chardonnay, Sauvignon Blanc, Riesling, Pinot Gris, Gewürztraminer, Late Harvest Riesling, Late Harvest Gewürztraminer, Noble Riesling, Pinot Noir, Merlot, Merlot/Cabernet Sauvignon

RECENT AWARDS
Most Successful Exhibitor Trophy: New Zealand Wine Society Royal Easter Wine Show 2004; Air New Zealand Wine Awards 2003: two trophies, 12 gold medals and four silver medals; Villa Maria Cellar Selection Marlborough Sauvignon Blanc 2003 – Trophy for Best Sauvignon Blanc: Cool Climate Wine Show 2004; Villa Maria Reserve Pinot Noir 2002 – Gold Medal & Trophy for Best Pinot Noir: Royal Hobart Wine Show 2003

Mahurangi Estate Winery

Ransom Wines

Twilight Vineyards

Kumeu River Wines

VINEYARD

Waikato & Bay of Plenty

Fotopress

WAIKATO/BAY OF PLENTY, south of Auckland in the North Island, is the country's smallest wine region, producing just 0.9 per cent of the national crop. Its vineyard plantings occupy scattered pockets amid the rolling dairying and horticultural belt of the Waikato and Bay of Plenty. The larger wineries, based here generally for proximity to markets, obtain most or all of their grapes from other regions. Most Waikato vineyards are north of the city of **Hamilton** around the rural towns of **Te Kauwhata** and **Mangatawhiri**, and some lie south of the city near **Te Awamutu**. Bay of Plenty vineyards are predominantly around the coastal city of **Tauranga**, with others near the seas not far from the city of **Whakatane**, and inland near the town of **Murupara**. Soft, mouth-filling wines with ripe fruit flavours are the hallmark of the region, including tropical fruit-flavoured Chardonnays and Sauvignon Blancs. Full-bodied Cabernet Sauvignons and botrytised dessert wines are also successfully produced.

Hamilton, with its river and gardens, is the centre of the Waikato region. Tauranga is a thriving city and gateway to the Bay of Plenty's beaches and horticultural areas.

For more information on the Waikato/Bay of Plenty region visit www.waikatonz.co.nz or www.tauranga.govt.nz. Or contact Hamilton Visitor Information Centre: Transport Centre, corner Bryce and Anglesea Streets, Hamilton, (07) 839 3580, hamiltoninfo@wave.co.nz, or Tauranga Visitor Information Centre: 95 Willow Street, Tauranga, (07) 578 8103, trgvin@tauranga.govt.nz.

HISTORY

The government's Viticultural Research Station was established at Te Kauwhata in 1897 (now the site of Rongopai Wines), giving an impetus to grape-growing in the region. In the 1960s, Montana established vineyards at Mangatangi in the northern Waikato and Cooks planted vineyards and developed a winery at Te Kauwhata. By the 1980s the region was producing close to six per cent of the national crop. However, since then there has been a steady decline in its importance as grape-growing has moved to drier regions in the south.

SOILS

Heavy loams over clay subsoils are common in the Waikato, their fertility demanding good management to control vine vigour. The Bay of Plenty vines grow chiefly in volcanic loams.

CLIMATE

Both Waikato and Bay of Plenty enjoy a moderately warm, mild climate and high sunshine hours. Humidity and rainfall are high, but most of the rain tends to fall after harvest in autumn. Inland Bay of Plenty sites near Murupara experience hot days and cold nights.

GRAPE VARIETIES AND WINE STYLES

The major varieties are Chardonnay, Cabernet Sauvignon and Sauvignon Blanc. Chardonnays produced feature tropical-fruit flavours and most undergo malolactic fermentation to soften their acidity. Cabernet Sauvignon and Sauvignon Blanc are made in full-bodied styles with ripe flavours. The region's relatively humid climate helps in the production of sweet botrytised dessert wines. Pinot Noir wines in berry fruit-flavoured styles are also showing promise in the region.

SUB-REGIONS

Waikato, on heavy loams among fertile farmlands, principally north of the city of Hamilton around Te Kauwhata and Mangatawhiri, as well as south of the city near Te Awamutu.

Bay of Plenty, on volcanic loams, includes vineyards around Tauranga and Whakatane, and inland at Galatea near Murupara.

Events

- **The International Food and Wine Festival.** The largest event showcasing the region's best produce. Held annually in Hamilton in May.
- **Jazz, Wine and Food Festival.** Inaugural festival held in Hamilton East in 2004. Planned to be held annually.

For more information contact the Hamilton Visitor Information Centre

Kinross Vineyard, Morton Estate

Vilagrad Wines

Colefield Vineyard, Morton Estate

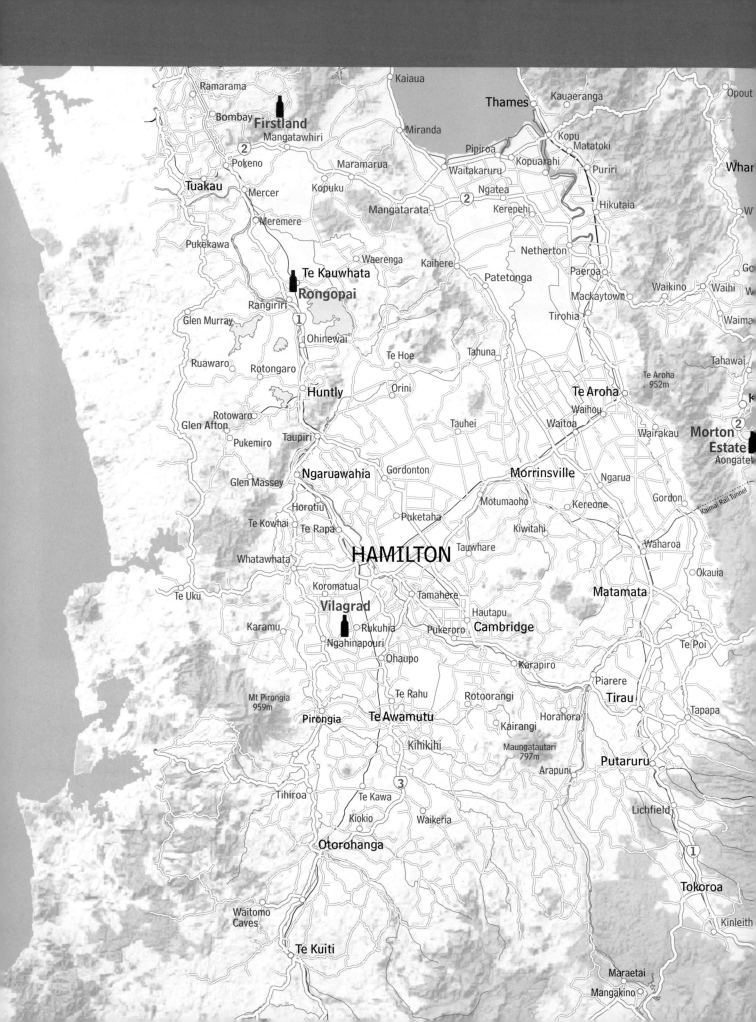

Mayor Island

Matakana
Island

TAURANGA Mt Maunganui
Omanu Beach
Vairoa Pa Kairua
Mills Reef Papamoa Beach

Motiti Island

BAY OF

Tauriko Welcome Bay Papamoa Maketu
Ohauiti (2) Te Puke

PLENTY

Pyes Pa
Pukehina

Paengaroa

Pongakawa Ohinepanea

Te Ranga Matata

Moutohora Island

Awakaponga
Thornton WHAKATANE
Paroa
Manawahe Edgecumbe
Okere Falls Otakiri Ohope
Otaramarae Rotoehu
Awahou Mourea Rotoiti Lake Rotoma
Te Teko Opotiki
naku Ngongotaha Lake Tikitere Onepu Kutarere
Rotorua
ROTORUA Kawerau Taneatua (2)
Uwhata Mt Edgecumbe
Whakarewarewa 821m
Ruatoki North
Lake Waimana
Tarawera Waikirikiri
Horohoro Mt Tarawera
. 1111m Waiohau
Te Whakaumu Ruatupapaku
765m . . 671m
Rerewhakaaitu
tiamuri Waiotapu
Kopuriki

RANGES

NGE

three

Three

naku

Three

500 Lyons Rd, Mangatawhiri
Tel: (09) 233 6314
Fax: (09) 233 6215
Email: info@firstland.co.nz
Website: www.firstland.co.nz

DIRECTIONS
45 minutes drive south of Auckland on
SH2. Turn left into Lyons Rd, Firstlands
is at the end of the road.

OPENING HOURS
Cellar Door: 7 days, 9.30am–5pm
Restaurant: 7 days for lunch and dinner

WINERY SALES
Cellar door, retail mail order, Internet

PRICE RANGE $20–$50

TASTING
Tasting is free of charge; group tastings
on application.

RESTAURANT
The Vineyard Restaurant offers superb
dining in an elegant setting. Diners also
have the option of the private Vintage
and De Redcliffe Rooms and the outside
terrace areas.

ACCOMMODATION
Peppers Hotel du Vin has 48 restful,
spacious chalets set in lush gardens
surrounding the original winery and
reception building.

ACTIVITIES
A wide range of leisure activities is
available at Peppers Hotel du Vin for
day vistors: pétanque, clay bird
shooting, croquet, tennis, Barrel-In-One
golf challenge, archery, volleyball,
cricket. These activities require advance
booking.

OWNERS
Ed & Barbara Aster

WINEMAKER
Dr John Forrest

DATE ESTABLISHED 1976

Firstland Vineyards

Firstland Vineyards is based at Peppers Hotel du Vin in the picturesque Mangatawhiri Valley, 45 minutes south of Auckland. With 85 per cent of the company's wines being produced from Marlborough fruit, the original winery on the premises has been decommissioned and will shortly reopen as a luxury day spa. Wines are now made in Marlborough from grapes grown on the company's Lauren Vineyard and also purchased from growers in Renwick and Gimblett Road in Hawke's Bay. The cellar door at the Peppers Hotel du Vin offers a full range of Firstland wines as well as several large-format bottles that are only sold here. As well as wine-tasting, day visitors to Firstlands Vineyards can also enjoy fine dining and a wide range of leisure activities (see left).

Firstland Vineyards is primarily an export company, with more than 90 per cent of the wines being sold in the USA, UK, Australia and Korea. In keeping with its export focus, the production of Sauvignon Blanc and Pinot Noir has been increased and they will release a Pinot Gris in 2006.

WINES
Firstland Marlborough Sauvignon Blanc, Riesling, Chardonnay, Pinot Noir; Hawke's Bay Cabernet/Merlot/Malbec, Firstland Reserve Hawke's Bay Cabernet Sauvignon, Marlborough Chardonnay

55 Te Kauwhata Rd, Te Kauwhata
Tel: (07) 826 3891
Fax: (07) 826 3462
Email: shop@rongopaiwines.co.nz
Website: www.rongopaiwines.co.nz

DIRECTIONS
30 minutes' drive south of Auckland on
SH1. Turn off at Te Kauwhata and
follow the signs.

OPENING HOURS
Mon–Fri, 9am–5pm
Weekends, 10am–4pm

WINERY SALES
Cellar door, retail, mail order, Internet

PRICE RANGE $12.95–$75

TASTING & TOURS
Tasting fee: $2 pp to taste the Seasonal
and Regional Range; refundable on
purchase. Tours by appointment only.
Tour fee: $5 (includes free tasting)

PICNIC AREA
Beautiful park-like area with picnic
tables.

OWNERS
D & J Reid, R Burney & E Bolliger

WINEMAKER
Emmanuel Bolliger

DATE ESTABLISHED 1932

Rongopai Wines

In the heart of the Waikato, above beautiful Lake Waikare, lies the small town of Te Kauwhata and the home of Rongopai Wines. A short half-hour drive south of Auckland and set in the picturesque research station built by Italian viticulturist Romeo Bragato in 1902, Rongopai is the birthplace of New Zealand winemaking research and one of our leading producers of botrytised wine.

With established vineyards in three key winegrowing regions — Hawke's Bay, Gisborne and Marlborough — Rongopai is both a familiar and reliable source of great wines. Numerous medals and awards have shown New Zealand and the world the quality and strength of their selection.

The evident beauty of the winery itself makes Rongopai Wines a popular place to visit. If you like truly great wines and beautiful, historic settings then you'll love Rongopai. Visitors are welcome to drop in, sample wines at the cellar door and relax in the park-like surroundings — or by telephoning in advance arrange a tour of the highest-classed historic winery in New Zealand.

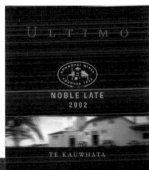

WINES
Labels: Seasonal Series, Regional Range,
ULTIMO Collection (premium range)
Wines Styles: Sauvignon Blanc,
Chardonnay, Viognier, Merlot, Malbec,
Pinot Noir, Sweet wines varieties include
Chardonnay, Riesling and Wurzer

RECENT AWARDS
ULTIMO Noble Late Harvest 2002 –
Gold: Royal Easter Wine Show 2004,
Gold: Challenge International du Vin
2004; ULTIMO Chardonnay 2002
Silver: Royal Easter Wine Show 2004,
Silver: Challenge International du Vin
2004; Reserve Merlot 2002 – Silver:
New World Wine Awards 2003; Reserve
Gisborne Chardonnay 2002 – Silver:
Liquorland Top 100 2003

702 Rukuhia Rd
R D 2, Ohaupo
Tel: (07) 825 2893
Fax: (07) 825 2093
Email: wines@vilagrad.co.nz
Website: www.vilagradwines.co.nz

DIRECTIONS
10 minutes south of Hamilton on SH3.
Turn off at Rukuhia Rd and follow for
7km — Vilagrad is on the right.

OPENING HOURS
Cellar Door: 7 days, 9am–4pm.
Restaurant: Sun, all year, 12pm–4pm

WINERY SALES
Cellar door, retail, mail order, Internet

PRICE RANGE
$16–$29

TASTING & TOURS
Tasting is free of charge. 1-hour
educational tasting and tour by
appointment: $10 pp. Tour, educational
tasting & nibbles platter: $15 pp.

RESTAURANT
Vilagrad Restaurant: open for Sunday
lunches. Available for conferences,
private functions and weddings.

EVENTS & ACTIVITIES
Harvest Festival held in April.

OTHER PRODUCTS
Personalised wine labels: personalise
your own bottle(s) of wine for a special
gift or event.

OWNERS
Pieter & Nelda Nooyen

WINEMAKER
Jacob Nooyen

CHEF
Kristian Nooyen

DATE ESTABLISHED 1922

Vilagrad Wines

Named after the Croatian word meaning place, Vilagrad Wines is the region's oldest winery, established over 80 years ago by Dalmatians, the Milicich family, whose vision was to transport a slice of their European cultural heritage to their new home in New Zealand. Still family owned and operated, Vilagrad now encompasses four generations of winemaking.

Set in the tranquil and picturesque Waikato countryside, Vilagrad captures the spirit of a traditional European lifestyle and offers this old-world experience to visitors. Sunday lunches in the cobbled courtyard under a canopy of vines are a relaxing casual affair where you can enjoy succulent meat off the spit, Mediterranean vegetable dishes, fresh salads and mouth-watering desserts accompanied by some of their award-winning wines. You can teach your taste buds and educate your palate on the tasting tour of the vineyard and cellar where you will learn about the art of viticulture and winemaking from grape to bottle. At Vilagrad, tried and true traditional methods of winemaking are still faithfully practised to produce their excellent range of regional wines.

VILAGRAD
V
2001
*Cabernet/Merlot
Malbec Reserve*
ALC/VOL 13%. 750mL
Product of New Zealand
and Australia

WINES
Vilagrad Mt Pirongia
Chardonnay, Mt Pirongia
Cabernet Merlot,
Chardonnay/Traminer,
Reserve Chardonnay,
Reserve Cabernet/
Merlot/Malbec, Méthode
Traditionnelle

RECENT AWARDS
Vilgrad's wines, all grown
and produced in the
Waikato, have won 31
awards over the last six
seasons.

Mills Reef Winery

Mills Reef Winery and Restaurant has established itself as a major Tauranga landmark — though the vineyards are situated in Hawke's Bay. With its Art Deco architectural style it has been acclaimed as one of the most stylish and attractive winery buildings in New Zealand. Set on expansive grounds, the winery is purpose-built for wine production and wine appreciation and has been recognised as a world-class facility. The complex has full winemaking and bottling capacity, a 500-barrel cellar, an aged wine cellar and spacious wine-tasting areas. An award-winning restaurant completes the picture with a relaxed outdoor dining area, pétanque courts and beautifully landscaped grounds.

WINES
Labels: Mills Reef, Reserve and Elspeth
Wine Styles: Chardonnay, Riesling, Sauvignon Blanc, Gewürztraminer, Syrah, Merlot, Cabernet Merlot, Cabernet Franc, Malbec and Mills Reef's

Icon Blend 'Elspeth One'

RECENT AWARDS
Wines have won over 250 medals, nine Champion Wine trophies and 'Champion Wine-maker' at the NZ Wine Society Royal Easter Wine Show 2003.

143 Moffat Rd, Bethlehem Tauranga
Tel: (07) 576 8800
Fax: (07) 576 8824
Email: info@millsreef.co.nz
Website: www.millsreef.co.nz

DIRECTIONS
From the north and Tauranga, take SH2 to Bethlehem, turn onto Moffat Road; Mills Reef is 500m on the right.

OPENING HOURS
Tasting room: 7 days, 10am–5pm. Restaurant: lunch 7 days, 10am–5pm, dinner by arrangement.

WINERY SALES
Cellar door, retail, Internet

PRICE RANGE $15–$50

TASTING & TOURS
Tasting is free of charge.

Tours by appointment.

RESTAURANT
Relaxed indoor and outdoor dining in a rural setting. Pacific Rim-style cuisine and wood-fired pizzas. Reservations: (07) 576 8800.

EVENT & ACTIVITIES
Winemakers dinners, Annual Mills Reef Concert on the lawn (in January, Auckland Anniversary Weekend), Tauranga Garden & Art Festival (8–14 November 2004)

OTHER FACILITIES
Available for weddings and functions.

OWNERS
The Preston family

WINEMAKERS
Paddy & Tim Preston

DATE ESTABLISHED 1989

Morton Estate

With estates in the prime winegrowing regions of Hawke's Bay and Marlborough, Morton Estate has built a reputation for consistently producing some of New Zealand's most exceptional wines, confirmed by numerous accolades in the most rigorous international wine competitions. Famous for its Chardonnays, Morton Estate is now making a name for itself with its Sauvignon Blancs and reds. Located on the main highway in Katikati, the distinctive Cape Dutch-style winery is a popular spot to spend a day, with cellar-door wine sales and tasting, and memorable dining at Mortons Restaurant. The menu features delectable game dishes, and after a leisurely lunch and sampling wines you can then visit the cellar door to make your purchases.

WINES
Labels: Coniglio, Morton Estate Black Label, Reserve Range, Individual Vineyard Series, Méthode Traditionnelle, White Label, Mill Road
Wine styles: Chardonnay, Sauvignon Blanc, Riesling, Sémillon/Chardonnay, Syrah, Merlot, Merlot/Cabernet, Sparkling, Pinot Gris, Pinot Noir

RECENT AWARDS
NZ Wine Producer of the year: International Wine & Spirit Competition 2002; Stone Creek Marlborough Sauvignon Blanc 2002 – Best Sauvignon Blanc Trophy: London International Wine Challenge 2003, Blue-Gold: Sydney International Wine Challenge 2003; Non Vintage Brut – Champion Sparkling Trophy: Air NZ Awards 2003

State Highway 2
Katikati
Tel: (07) 552 0795
Fax: (07) 552 0651
Email: auckland@mortonestatewines.co.nz
Website: www.mortonestate.co.nz

DIRECTIONS
In Katikati, 15 minutes north of Tauranga on SH2.

OPENING HOURS
Cellar door: 7 days, 9.30am–5pm (closed Christmas Day). Restaurant: lunch: 7 days, 11.30am–3pm, dinner: Thurs–Sat from 6pm

WINERY SALES
Cellar door, retail, mail order, Internet

PRICE RANGE $10–$80

TASTING & TOURS
Tasting is free of charge. Tours available on request.

RESTAURANT
Morton Restaurant. Reservations: (07) 552 0620.

OTHER FACILITIES
State-of-the-art Méthode Traditionnelle Centre. Available for functions.

OWNER John Coney

WINEMAKERS
Evan Ward & Chris Archer

DATE ESTABLISHED 1978

Gisborne

GISBORNE, on the eastern tip of the North Island, with the first vines in the world to see the sun each day, is New Zealand's third largest wine region, comprising 10.7 per cent of the national crop. Spreading out behind the coastal city of **Gisborne**, the Gisborne Plains form a sheltered triangle of land bordered by mountain ranges and the sea in Poverty Bay. Most plantings occur in the Ormond Valley in the northern apex of the triangle, and along plains bordering the Waipaoa River that runs the length of the region. Some vineyards are creeping into hillside areas. Chardonnay is the key grape, comprising over half of all plantings, produced with the soft, lush, tropical-fruit flavours that characterise most of Gisborne's white wines, including Gewürztraminer, Sémillon and Chenin Blanc. Warm, soft, fruity Merlots are also made, and Pinot Noir finds its way into méthode traditionnelle wines. The region is one of the country's sunniest and warmest, with grapes ripening relatively early.

Gisborne is the gateway to the unspoilt East Coast region and the city offers popular surf beaches, wine trails, restaurants and historical sites.

For more information on the Gisborne region visit www.gisborne.co.nz or www.gisbornewine.co.nz. Or contact Gisborne Visitor Information Centre: 209 Grey Street, Gisborne, (06) 868 6139, info@gisbornenz.com.

The Millton Vineyard

HISTORY

The first wines in Gisborne were planted by Marist priests in the 1850s. German winemaker Friedrich Wohnsiedler pioneered commercial winemaking in the region, establishing vines at Waihirere and releasing his first wine in 1921. (Wohnsiedler's winery was eventually purchased by Montana in 1973.) The modern era of grapegrowing began in the late 1960s when Corbans and Montana began contracting local farmers to raise grapes for processing at their Auckland wineries. Vineyards spread rapidly and bulk wine production dominated the region in the 1970s and 1980s. This was followed by some downsizing and shifting of varietal focus. Montana has invested heavily in the region's vineyards and its hugely popular Montana Gisborne Chardonnay, first made in 1973, is one of its biggest-volume wines.

SOILS

Gisborne's soils are chiefly alluvial clay loams of moderate to high fertility, requiring vine vigour to be kept in check. Soils do not vary greatly across the region, so different rootstocks and clones are used to produce fruit with a range of flavours. Newer hillside sites outside of the plains areas have lower-fertility soils.

CLIMATE

Gisborne is very sunny, and warm temperatures lead to early grape harvest. The region is relatively sheltered from strong winds, and coastal areas are cooled by sea breezes, helping grapes retain their crispness. Frequent autumn rainfall can cause strong risk of fungal disease.

GRAPE VARIETIES AND WINE STYLES

Chardonnay occupies around half of Gisborne's vineyards and white varieties make up most of the balance. Chardonnay is produced in soft, fruit-forward styles. Müller-Thurgau, often used in blends, shows floral, citrus characters. Most Muscat produced is used in Montana's popular sparkling wine, Bernadino. Gisborne is also one of the best region's in the country for crisp Sémillons and Gewürztraminers that range from elegant, floral wines to rich,

spicy complex examples. Soft, plummy and fruity Merlot is the key red while Pinot Noir is used mainly for sparkling wine production.

SUB-REGIONS

Patutahi, in the west, has around a third of the region's vines, mainly Chardonnay along with Gewürztraminer, and produces premium, richly flavoured wines.

Ormond, in the northern end of the plains, has produced superb Chardonnays since the 1980s.

Manutuke, the oldest sub-region, closer to the coast south of the Waipaoa River, produces mainly Chardonnay, Chenin Blanc, Malbec, varietal Muscat and Pinot Noir.

Hexton, on the north-eastern edge of the plains, is known for its Chardonnay, along with Gewürztraminer, Merlot, Malbec and Viognier.

Matawhero, alongside the Waipaoa River nearer the coast, produces mostly Chardonnay and Gewürztraminer.

Waihirere, in the north of the plains, is home to the first commercial vineyard and to Montana Gisborne Chardonnay, produced from the sub-region's key variety.

Makauri/Bushmere, in the centre of the plains, produces mainly Chardonnay, Merlot, Sémillon, Muscat and Müller-Thurgau.

Waipaoa Valley, at the northern end of the plains, on free-draining soils close to the Waipaoa River, is a newer sub-region planted mainly in Chardonnay, Sémillon and Pinot Noir.

The Millton Vineyard

TW Wines

Events

● **Taste Gisborne Festival.** Wine, art, food and music. Six hours of non-stop entertainment at the historic Waiohika Estate Vineyard. Held annually in January.

● **Gisborne Wine and Food Week.** A festival of wine-related activities, incorporating a wine and food festival and International Chardonnay Challenge. Held annually over Labour Weekend (October).

For more information visit www.gisbornewine.co.nz

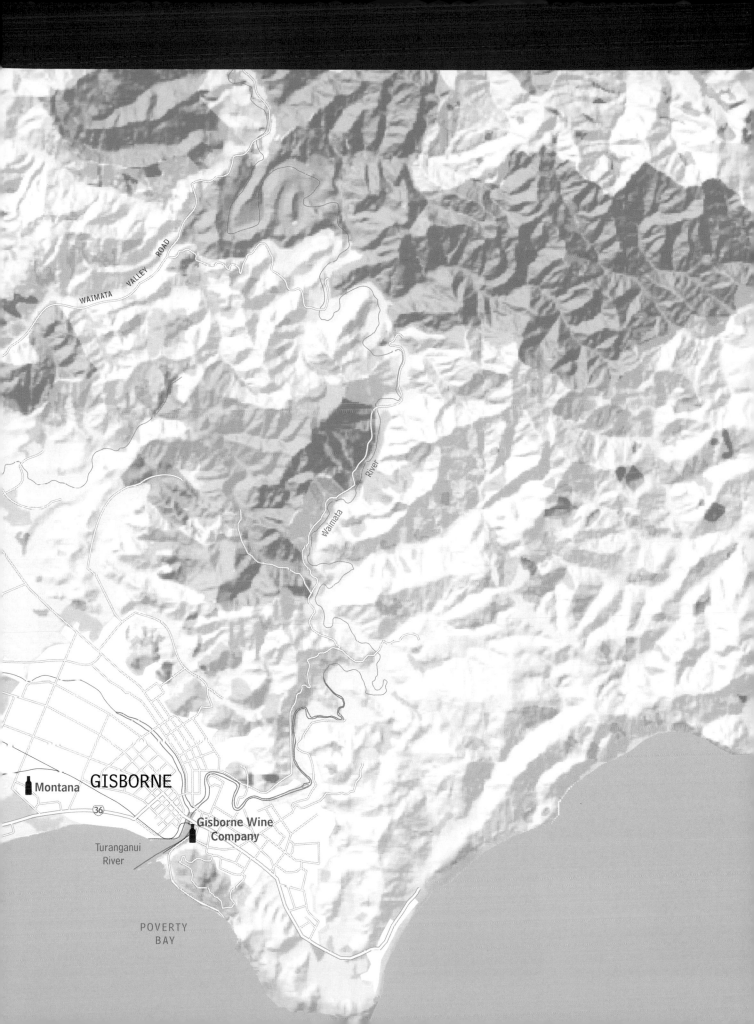

Gisborne Wine Company

The Gisborne Wine Company is located in a former freezing works, built in 1906 and once the largest brick façade in the Southern Hemisphere. Since 1998 it has become the Works Café and Winery with winemaker John Thorpe processing over 200 tonnes of grapes each year for a range of different local wines. The rear of the building houses the cellar, with thick brick walls and concrete ceilings maintaining perfect cellaring conditions. Over 80 per cent of the barriques in the cellar hold Merlot, Malbec and Cabernet Franc wines, which challenges the traditional white-wine dominance of this region. John Thorpe is also trained as a chef and inspires a menu that focuses on local produce including Waimata Cheeses, truffles, paua, kina and a huge range of local seafood.

TW Wines

Gisborne Wine Company

Montana Gisborne Winery and Lindauer Cellars

LONGBUSH
GISBORNE

CHARDONNAY
2002

WINES

Longbush Chardonnay, Merlot, Gewürztraminer, Vintage Brut Méthode Traditionnelle (12 years old) Works Chardonnay, Sauvignon Blanc, Rosé, Cabernet Franc, Merlot

The Esplanade, Gisborne
Tel: (06) 863 1285 or
0800 gizwine
Fax: (06) 863 0973
Email:
info@gisbornewinecompany.co.nz
Website:
www.gisbornewinecompany.co.nz

DIRECTIONS On Gisborne's inner harbour, The Esplanade is off the main road heading north.

OPENING HOURS
Sales and tastings during café hours: 7 days, 10am–late

WINERY SALES Cellar door, retail, Internet

PRICE RANGE $12–$38

TASTING & TOURS
Tasting fee: $10, includes a platter of Waimata cheeses. Local vineyard tours: $60 pp, minimum of 3 people, departing daily 10am & 2pm.

CAFÉ
The Works Café: (06) 863 0973

OTHER FACILITIES
The Works Café is available for group functions.

OWNER
John Thorpe

WINEMAKER
John Thorpe

DATE ESTABLISHED 1998

Solander St, Gisborne
Phone: (06) 868 2757
Fax: (06) 867 9817
Email:
GisborneCellarDoor@montanawines.co.nz
Website: www.montanawines.co.nz

DIRECTIONS
Situated on Solander Street in the heart
of Gisborne.

OPENING HOURS
7 days, 10am–5pm

WINERY SALES
Cellar door, retail

PRICE RANGE $14–$80

TASTING & TOURS
Tasting is free of charge. Museum tours
daily at 10.30am & 2pm.

CAFÉ
7 days, lunch from 11.30am.
Cheeseboards available all day.

OTHER FACILITIES
There is a shade sail, pétanque court
and grass area to enjoy. The Lindauer
Cellars can cater for private functions
for up to 80 people.

OTHER PRODUCTS
Premium Montana wines, quality gifts
and accessories.

OWNERS
Montana Wines

WINEMAKERS
Steve Voysey & Brent Laidlaw

DATE ESTABLISHED 2002

Montana Gisborne Winery & Lindauer Cellars

The former Corbans Winery in Gisborne has been transformed into a striking, modern cellar door, complete with an extensive wine shop, a private tasting room, a shady courtyard and a winery museum. Visitors walk through an imposing colonnade with a pétanque court and grassy area to their left, a large outdoor fire directly ahead of them and the extensive cellar door to their right. With its exposed wooden beams and pebble stone flooring, the cellar door opens onto the courtyard. An extensive selection of Montana wines are available to taste, purchase, or enjoy in the sheltered courtyard. Lunches are also available in the winery café.

A feature of the tastings is a winery tour and the opportunity to venture into the winery museum that highlights the production of méthode traditionnelle wines such as Lindauer and the history of winemaking in the region. Housed in a former cuve room, the museum is dark and cavernous with lots of uplighting to try and replicate the feeling of being underground in the Champagne caves of France.

WINES
Lindauer Special Reserve, Fraise
Montana Gisborne Chardonnay,
Ormond Estate Chardonnay,
Patutahi Estate Gewürztraminer
Corbans Chardonnay, Pinot Gris

RECENT AWARDS
Lindauer Special Reserve —
Gold: InterVin 2002, Best Value
Sparkling & Top Gold: 1999
WINPAC Wine Show Hong
Kong; Lindauer Brut — Gold:
InterVin 2002, Gold: Japan
International Wine Challenge
2002

119 Papatu Road, Manutuke
Tel: (06) 862 8680
Fax: (06) 862 8869
Email: info@millton.co.nz
Website: www.millton.co.nz

DIRECTIONS
From Gisborne, follow SH2 to Napier for 10 minutes. Papatu Rd is just before Manutuke. Turn up Papatu Rd for 1.5km.

OPENING HOURS
Summer: Mon–Sat, 10am–5pm.
Winter: by appointment

WINERY SALES
Cellar door, mail order, Internet

PRICE RANGE $17–$45

TASTING & TOURS
Tasting is free of charge. Tours by appointment.

PICNIC AREA
In summer months only.

OWNERS
James & Annie Millton

WINEMAKER
James Millton

DATE ESTABLISHED 1984

The Millton Vineyards

In 1984 James and Annie Millton established their winery on the banks of the Te Arai River near Manutuke where the early settlers first planted grapevines in 1871. The Millton Vineyards is New Zealand's first fully certified commercial organic vineyard and winery. Following the indications given by Dr Rudolf Steiner, bio-dynamic techniques are used in all areas of production. Their philosophy is to produce a selection of specialised table wines expressive of the natural flavours found in the grapes harvested from their vineyards, all located in the Gisborne region. As well, they wish to enhance the life quality of the land they are responsible for and leave it in an improved state for future generations. In 2003 James was one of two Southern Hemisphere wine-growers invited to attend the first Bio-dynamic Winegrowers exhibition, in conjunction with the Vinexpo Exhibition, in Bordeaux, France.

At the cellar-door sales area at the winery visitors can taste and discuss the wine styles while enjoying a tranquil traditional garden setting. Tours of the bio-dynamic vineyards and tutored tastings of library stocks are also available by prior appointment.

WINES
Millton Chardonnay Opou Vineyard, Riesling Opou Vineyard, Chenin Blanc Te Arai Vineyard, Merlot Te Arai Vineyard, Gisborne Chardonnay
The Growers Series: Gewürtztraminer McIldowie Vineyard, Viognier Briant Vineyard
Clos de Ste Anne: Chardonnay, Pinot Noir and Viognier
All wines are certified organic except The Growers Series where each grower is a member of the Sustainable Wine Growing scheme.

RECENT AWARDS
Recognition has been achieved by winning numerous Gold and Silver medals, and trophies at national and international wine competitions.

TW Wines

Gisborne is well known as New Zealand's Chardonnay capital. A narrow 20-kilometre strip of this area, from Ormond to Hexton (just northwest of Gisborne), known as 'The Golden Slope' has given rise to most of Gisborne's gold medal-winning Chardonnays. This is Gisborne's very own Côte D'Or, paralleling France's great wine region of Burgundy. The name TW stands for Tietjen Witters — two good friends, Paul Tietjen and Geordie Witters, both respected grape-growers who each have a vineyard on these golden slopes. The TW wines — that combine the best hand-picked grapes from both vineyards — have a unique character with forward fruit flavours arising from the distinctive terroir.

A visit to the vineyard is also a unique and memorable experience, where by a simple phone call you can undertake a personalised tour with either Paul or Geordie. Because they do not have a winery, the tour through the vineyard is an introduction to the vines and grapes, and is then followed by a tutored tasting. Or you can make an appointment to just taste and purchase.

Back Ormond Rd, Gisborne
Tel: 021 864 818 (Paul) or 0274 502 339 (Geordie)
Email: info@twwines.co.nz
Website: www.twwines.co.nz

DIRECTIONS
The vineyard is approximately 5 minutes' drive along Back Ormond Rd, one of the main roads running north from Gisborne City.

WINERY SALES
Cellar door, retail, mail order, Internet

PRICE RANGE $16–$27

TASTING & TOURS
Tasting is free of charge. Tours by appointment.

PICNIC AREA
Visitors are welcome to bring a picnic and enjoy the vineyard setting.

OWNERS
The Tietjen and Witters families

WINEMAKER
Anita Ewart-Croy

DATE ESTABLISHED 1973

WINES
TW Gisborne Viognier, Estate Chardonnay, Chardonnay, Botrytis Sémillon, Botrytis Chardonnay, Makauri (Malbec/Merlot blend)

AWARDS
Since the 1989 vintage, grapes from the two vineyards have won 45 national and international medals, including nine golds and two trophies at the 1997 National Wine Show of Australia and the 1998 Air New Zealand Wine Awards.

Hawke's Bay

HAWKE'S BAY, on the sheltered east coast of the North Island, is the country's second largest wine region, producing 23.5 per cent of the national crop. Grape-growing takes place from Mahia Peninsula in the north to Cape Kidnappers in the south of Hawke's Bay. There is a diversity of sites within the region, with vineyards spread from high-country foothills in the west, down warmer inland flats and along the cooler coastal plains around the cities of **Hastings** and **Napier**. With a range of soils and climatic influences, there are almost a dozen sub-regions, from **Esk Valley** in the north, inland in the west to **Crownthorpe**, and south to **Central Hawke's Bay**. These produce a wide diversity of varieties and styles, although Hawke's Bay has made its name with soft, fruit-flavoured Sauvignon Blancs, well-rounded Chardonnays and robust reds, including Merlot and Cabernet Sauvignon.

The warm, sunny Hawke's Bay, with the Art Deco city of Napier at its centre, draws visitors to its seaside boulevards and beaches, historical cities, wine trails and restaurants.

For more information on the Hawke's Bay region visit www.hawkesbaynz.com or contact Napier Visitor Information Centre: 100 Marine Parade, Napier, (06) 834 1911, info@napiervic.co.nz, or Hastings Visitor Information Centre: Russell Street, Hastings, (06) 873 5526, vic@hastingstourism.co.nz.

Black Barn Vineyard

Esk Valley Estate

Church Road Winery

HISTORY

Hawke's Bay has a 150-year heritage in wine. Marist missionaries planted the first vines at Pakowhai south of Napier in 1851, and by the 1890s the Mission was selling wines, as were several wealthy landowners. Spanish-born Anthony Vidal was the first commercial winemaker to begin operation, in 1905. The industry languished through the Depression and world wars but several pioneers were producing fortified wines. McWilliam's, established in 1947, was the major winery for many years, producing well-known white and red wines. In the 1960s contract grape-growing helped Hawke's Bay onto the wine map but it was not until the 1990s that the area under vines mushroomed, and careful selection of sites and varieties saw superior wines being produced.

SOILS

There is a diverse range of soil types, from fertile, silty loams with a high water table to free-draining shingle. There are 22 categories of soil types on the Heretaunga Plains alone, from stones to hard pans to heavy silts. Most districts have alluvial flood-plain soils of moderate fertility. Three meandering rivers in the region have laid down deposits over a long period of time. Generally, soils become more fertile the further they are from old riverbeds.

CLIMATE

Hawke's Bay enjoys high sunshine hours, with warm summer temperatures and dryish autumns, but it is frost-prone in cooler months. Shelter from the western mountains means the Bay is less windy than many other regions. Its east coast location also means rainfall is moderate.

GRAPE VARIETIES AND WINE STYLES

Major varieties are Chardonnay, Merlot, Cabernet Sauvignon, Sauvignon Blanc, Pinot Noir and Cabernet Franc. Sweet dessert wines and sparkling wines are also produced. The Chardonnays display rich flavours of stone-fruit and citrus, while Merlot and Cabernet Sauvignon produce wines with rich fruit flavours, among them some of the country's finest reds. The Bay's soft Sauvignon Blancs with melon and stone-fruit flavours are becoming well known. Pinot Noir does not generally ripen well enough in the region's warmth to make premium stand-alone wines, although they do produce good sparkling wine.

SUB-REGIONS

Esk Valley, near the coast north of Napier, cooled by sea breezes.

Dartmoor Valley, based around the Tutaekuri River, often experiences high temperatures, known for both reds and whites.

Crownthorpe (Matapiro), a new sub-region in the west, thought to suit early-ripening varieties.

Mangatahi, in the western foothills, higher than the plains, produces excellent Chardonnay.

Korokipo and Fernhill, including warm sites around the Tutaekuri River that produce excellent Chardonnay. Fertile plains land produces mainly Sauvignon Blanc.

Gimblett Gravels, an area of free-draining alluvial gravels on the inland edge of the Heretaunga Plains, known especially for its late-ripening reds and Chardonnay.

The Red Metal Triangle, also on the edge of the Heretaunga Plains, named for its red metal subsoils that suit earlier-ripening red varieties like Merlot.

Havelock Hills and Te Mata, around the town of Havelock North, has some of the sunniest sites in the region, producing great reds and whites.

Te Awanga, on the southern coastal edge of the Bay, cooled by sea breezes, is producing excellent Chardonnay and early-ripening reds.

Central Hawke's Bay, around the towns of Waipukurau and Waipawa, are new grape-growing areas, higher and cooler than the plains, with free-draining soils.

Church Road Winery

Events

- **Harvest Hawke's Bay**. A celebration of wine, food, music and art. Held annually in early February at various sites.
- **Hawke's Bay Blossom Festival**. Food, wine and fun to celebrate the bounty of Hawke's Bay's orchards. Held annually In mid-September al various sites.
- **A Month of Wine & Roses**. Held in November.

For more information visit www.hawkesbaynz.com/events

Vidal Estate

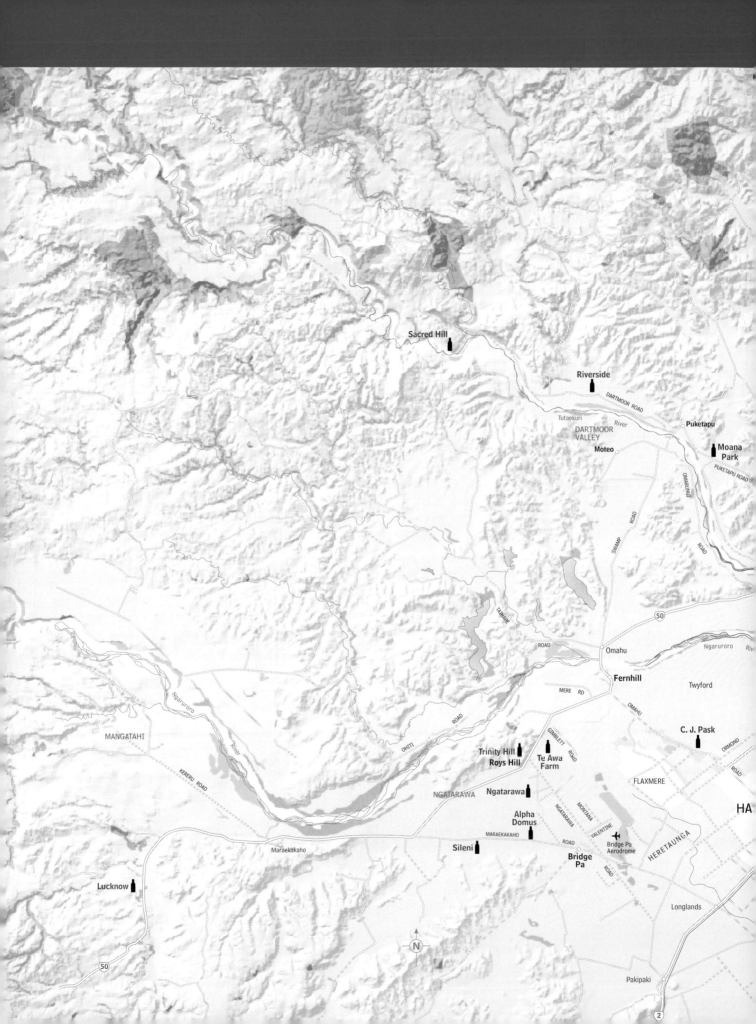

Sacred Hill

Riverside

DARTMOOR ROAD

Tutaekuri   River

Puketapu

DARTMOOR
VALLEY   Moana
Moteo   Park

PUKETAPU ROAD

OMARUNUI

SWAMP

ROAD

50

TAIHAPE   ROAD

Omahu   Ngaruroro   Riv

Fernhill   Twyford

MERE   RD

OMAHU

Ngaruroro   C. J. Pask

MANGATAHI   GIMBLETT

River   FLAXMERE

KERERU ROAD

Trinity Hill   ORMOND
Roys Hill   Te Awa
Farm

ROAD

OHITI

NGATARAWA   Ngatarawa

NGATARAWA

Alpha   MONTANA
Domus

VALENTINE

MARAEKAKAHO

Maraekakaho   Sileni   Bridge   Bridge Pa   HERETAUNGA   HA
Pa   Aerodrome

ROAD

Lucknow

Longlands

N

50

Pakipaki

2

Alpha Domus

Black Barn Vineyards

Ngatarawa Wines

Kim Crawford Wines

Moana Park Winery

The Alpha Domus vineyard and winery is managed and operated by two generations of the Ham family. The name represents how the venture came into being: 'Alpha' represents the Ham family as it is a grouping of each family member's first initial and 'Domus' is the Latin word for house or home.

Located just near the Bridge Pa aerodrame, the logo uses the image of a Tiger Moth aeroplane, often seen flying over the vineyard. All wines are made from estate-grown grapes with 35 hectares under vines. The alluvial soils characteristic of this area combined with low rainfall and high summer temperatures provide ideal growing conditions for high-quality fruit.

WINES

Alpha Domus Sauvignon Blanc, Chardonnay, Sémillon, Pinot Noir, Merlot, Merlot/Cabernet, The Navigator (Merlot/Cabernet Sauvignon/Cabernet Franc/Malbec), Leonarda Late Harvest Sémillon
AD Sémillon, Chardonnay, The Aviator (Merlot/Cabernet Sauvignon/Cabernet Franc/Malbec), Noble Selection

ALPHA DOMUS
HAWKES BAY
2001
THE NAVIGATOR
52% CABERNET, 35% MERLOT, 13% MALBEC

750ML ALC 13.5% by VOL
Produced by Alpha Domus Limited
Maraekakaho Road, Hastings, New Zealand
WINE OF NEW ZEALAND

1829 Maraekakaho Road, Hastings
Tel: (06) 879 6752
Fax: (06) 879 6952
Email: wine@alphadomus.co.nz
Website: www.alphadomus.co.nz

DIRECTIONS Driving south out of Hastings on Maraekakaho Road from Stortford Lodge, turn right at the roundabout, where Maraekakaho Road continues. Drive through Bridge Pa and Alpha Domus is 1km on the right.

OPENING HOURS
Summer: 7 days, 10am–5pm
Winter: Fri–Mon, 10am–4pm

WINE SALES
Cellar door, retail, mail order

PRICE RANGE $16–$50

TASTING & TOURS
Tasting is free of charge. Tours by appointment.

PICNIC AREA
Tables with umbrellas by the cellar door with vineyard views.

OWNERS
The Ham family

WINEMAKER
Evert Nijzink

DATE ESTABLISHED 1995

Black Barn Vineyards

Black Barn is a small vineyard focusing on premium Bordeaux-style red varieties such as Merlot, Cabernet Sauvignon and Cabernet Franc; their award-winning whites include Chardonnay and Sauvignon Blanc. All wines are estate-grown and the fruit is hand-picked. With just over 20 acres of vines many of the wines are only available through the cellar door.

Its spectacular location on the warm north-facing slopes of the Te Mata foothills is not only an excellent location for grapegrowing, it also provides stunning views across Hawke's Bay to the ocean and mountains, a warm sheltered microclimate and a perfect situation for visitors to spend a few hours, a night, or even a week or two. You can taste wines, have lunch in the Bistro, spend a summer Saturday morning at the Village Growers Market, visit the Art Gallery, watch an evening concert in the amphitheatre, or all of the above by staying in one of their luxuriously appointed properties.

WINES
Black Barn Sauvignon Blanc, Rosé, Unoaked Chardonnay, Barrel-Fermented Chardonnay, Merlot Cabernet Franc (estate blend), Reserve Merlot

RECENT AWARDS
Although the vines are now 10 years old the Black Barn brand was only launched in 2003. It is only starting to enter award rounds now.

OTHER ACTIVITIES
Village Growers Market: open Saturday mornings during the summer. Black Barn Gallery: features smaller works by leading New Zealand artists. Large purpose-built terraced amphitheatre for summer concerts.

Black Barn Rd, Havelock North
Tel: (06) 877 7935
Fax: (06) 877 7816
Email: blackbarn@blackbarn.com
Website: www.blackbarn.com

DIRECTIONS
Follow Te Mata Rd out of the Havelock North village. Soon after you reach the 70kph zone you will find Black Barn on the right.

OPENING HOURS
Cellar door: 7 days, 10am–5pm. Bistro: Wed–Sun, 12pm–3pm for lunch. Functions by arrangement.

WINERY SALES
Cellar door, retail, Internet

PRICE RANGE
$20–$60

TASTING & TOURS
Tasting fee: $2, refundable on purchase. Tours by appointment.

CAFÉ
Black Barn Bistro: Open airy restaurant with beautiful views, a sheltered vine-covered courtyard for outdoor dining and innovative seasonal menu. Reservations: (06) 877 7985.

OTHER FACILITIES
Private functions and dinners can be held in the Bistro, Art Gallery, Underground Cellars and the Growers Market.

PICNIC AREA
The vineyard has walkways and park-like grounds to explore and find your own picnic spot.

ACCOMMODATION
The Black Barn private retreats are Hawke's Bay's most sought after accommodation. In spectacular locations and luxuriously appointed, they sleep from 1–6 couples. Two of the six properties are on the vineyard; the others are at a nearby beach, a river and Cape Kidnappers. View at www.blackbarn.com.

OWNERS
Andy Coltart & Kim Thorp

WINEMAKER
Dave McKee

DATE ESTABLISHED 2003

Brookfields Road, Meeanee
Napier
Tel: (06) 834 4615
Fax: (06) 834 4389
Email: brookfields.vineyards@xtra.co.nz
Website: www.brookfieldsvineyards.co.nz

DIRECTIONS
Turn off SH2 10 minutes south of
Napier into Awatoto Road; turn left into
Brookfields Rd. The winery is on the
left.

OPENING HOURS
7 days, 11am–4.30pm (closed
Christmas Day and Good Friday)

WINERY SALES
Cellar door, retail, mail order, Internet

PRICE RANGE $18+

TASTING AND TOURS
Tasting is free of charge. Tours by
appointment.

RESTAURANT
Open daily for lunches; evening
functions by prior arrangement:
(06) 834 4389

OTHER FACILITIES
Available for private functions, from
corporate and promotional events to
weddings or intimate gatherings.

OWNER
Peter Robertson

WINEMAKER
Peter Robertson

DATE ESTABLISHED 1937

Brookfields Vineyards

Brookfields Vineyards is situated alongside the glistening waters of the Tutaekuri River, between Napier and Hastings. Their winemaking philosophy is to make fruit-driven wines that are enjoyable in their youth, go well with food, and for those that can resist temptation, wines that respond well to cellaring.

Brookfields is an impressive venue during the day with its beautiful rose gardens, views of the vineyard, handmade brick winery and tasting room, and the pétanque court. For visitors, a glass of Brookfields wine with lunch at the winery is an experience not to be missed. The pairing of fine cuisine using only the best Hawke's Bay produce and a quality Brookfield wine is perfect. Having lunch amidst the gardens or indoors where you will be surrounded by barrels of wine maturing in the racks and an outstanding collection of Piera McArthur paintings all forming a unique series called 'Aspects of Music', is an idyllic experience. Centre stage is the inglenook fireplace that provides a cosy ambience throughout the winter months.

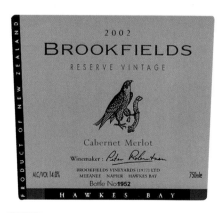

WINES
Brookfields Riesling, Sauvignon Blanc,
Gewürztraminer, Bergman Estate
Chardonnay, Marshall Bank Chardonnay,
Ohiti Cabernet Sauvignon, Hillside Syrah
Cabernet Merlot

RECENT AWARDS
2002 Hillside Syrah Reserve – Top 100,
Blue-Gold & Trophy: Sydney International
Wine Challenge 2004; 2000 Hillside Syrah
Reserve – Gold: Air NZ Wine Awards
2003; 2000 Gold Label Cabernet Merlot –
5 Stars: *Winestate* magazine; 2001 Marshall
Bank Chardonnay – 4½ Stars: Michael
Cooper's *Buyer's Guide to NZ Wines* 2004

150 Church Road, Taradale
Napier
Tel: (06) 844 2053
Fax: (06) 844 3378
Email: thecellardoor@churchroad.co.nz
Website: www.churchroad.co.nz

DIRECTIONS
The Church Road Winery is on Church Road in Taradale, just 15 minutes from the Napier and Hastings town centres.

OPENING HOURS
7 days, 9am–5pm

WINERY SALES
Cellar door, retail, mail order (through the winery newsletter Church Road Cellar Notes)

PRICE RANGE $15–$99

WINE TASTING
Sample the wines that have been specially selected (no charge for these samples) or buy a Cellarmaster's Tasting Tray.

WINERY TOURS
Daily at 10am, 11am, 2pm and 3pm: small charge applicable; bookings for groups essential.

RESTAURANT
Church Road Restaurant. Lunch from 11.30am daily. Bookings advisable. Reservations: (06) 844 2053.

OTHER PRODUCTS
Older vintage Church Road wines and the limited-edition Church Road Cuvée Series, other premium wines and quality gifts and accessories.

OTHER FACILITIES
The historic Church Road Winery offers superb function and conference facilities, and is an ideal venue for business meetings, social events or special private celebrations.

OWNERS
Church Road Winery

WINEMAKERS
Tony Prichard & Chris Scott

DATE ESTABLISHED 1897

Church Road Winery

Founded in 1897, the historic Church Road Winery offers a uniquely New Zealand wine tourism experience. Trace a fascinating journey through winemaking history with a tour of the country's first wine museum and visit the magnificent Tom McDonald Cellar, created in memory of the father of quality red-winemaking in New Zealand. The museum, opened in 1998, celebrates the history of wine. Housed underground in wine tanks once used by Tom McDonald, some of the exhibits on display date back to Roman times. Others are among the oldest winemaking relics in the country, while local sculptor Owen Yeomans' lifelike mannequins bring the scene alive. The Tom McDonald Cellar contains hundreds of oak barrels used for the maturation of premium wines.

Sample the wines that have been specially selected or buy a Cellarmaster's Tasting Tray. For those who just want to relax in an elegant rustic setting, modern European-style food can be enjoyed indoors in the charming Tiffen Room or served alfresco in the picturesque garden.

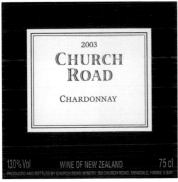

WINES
Tom, Virtu, Church Road Reserve Merlot Cabernet and Chardonnay, Noble Sémillon; Church Road Chardonnay, Sauvignon Blanc, Merlot Cabernet

RECENT AWARDS
Tom 1998 – 5 stars: Michael Cooper, *Sunday Star-Times* (22 Dec 02); Church Road Reserve Chardonnay 2002, Church Road Reserve Noble Sémillon 1999, Church Road Reserve Hawke's Bay Merlot Cabernet 2000 – All 5 stars: Michael Cooper, *Buyer's Guide to New Zealand Wines 2004*

Main Road, Bay View
Napier
Tel: (06) 836 6411
Fax (06) 836 6413
Email: enquiries@eskvalley.co.nz
Website: www.eskvalley.co.nz

DIRECTIONS
12km north of Napier on SH2. Ten mins
from Napier Airport.

OPENING HOURS
7 days, 10am–5pm

WINERY SALES
Cellar door, retail, mail order and
Internet

PRICE RANGE From $18.95

TASTING & TOURS
Tasting is free of charge. Tours by
appointment only ($5 pp).

OTHER FACILITIES
Picnic area with tables

OWNER
George Fistonich

WINEMAKER
Gordon Russell

DATE ESTABLISHED 1933

Esk Valley Estate

Esk Valley Estate is one of Hawke's Bay's leading boutique wineries specialising in creating exceptional hand-crafted wines. Winemaker Gordon Russell places emphasis on quality rather than quantity and his quirky yet fun character helps give Esk Valley wines their uniqueness. Wine writer Joëlle Thompson named Gordon as one of the top ten winemakers in the country in *Panorama* magazine: 'Red-wine lovers should thank their lucky stars that Russell eschewed a career in town planning for one in wine,' enthused Thompson.

A trip to Esk Valley is an opportunity to taste and buy wines that are only sold through the cellar door, with limited-quantity wines including Riesling, Rosé, Chenin Blanc, Pinot Gris, Syrah, and Verdelho usually available. One of the most attractive vineyard sites in New Zealand, winery, cellar shop and famed terraced Vineyard are nestled in a small picturesque valley with stunning views over the Hawke's Bay coastline.

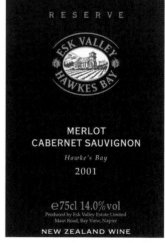

WINES

Black Label Range: Exhibit classic Hawke's Bay characteristics, with a unique richness and depth of flavour, and designed to complement a wide range of foods. Key varietals include Chardonnay, Sauvignon Blanc, Merlot and Merlot/Cabernet Sauvignon.

Reserve Range: Only produced when vintage conditions are ideal. Includes a Chardonnay and a Merlot/Malbec/Cabernet blend (consistently awarded gold medals and trophies).

Terraces: In outstanding vintage years, Esk Valley produces 'The Terraces'. Grapes for this extraordinary wine are sourced from the terraced Vineyard and it is only available for sale 'en primeur' (prior to bottling to registered purchasers) or by exception from the cellar door.

RECENT AWARDS

Esk Valley's position as one of New Zealand's most unique boutique wineries is reinforced by the awards it receives and in positive press comments both nationally and internationally. Four of the last five vintages of Esk Valley's Reserve Red have received 5 Stars from *Cuisine* magazine. Two of the last five vintages have been trophy winners in prestigious competitions.

C.J. Pask Winery

C.J. Pask has an impressive record of award-winning wines from some of New Zealand's oldest vines. One of the pioneers of the Gimblett Gravels appellation, they own 100 hectares of vineyards on Gimblett Road and are well known internationally for the production of Merlot, Chardonnay, Syrah and Bordeaux blends. The original production of one barrel of Cabernet Sauvignon has now increased to over 45,000 cases and the 2004 vintage has been one of the best, harvesting around 550 tonnes. At the Mediterranean-style winery they produce three tiers of wine in the Roy's Hill, Gimblett Road and Reserve ranges. Each offers a different style, from the fruit-driven, easy-drinking style of Roy's Hill, to the concentrated, full-bodied Reserve wines.

WINES
Roy's Hill Sauvignon Blanc, Chardonnay, Merlot and Cabernet Merlot, Gimblett Road Sauvignon Blanc, Chardonnay, Syrah, Merlot, Cabernet Merlot, Reserve Chardonnay, Syrah, Merlot, Declaration (Bordeaux blend)

RECENT AWARDS
Reserve Merlot 1998 – Bordeaux & Cabernet Trophy: International Wine Challenge, London 2000, Champion Wine of Show: Air New Zealand Wine Awards 2000; Kate Radburnd – Hawke's Bay Winemaker of the Year 2001

1133 Omahu Road, Hastings
Tel: (06) 879 7906
Fax: (06) 879 6428
Email: info@cjpaskwinery.co.nz
Website: www.cjpaskwinery.co.nz

DIRECTIONS On the Fernhill side of the Napier–Hastings Expressway/Omahu Rd Intersection, approx. 10 mins from Hastings City centre. Omahu Rd is a key arterial road running from Hastings.

OPENING HOURS
All year: Mon–Fri, 9am–5pm; Sat & public holidays, 10am–5pm; Sun, 11am–4pm

WINERY SALES Cellar door, retail, mail order, Internet

PRICE RANGE $14.50–$45

TASTING & TOURS Tasting is free of charge. Tours by appointment only.

OWNERS
Chris Pask, Kate Radburnd & John Benton

WINEMAKERS
Kate Radburnd & Russell Wiggins

DATE ESTABLISHED 1985

Kim Crawford Wines

Kim Crawford Wines is located in the quiet coastal settlement of Te Awanga in Hawke's Bay. The modern tasting room has sweeping views from Mahia Peninsula across the Bay to Cape Kidnappers, taking in rural farmland and the immaculately tended Te Awanga vineyards. Visitors are welcome to try the range of award-winning wines made from grapes sourced from vineyard sites in Hawke's Bay, Marlborough and Gisborne, where Kim believes the grapes grow best. There is a widely held belief at this winery that a happy working environment is transferred to the bottle … you can almost taste it in the wine!

WINES
Kim Crawford Marlborough Sauvignon Blanc, Unoaked Marlborough Chardonnay, Marlborough Dry Riesling, Marlborough Pinot Gris, Tietjen Briant Gisborne Chardonnay, Te Awanga Pinot Noir, Te Awanga Merlot, Tané

RECENT AWARDS
Kim Crawford Wines received over 60 awards in 2003.

ACCOMMODATION
Above the cellar door is a self-contained, 1 bedroom apartment. Includes ingredients for a Kiwi breakfast, antipasto platter and a bottle of wine per day. $200 per night for a 2-night stay. *Regrettably not suitable for children.*

Clifton Road, Te Awanga
Tel: (06) 875 0553
Fax: (06) 875 1188
Email: info@kimcrawfordwines.co.nz
Website: www.kimcrawfordwines.co.nz

DIRECTIONS
Just south of Clive, turn into Mill Road, follow the road to Haumoana and on to Clifton Road. Kim Crawford Wines is right next to Clearview.

OPENING HOURS
Dec–Easter: 7 days, 11am–6pm; Easter–Nov: Sat, Sun, Mon, 11am–5pm

WINERY SALES
Cellar door, retail, mail order

PRICE RANGE $15–$40

TASTING
Tasting is free of charge.

OTHER FOOD OPTIONS
Picnics and tasting platters made from locally sourced ingredients.

PICNIC AREA
Visitors are welcome to picnic on the lawn, enjoy the stunning view and the peace and tranquillity of this site. Tables and picnic blankets are supplied.

OWNERS
Vincor International

WINEMAKER
Kim Crawford

DATE ESTABLISHED 1996

Lucknow Estate Winery

This boutique Hawke's Bay winery is set on the terraces overlooking the Maraekakaho Stream, with views to the ranges beyond. Plantings are 90 per cent red wine, with vines split over two terrace sites that have very different soil types. Wherever possible, the handcrafted wines are 'single' vineyard, reflecting the character of each site and its fruit. The winery was designed to reflect the rural heritage of the region: untreated rough-sawn timber for the tasting room and plastered straw bales for the barrel room. Wine tasting and sales are available at the cellar door as well as vineyard platters in the terrace garden. Visitors are welcome and encouraged to bring a picnic.

WINES
Quarry Bridge Vineyard Merlot, Halterman (Merlot/Malbec), Gamay Noir, Pinot Gris Lomond BridgeVineyard Syrah Two Bridges Merlot/Malbec/Syrah

OTHER PRODUCTS
Ellesgrove olive oils and olives — Maraekakaho grown and produced.

3764 SH50, Maraekakaho, Hastings
Tel: (06) 874 9007
Fax: (06) 874 9008
Email: info@lucknowestate.com
website: www.lucknowestate.com

DIRECTIONS
On SH50, 2.7km past the Maraekakaho junction and 25km southwest of Hastings.

OPENING HOURS
Summer: 7 days, 10.30am–5.30pm; Winter: Mon–Fri, 10.30am–4pm

WINERY SALES Cellar door, retail, mail order, Internet

PRICE RANGE $16–$32

TASTING Tasting is free of charge. Large groups by appointment.

FOOD OPTIONS Delicious platters with a selection of local produce that includes cheeses, fruit pastes, olives and breads. Available summer months only.

PICNIC AREA Visitors are welcome to bring a picnic or purchase one of the vineyard platters to enjoy in the terrace garden or rustic shaded glade. Facilities: Tables, barbecue, pétanque.

OTHER FACILITIES
The terrace garden is the perfect spot for functions. Grassed marquee sites are available.

OWNERS Bruce Nimon, Colin Wylie & Lance Dear

WINEMAKER Bruce Nimon

DATE ESTABLISHED 1998

Moana Park Winery

In 1979 Ron Smith planted his first vines in Hawke's Bay's Dartmoor Valley. In 2000 (over two decades and 200,000 vines later) he began producing wines under his own label. Moana Park is now a successful privately owned boutique winery with an American-style barn for its cellar door along with a newly completed winery and barrel room. There is a friendly atmosphere and visitors are encouraged to bring a picnic and enjoy their wines in a charming rural setting. Wines are mostly single varietals that express the characteristics of the grapes sourced exclusively from their two family-owned vineyards: in Puketapu, where the winery and cellar door are situated, and nearby in the heart of the Dartmoor Valley.

WINES
Moana Park Pascoe Series (entry level) Sauvignon Blanc, Chardonnay, Rosé, Merlot Cabernet, Syrah Vineyard Tribute Pinot Gris, Chardonnay, Merlot, Malbec, Cabernet Franc, Syrah Symphony (top red blend)

RECENT AWARDS
Pascoe Series Sauvignon Blanc 2002 – 85/100: *Wine Spectator* (Sept 2003); Vineyard Tribute Cabernet Franc 2002 – Silver: Air New Zealand Wine Awards 2003; Dartmoor Valley Pinot Gris 2003 & Barrique Fermented Chardonnay 2001 – Silver: Bragato Wine Awards 2003

530 Puketapu Rd, Napier
Tel: (06) 844 8269
Fax: (06) 844 0923
Email: sales@moanapark.co.nz
Website: www.moanapark.co.nz

DIRECTIONS
From Taradale the winery is just 5km along Puketapu Rd (5 mins from Church Rd).

OPENING HOURS
Labour Weekend–Easter: 7 days, 11am–5pm; Easter–Labour Weekend: 7 days, 1pm–3pm

WINERY SALES Cellar door, retail, mail order

PRICE RANGE $11–$35

TASTING & TOURS
Tasting is free of charge. Tours by appointment.

FOOD OPTIONS Cheese platters available by arrangement.

PICNIC AREA BYO picnic. Picnic facilities: tables, pétanque.

OTHER FACILITIES
Marquee sites are available for weddings and functions.

OWNER
Ron Smith

WINEMAKER
Derek Clarke

DATE ESTABLISHED 2000

Mission Estate Winery

Mission Estate Winery is New Zealand's oldest wine producer. In 1838 a group of French missionaries established a Marist mission in New Zealand. Besides being a teaching order, the Fathers followed the tradition of winemaking and grapes were planted to produce both sacramental and table wines. The first commercial sale was in 1870 when a parcel of mostly dry reds was sold. Mission has never lost sight of its French heritage, as over the years the Brothers of the Order have travelled to France to study and learn viticultural and winemaking techniques.

Today Mission Estate is one of Hawke's Bay's largest established wineries, with a well-earned reputation in New Zealand and overseas as a producer of consistent quality, value-for-money wines. The beautiful old seminary building has been faithfully restored and is home to the cellar door, where you walk through time and history in a setting that complements the old and new. The world-class restaurant offers both indoor and outdoor dining and you can enjoy fabulous vineyard and city views, delicious cuisine, discerning service and award-winning wines

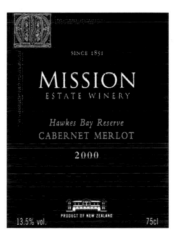

WINES
Labels: Mission Estate, Mission Reserve, Mission Jewelstone (super-premium)
Wine styles: Chardonnay, Sauvignon Blanc, Riesling, Gewürztraminer, Pinot Gris, Ice wine, Sémillon, Merlot, Cabernet Merlot, Cabernet Sauvignon, Syrah

RECENT AWARDS
Mission Estate wines regularly receive awards at the major New Zealand wine shows.

OTHER ACTIVITIES
Gallery at the Mission: Stocks an extensive range of local art and craft including pottery, jewellery, woodwork, furniture, paintings, and hand-woven woollen rugs and scarves.

198 Church Road, Taradale
Napier
Tel: (06) 845 9350
Fax: (06) 844 6023
Email: missionwinery@clear.net.nz
Website: www.missionestate.co.nz

DIRECTIONS
Mission Estate is on Church Rd in Taradale, just 15 mins from Napier and Hastings town centres.

OPENING HOURS
Cellar door: Mon–Thurs, 8.30am–5.30pm; Fri–Sat, 8.30am–7pm; Sun, 10am–4.30pm. Restaurant: 7 days, 10am–late. The Gallery at the Mission: 7 days, 10am–5pm

WINERY SALES
Cellar door, retail, mail order, Internet

PRICE RANGE $14.95–$35.00

TASTING & TOURS
Tasting is free of charge. Groups larger than 10 persons by appointment. Winery history and underground barrel room tours: Mon–Sat, 10.30am & 2pm. Private tours & tasting: $2 pp.

RESTAURANT
Reservations: (06) 845 9354

EVENTS
The annual Mission Estate concert is held in February. A unique event set outdoors in a natural amphitheatre with a line-up of memorable acts. For information: www.missionconcert.co.nz.

OWNERS
Marist Holdings (Greenmeadows) Ltd

WINEMAKER
Paul Mooney

DATE ESTABLISHED 1851

Ngatarawa Wines

Ngatarawa (pronounced Naa-taa-ra-wa) is owned by the Corban family whose winemaking heritage spans over 100 years in New Zealand. Established in 1981 on ancient riverbed soils, Ngatarawa is the key pioneer in The Triangle, west of Hastings at Bridge Pa, and is acclaimed for Sauvignon Blanc, Chardonnay, Bordeaux-style Merlot-based reds and Noble Harvest Riesling. The winemaking philosophy of 'best grapes from best regions' sees Ngatarawa also source grapes from Gisborne, Martinborough and Marlborough. The Ngatarawa style is a fusion of new world flavour and old world structure; the wines have palate texture, flavour intensity and complexity. A visit to Ngatarawa is an opportunity to enjoy award-winning wines and renowned hospitality in their historic racing stables.

NGATARAWA
Life, times told in wine.

WINES
Label: Stables (softer, everyday range), Glazebrook (regional reserve), Alwyn (winemakers' selection). Wine styles: Sauvignon Blanc, Chardonnay, Merlot, Merlot and Cabernet blends, Syrah, Pinot Noir and Riesling for dessert wine.

RECENT AWARDS
Alwyn Chardonnay 2002 – 5 Stars: Michael Cooper, *Sunday Star-Times* (Feb 2004), 5 Stars: Peter Saunders, *Winestate* (May/Jun 2004); Glazebrook Marlborough Sauvignon Blanc 2003 – Silver: Air NZ Wine Awards 2003

305 Ngatarawa Road
Bridge Pa, Hastings
Tel: (06) 879 7603
Freephone: 0508 STABLES
Fax: (06) 879 6675
Email: info@ngatarawa.co.nz
Website: www.ngatarawa.co.nz

DIRECTIONS Driving south out of Hastings from Stortford Lodge, turn right into Marae-kakaho Rd at the roundabout. Continue approx 3 km and turn right into Ngatarawa Rd.

OPENING HOURS
7 days, 10am–5pm (except Christmas Day and Good Friday)

WINERY SALES Cellar door, retail, mail order, Internet

PRICE RANGE $14.95–$100

TASTING & TOURS
Tasting is free of charge. Groups and tours by appointment only.

FOOD OPTIONS Platters arranged if booked in advance.

PICNIC AREA In picturesque landscaped grounds, with views over the vines. Picnic tables, gas BBQ, pétanque.

OWNERS Cousins, Alwyn and Brian Corban

WINEMAKERS
Alwyn Corban and Peter Gough

DATE ESTABLISHED 1981

Riverside Wines

Rachel and Ian Cadwallader established Riverside Wines in 1989 on Ian's family farm, 'Rosemount', settled by his great-great-grandparents in 1851. The farm now runs sheep and cattle along with a 33-hectare vineyard and winery. The nearby Tutaekuri River and its trout-fishing reputation prompted the name and the logo of the leaping trout. Committed to producing premium wines that are affordable and enjoyable, Riverside uses almost entirely estate-grown grapes to ensure the high quality of their product. A visit to this working vineyard/winery/farm is a real Kiwi country experience and visitors are welcome to picnic in the grounds, taste the wines and take in the beautiful views across the vineyards and the Dartmoor Valley.

WINES
Riverside Wines produces two tiers of wines: the super-premium Stirling Reserve range and the premium range, ideal for everyday consumption. Stirling Reserve range: Merlot Cabernet, Chardonnay, Pinotage. Premium range: Chardonnay, Sauvignon Blanc, Rosé, Merlot, Cabernet Sauvignon

CADWALLADERS
Riverside
NEW ZEALAND
SAUVIGNON BLANC
750 ML · 2004 · 12.5% ALC. BY VOL.
Product of New Zealand

434 Dartmoor Rd
Puketapu, Napier
Tel: (06) 844 4942
Fax: (06) 844 4671
Email: info@riversidewines.co.nz
Website: www.riversidewines.co.nz

DIRECTIONS
4.3km from Puketapu, on right-hand side of Dartmoor Rd.

OPENING HOURS Labour Weekend & 27 Dec–28 Feb: 7 days, 11am–4pm (closed New Year's Day)

WINE SALES Cellar door, retail, mail order, Internet

PRICE RANGE $15–$28

TASTING & TOURS
Tasting is free of charge. Tours by appointment.

FOOD OPTIONS
Cheeses, antipasti, patés.

PICNIC AREA Tables and chairs with umbrellas and barbecue are in the winery garden. You can also picnic in a shady tree area near the vineyard.

OTHER PRODUCTS
'Simply Lavender' body products, Capercaillie Wine from Hunter Valley, NSW

EVENTS & ACTIVITIES
Scarecrow Day in March. A fun family day where scarecrows are made for a competition and auctioned for charity. Quilt exhibition by local quilters at Labour Weekend (on even years).

OWNERS
Rachel & Ian Cadwallader

WINEMAKER Mark Cairns

DATE ESTABLISHED 1989

2016 Maraekakaho Rd
Bridge Pa, Hastings
Tel: (06) 879 8768
Fax: (06) 879 7187
Email: info@sileni.co.nz
Website: www.sileni.co.nz

Sileni Estates

Sileni Estates offers the visitor a total wine and food destination experience in a spectacular setting. The winery is named after the Sileni who featured in Roman mythology alongside Bacchus, the God of Wine — together they celebrated good wine, good food and good company — now the mission of Sileni Estates.

The Cellar Store, incorporating the Wine Discovery Centre, is dedicated to tasting Sileni Estates' wines and to wine education in general. You will also find an amazing gourmet food store and a comprehensive display of French winemaking antiques. Sileni Estates Restaurant showcases the best Hawke's Bay produce matched with your choice of Sileni wines, and you can choose between an intimate dining room or the alfresco courtyard terrace.

Sileni's modern new winery is committed to providing ultra-premium quality wines that achieve world status. Crafted using traditional techniques, wines are based on classic varieties including Merlot, Cabernet Franc, Malbec and Sémillon from Bordeaux, as well as Pinot Noir and Chardonnay from Burgundy.

WINES
Labels: Sileni Estates Cellar Selection (CS), Estate Selection (ES), Exceptional Vintage (EV)
Wine Styles: Merlot/Cabernet Franc/Malbec, Pinot Noir, Sémillon, Chardonnay

RECENT AWARDS
Sileni Estates' flagship varietals (Merlot, Chardonnay and Sémillon) are consistently multi-award-winning wines. Recent awards for the Estate Selection wines include:

Sileni Estates Estate Selection Sémillon 2002 – Gold: Japan International Wine Challenge 2003; Sileni Estates Estate Selection Chardonnay 2002 – Gold: International Chardonnay Challenge Gisborne 2003; Sileni Estates Estate Selection Merlot Cabernets 2000 – Gold: Air New Zealand Wine Awards 2003, Gold: Hong Kong International Wine Challenge 2003

OTHER ACTIVITIES
The Sileni Culinary School offers excellence in instruction, within a total culinary learning experience. Day and evening classes are offered for both the enthusiast interested in

good food and the professional chef wishing to hone their skills.

The Gourmet Cellar Store has a controlled-environment cheese larder, stocks gourmet food products from around the world and supports and showcases Hawke's Bay producers along with a wide range of wine paraphernalia.

The Wine Discovery Centre has a variety of tours and tastings to accommodate a range wine and food interests.

DIRECTIONS
Head south out of Hastings along Maraekakaho Road. Follow the signs to Bridge Pa and Sileni is 3km further on.

OPENING HOURS
Cellar shop: 7 days, 10am–5pm.
Restaurant: 7 days, lunch from 11am, evenings for group bookings (see below).

WINERY SALES
Cellar door, retail, mail order, Internet

PRICE RANGE $19.50–$99

TASTING & TOURS
Tasting fee: $5 pp, refundable on purchase. Tours available 7 days, 11am & 2pm: $12 pp (includes wine tasting).

RESTAURANT
Open for casual lunches, and for private dining and functions for groups of 10 or more. Bookings essential. Reservations: (06) 879 4831.

OTHER FACILITIES
There is a range of facilities for private functions, meetings, conferences and weddings for groups of 10–120 people.

OWNER
Graeme Avery

WINEMAKER
Grant Edmonds

DATE ESTABLISHED 1998

Sacred Hill

Te Awa Winery

Sacred Hill was established in 1986 by the Mason family, who have farmed in Hawke's Bay for over 30 years. The name is derived from the translation of Puketapu ('Sacred Hill'), the small village close to the Mason family's property. Their focus is on producing multi-award-winning handcrafted wines from vineyards in the Dartmoor Valley and Gimblett Gravels area of Hawke's Bay and Marlborough. The picturesque cellar door has spectacular views over the Dartmoor Valley. This is an idyllic country setting in which to experience Sacred Hill's wonderful array of wines. The staff are renowned for their friendly and informative approach to wine-tasting, making Sacred Hill one of Hawke's Bay's more popular winery destinations.

Te Awa is a unique place. The full name in Maori — Te Awa o Te Atua — means River of God, a reference to the subterranean stream over which Te Awa is sited. The winery is situated in the heart of the Gimblett Gravels winegrowing region and considerable care is taken in the growing, making, and blending of their single-estate wines. Te Awa's rustic charm is complemented by its tranquil garden setting, and reflects the rural New Zealand landscape. Along with fine wines to taste and purchase in their cellar door, Te Awa's highly acclaimed winery restaurant offers an outstanding New Zealand wine and food experience.

WINES
Labels: Whitecliff, Reserve, Special Selection
Wine styles: Sauvignon Blanc, Chardonnay, Riesling, Pinot Gris, Nobel Selection Riesling, Botrytis Semillon, Merlot, Merlot/Malbec, Cabernet/Merlot, Pinot Noir

RECENT AWARDS
Sacred Hill Riflemans Chardonnay 2002 – New Zealand Wine Society Trophy, Champion Wine of Show: NZ Wine Society Royal Easter Show 2004; Sacred Hill Helmsman Cabernet Merlot 2000 – Gold: London International Wine Challenge 2003

WINES
Te Awa: Sauvignon Blanc, Chardonnay, Syrah, Pinotage, Boundary (Merlot predominant Bordeaux blend) and Zone 10 Cabernet Sauvignon
Longlands: Chardonnay, Rosé, Syrah, Cabernet Merlot, Merlot

RESTAURANT
The winery's restaurant features dishes inspired by fresh local Hawke's Bay produce and offers a comprehensive à la carte lunch menu that pairs dishes with Te Awa's estate-grown wines. Rustic outdoor tables in the tranquil garden are popular over summer or over winter choose a table close to the glowing open fire.

1033 Dartmoor Road, Puketapu
Tel: (06) 844 0138
Tel: (06) 879 8760 (admin)
Fax: (06) 879 4158 (admin)
Email: enquiries@sacredhill.com
Website: www.sacredhill.com

DIRECTIONS 10km from Puketapu on Dartmoor Rd.

OPENING HOURS Dec–Feb: 7 days, 11am–5pm

WINERY SALES Cellar door, retail, mail order, Internet

PRICE RANGE $15–$50

TASTING Tasting is free of charge. But for groups of over 10 people there is a small fee, refundable on purchase.

RESTAURANT
Sacred Hill Cellar Door specialises in French-style picnic boxes containing locally sourced fresh produce and breads.
Reservations: (06) 844 0138.

PICNIC AREA
There are plenty of beautiful picnic spots with tables and a pétanque court.

OWNERS
The Mason family

WINEMAKER
Tony Bish

DATE ESTABLISHED 1986

2375 State Highway 50
RD 5, Hastings
Tel: (06) 879 7602
Fax: (06) 879 7756
Email: winery@teawa.com
Website: www.teawa.com

DIRECTIONS On SH50, approx 3km south of the Fernhill/Omahu Rd intersection; or heading north, 5km from the SH50 Maraekakaho Rd junction (almost opposite Trinity Hill winery).

OPENING HOURS
Cellar Door: 7 days, 9am–5pm.
Restaurant: Summer, 7 days, 12pm–2.30pm; Winter, Thurs–Mon, 12pm–2pm

WINERY SALES Cellar door, retail, mail order, Internet

PRICE RANGE $17.95+

OTHER FACILITIES Te Awa offers a premier venue in a unique vineyard setting. Its versatile facilities are perfect for small conference meetings through to large private dinners and celebrations. Pétanque court available.

OWNERS
Julian Robertson and Reg Oliver

WINEMAKER
Jenny Dobson

DATE ESTABLISHED 1992

Trinity Hill

Trinity Hill is consistently rated in the elite 'Top Ten' New Zealand wineries. A medium-sized company, with a focus on quality rather than quantity, its wines are known for their great elegance, power, complexity and balance.

John Hancock and his partners chose the barren, stony Gimblett Road site in 1987 with a vision to produce wines that reflected the unique 'terroir'. The warm, free-draining and sheltered site was planted with mainly Bordeaux-style varieties plus Chardonnay. Another site in the Gimblett Gravels was added in 2001. Varieties now include those from Burgundy, Northern Rhône, Spain and Italy.

The stunning modern winery sits against rugged Roy's Hill, surrounded by award-winning gardens and manicured lawns. It has been recognised with a 'stand-out' building award by the New Zealand Institute of Architects. The cellar door is stylish and art exhibitions adorn the five-metre high walls. The staff are knowledgeable and friendly and make it their business to ensure you enjoy tasting the wines as you learn the stories behind them.

WINES
Wines are produced under two labels: Shepherds Croft (reflecting earlier-drinking styles) and Gimblett Road/Gimblett Gravels (full, elegant and powerful wines, benefiting from cellaring). Shepherds Croft: Sauvignon Blanc, Chardonnay, Merlot/Cabernet/Syrah; Hawke's Bay Pinot Noir, Rosé; High Country Pinot Noir; Wairarapa Riesling; Trinity Hill Gimblett Road: Merlot, Cabernet Sauvignon, Cabernet Sauvignon/Merlot, Syrah, Tempranillo, Montepulciano, Chardonnay; Gimblett Gravels Pinot Gris, Viognier

RECENT AWARDS
Trinity Hill wines have won the acclaim of wine writers, judges and enthusiasts around the world. Of recent significance: 2001 Gimblett Road Syrah & 2001 Cabernet Sauvignon/Merlot – Top 10 NZ Reds 2003 (#2 & #7): *Cuisine* magazine, Gold Medal: Air New Zealand Wine Awards 2003; 2001 Cabernet Sauvignon/Merlot – Trophy for Best Cabernet Sauvignon/Merlot: Air New Zealand Wine Awards 2003, Gold: Royal Easter Wine Show 2004.

OTHER ACTIVITIES
Beautiful gardens include the Persian courtyard with fountain, and a lushly planted valley with trickling stream. There are picnic tables throughout. Ongoing art exhibitions from local and visiting artists also feature.

2396 State Highway 50, Hastings
Tel: (06) 879 7778
Fax: (06) 879 7770
Email: enquiries@trinityhill.com
Website: www.trinityhill.com

DIRECTIONS
On SH50, approx 3km south of the Fernhill/Omahu Rd intersection, or, heading north, 5km from the SH50 Maraekakaho Rd junction. (Almost opposite Te Awa winery.)

OPENING HOURS
All year except major statutory holidays. Labour Weekend (Oct)–Easter: 7 days, 10am–5pm. After Easter–Labour Weekend: 7 days, 11am–4pm

WINERY SALES
Cellar door, retail, mail order, Internet

PRICE RANGE $18.95–$39.95

TASTING & TOURS
Tasting is free of charge for individuals; tour groups by prior arrangement. Tours by appointment.

OTHER PRODUCTS
Extensive range of artworks and stylish wine accessories

PICNIC AREA
Facilities available: picnic tables, BBQ (gas — by arrangement), children's play area

OWNERS
John Hancock, Trevor & Hanne Janes (Auckland), Robert & Robyn Wilson (London)

WINEMAKER
Warren Gibson

DATE ESTABLISHED 1987

913 St Aubyn Street East, Hastings
Phone: (06) 876 8105
Fax: (06) 876 5312
Email: enquiries@vidalestate.co.nz
Website: www.vidal.co.nz

DIRECTIONS

From Napier Airport head south to Hastings on the expressway. Turn left at the intersection after the Meanee Bridge on to Pakowhai Rd. Follow for approx 5km; turn left into St Aubyn St and follow to the end.

OPENING HOURS

Cellar door: Labour Weekend–Easter Sunday, Mon–Sat, 10am–6pm; Sun, 10am–5pm; rest of year: 7 days, 10am–5pm. Restaurant: 7 days, lunch 12–3pm, dinner from 6pm. Platter menu and bar: 12pm till late.

WINERY SALES

Cellar door, retail, mail order, Internet

PRICE RANGE $16.50+

TASTING & TOURS

Tasting by appointment, a small tasting fee for groups of 10 or more, refundable on purchase. Tours by appointment.

RESTAURANT

Reservations recommended: (06) 876 8105.

OTHER FACILITIES

Two private function rooms are available for conferences, events and weddings.

OWNER George Fistonich

WINEMAKER Rod McDonald

DATE ESTABLISHED 1905

Vidal Estate

Vidal Estate in the acclaimed Hawke's Bay winegrowing region produces premium contemporary wines which truly reflect the region and vineyards from which they are sourced. A trip to Vidal Estate not only allows you to try their award-winning wines but also to dine at the renowned Vidal Restaurant, that is fast developing a reputation as one of the top spots in Hawke's Bay. Its seasonal menu utilises fresh local produce and all meals have a suggested wine match from Vidal's superb range.

Vidal Estate was established in 1905 and named after its founder — Spanish-born Anthony Joseph Vidal, who purchased a property in Hastings and converted the stables on it into wine cellars. This site and many of its original features remain, although they are infused with the benefits of modern technology — an approach that extends through to winemaker Rod McDonald's winemaking philosophy.

WINES

The Estate Range: A premium varietal selection for immediate enjoyment. Includes Chardonnay, Sauvignon Blanc, Riesling, Pinot Noir, Syrah and a Merlot/Cabernet Sauvignon blend.

The Reserve: Only produced when vintage conditions are ideal. Includes the classic varietals Chardonnay, Cabernet Sauvignon/Merlot, Noble Sémillon.

Joseph Soler: One of New Zealand's pioneering winemakers, Joseph Soler was the key influence in Anthony Joseph Vidal's decision to migrate to this country. During the 1998 vintage, winemaker Rod McDonald saw a small parcel of Cabernet Sauvignon as being particularly distinctive. Released under the Joseph Soler label it has become a truly exceptional wine that critics applaud as one of the best reds in New Zealand.

RECENT AWARDS

Air New Zealand Wine Awards 2003 – all 15 Vidal Estate wines that competed received medals, including: Vidal Soler Syrah 2002 – Gold Medal and Trophy Champion Syrah; Vidal Soler Syrah 2002 – Trophy: Reserve Wine of the Show

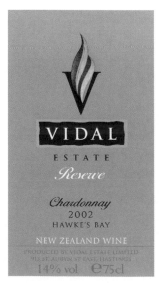

C.J. Pask

Te Awa Winery

Sileni Estates

Black Barn Vineyards

Wairarapa

WAIRARAPA, occupying a large area in the south-eastern North Island, is New Zealand's sixth largest wine region, producing some 3.6 per cent of the national crop. Its vineyards are scattered from near the city of **Masterton** south to around the town of **Martinborough**, the oldest and best-known sub-region. Sheltered in the west by the Rimutaka and Tararua ranges, and in the east by rolling hills, the broad valley of the Wairarapa enjoys a sunny, dry climate with vines planted on free-draining, low-vigour soils. This results in intensely flavoured grapes, especially powerful Pinot Noirs, the variety that makes up 60 per cent of plantings. Sauvignon Blanc, Chardonnay and Pinot Gris are also key wines. Most of the vineyards are boutique owner-operated businesses producing small quantities. The reputation of their wines, however, is impressive. The Wairarapa's location just over the Rimutaka Range from Wellington has made it a great weekend getaway for city dwellers keen on the restaurants and wine trails of this booming area.

For more information on the Wairarapa region visit www.wairarapanz.com or www.martinborough.com or contact Masterton Visitor Information Centre: 316 Queen Street, Masterton, (06) 370 0900, info@wairarapanz.com, or Martinborough Visitor Information Centre: 18 Kitchener Street, Martinborough, (06) 306 9043, martinborough@wairarapanz.com.

Jeff Barber

Springrock Vineyard, Te Kairanga Wines

Fairmont Estate

HISTORY

Wairarapa's first vines were planted in Masterton in 1883 by wealthy landowner William Beetham, and although the region showed early promise, little planting occurred until the 1970s. Publisher Alister Taylor established the first commercial venture on river terraces in Martinborough, and the following year Dr Neil McCallum of Dry River planted his small Martinborough vineyard. Others soon followed.

SOILS

Preferred sites in the region have free-draining, shallow loams with gravelly subsoils. The Masterton vineyards sit on light loams and heavy gravels. The sub-region of Gladstone and East Taratahi south of Masterton are chiefly free-draining river terraces. The best-known soils are those of the Martinborough Terraces, containing shallow loam topsoils above deep alluvial gravel subsoils laid down by the Huangarua River. The Te Muna sub-region south of Martinborough has similar soils.

CLIMATE

Climatically Wairarapa is more aligned to Marlborough than to any of the North Island regions. It has warm summer temperatures and a cool, dryish autumn. Cool nights help preserve the grapes' acidity and fruity characters. Exposure to strong north-westerly winds reduces yields, and spring frosts are a danger.

GRAPE VARIETIES AND WINE STYLES

Pinot Noir is Wairarapa's most planted and certainly most acclaimed grape variety, its success having helped drive the region's rapid development. Wairarapa Pinots are powerful wines with concentrated fruit flavours. Sauvignon Blanc is the next most planted variety and is produced in styles similar to Marlborough's aromatic wines. Rich styles of Chardonnay are produced along with Pinot Gris in a range of styles from light to rich.

SUB-REGIONS

Martinborough, in and around the township, with vineyards (including the earliest) planted on silty loams over gravelly river terrace soils. Produces acclaimed Pinot Noir and excellent

Sauvignon Blanc, Riesling, Chardonnay and Pinot Gris.

Te Muna, south-east of Martinborough, sharing similar soils, is a new sub-region, chiefly producing Pinot Noir.

South Martinborough, further south than Te Muna, sitting up against the foothills, produces mainly Pinot Noir.

Masterton, with chiefly silt loam soils over gravelly river terraces, is producing Pinot Noir, Sauvignon and Riesling. Many new vineyards are planted here.

Gladstone and East Taratahi (Dakins Road), south of Masterton and the site of some of the Wairarapa's earliest plantings, is expanding rapidly, with many new vineyards set to come on stream. Chief varieties are Sauvignon Blanc, Riesling, Pinot Noir and Pinot Gris.

Palliser Estate Wines

Te Kairanga Wnes

Margrain Vineyard

Murdoch James

Events

- **Toast Martinborough.** Wairarapa's premier wine and food festival, with various events centred on the township. Held annually in November.
- **Wairarapa Wine and Food Festival.** Music, entertainment, wine and food. Held in Masterton in February.

For more information visit www.wairarapanz.com/events

Kaituna

LOOPLINE RD Opaki

Ruamahanga River

Matahiwi

2

52

MASTERTON

SOLWAY CRESC

Te Ore Ore

Waingawa

Solstone

Aerodrome

Homebush

MANAIA ROAD

Waingawa River

CORNWALL ROAD

EAST TARATAHI ROAD

Clareville

Whangaehu River

Carterton

BRISTOL ROAD

DAKINS ROAD

PARK ROAD

Te Whanga

MORETON ROAD

CARTERS ROAD

GLADSTONE ROAD

Gladstone Vineyard

Fairmont Estate

River

Palliser

Margrain

Martinborough Vineyard

HUANGARUA RD

Huangarua River

PRINCESS STREET

DUBLIN STREET

CAMBRIDGE ROAD

PURUATANGA

Martinborough

NEW YORK STREET

ROAD

JELLICOE STREET

REGENT STREET

LAKE FERRY ROAD

To Coney

OXFORD STREET

Murdoch James

DUBLIN STREET

BOUNDARY ROAD

HINAKUR

Te Kairanga

Waikar

1

UPPER HUTT

Fairmont Estate

Fairmont Estate is a family business with a strong emphasis on creating handcrafted wines which reflect the best regional wine styles the area has to offer.

Situated in the sub-region of the Wairarapa known as Gladstone, it nestles amongst rolling hillsides with panoramic views of the Tararua Ranges. The vineyard lies on the free-draining alluvial Ruamahanga River terrace, which with its unique microclimate produces low-yielding, rich, concentrated grapes and wines that are distinctive and intense. Visitors are welcome at the cellar door and to enjoy the wines with a picnic in the grounds. There is a beautifully restored bungalow on the estate where you can stay and enjoy the peaceful surroundings.

WINES
Fairmont Estate Block One Chardonnay, Block One Pinot Noir, Pinot Noir, Chardonnay, Oaked Sauvignon Blanc, Sauvignon Blanc, Riesling

RECENT AWARDS
Fairmont Estate Sauvignon Blanc – 5 stars & Fairmont Estate Block One Pinot Noir 2001 – 4½ stars: *Winestate* magazine (Mar/Apr 2003); Jon McNab – New Zealand Winemaker of the Year 2003 finalist: *Winestate* magazine

Gladstone Rd, Gladstone
Tel: (06) 379 8498
Fax: (06) 379 5498
Email: pinot@xtra.co.nz
Website: www.fairmontestate.co.nz

DIRECTIONS
10 minutes east of Carterton and next door to Gladstone Estate.

OPENING HOURS
Sept–March: 7 days, 9am–5pm

WINERY SALES
Cellar door, retail, mail order, Internet

PRICE RANGE $15–$30

TASTING & TOURS
Tasting is free of charge. Tours by appointment.

PICNIC AREA
Outside the cellar door is a shady grassy area with a view over the vines.

ACCOMMODATION
Self-contained traditional bungalow that sleeps six with a B&B option, plus two B&B guest rooms in the homestead: $140 night for two people.
www.countrycottage.co.nz

OWNERS
The McNab family

WINEMAKER
Jon McNab

DATE ESTABLISHED 1992

Gladstone Vineyard

Gladstone Vineyard is one of the most beautiful vineyards in New Zealand — a restful spot where visitors can enjoy fine wines. Mature trees and landscaped grounds surround this charming winery with its elegant historic homestead nearby. Over the summer the wine garden and café is the perfect spot to spend a day out, where you can enjoy great food and a glass of wine followed by a game of pétanque or a walk round the vineyard or the pond. This is the ideal romantic setting for a wedding or special celebration. And for a complete vineyard experience, a quiet apartment for two above the winery provides a unique and luxurious place to stay.

Gladstone
SAUVIGNON BLANC 2003
Wairarapa

WINES
Gladstone Vineyard Sauvignon Blanc, Riesling, Pinot Gris, Chardonnay, Pinot Noir, Merlot & Cabernet Sauvignon

RECENT AWARDS
In recent years, Gladstone has won several Gold, Silver and Bronze medals at the Air New Zealand Wine Awards and the Royal Easter Show; Gladstone Pinot Gris 2003 – Top of Class: Winewise Small Vigneron Awards 2003

Gladstone Road
RD 2, Carterton
Tel: (06) 379 8563
Fax: (06) 379 8564
Email: info@gladstone.co.nz
Website: www.gladstone.co.nz

DIRECTIONS 1 hour 15 min from Wellington. In Carterton, turn right at the Westpac Bank if travelling north and follow the sign.

OPENING HOURS Cellar door: all year, Tues–Sun & public holidays: 11am–5pm. Wine Garden & Café: Labour Weekend–end March: Fri–Sun, 11am–4pm

WINERY SALES Cellar door, retail, mail order, Internet

PRICE RANGE $18–$39

TASTING & TOURS
Tasting is free of charge. Tours by appointment only.

GARDEN CAFÉ Outdoor and sheltered dining, from brunch through to afternoon teas. Bookings recommended.

PICNIC AREA Amongst the vines, down by the pond, or at a picnic table beside the winery.

ACCOMMODATION Apartment above the winery; tariff includes breakfast supplies, complimentary wine and a winery tour.

OTHER FACILITIES Functions by arrangement.

EVENTS Victoria University's Outdoor Summer Shakespeare season, held last week in February.

OWNERS
Christine & David Kernohan

WINEMAKER
Christine Kernohan

DATE ESTABLISHED 1986

Solstone Estate Winery

Solstone Estate is a boutique vineyard established on stony river terraces. Here the vines are low-trellised and closely planted, modelling the Bordeaux-style vineyards of France. Heat retained and reflected by the river stones aids ripening and helps grow concentrated full-flavoured grapes that are hand-picked and handcrafted into award-winning wines. Solstone's restaurant 'Seasons' offers hearty lunches and fine evening dining. Long summer sunsets and warm winter fires attract year-round visitors. Stunning country views add to the perfect surroundings while the close proximity of Wairarapa's major accommodation facilities and town centre makes Solstone an easy place to visit.

WINES
Solstone Cabernet Franc, Merlot, Cabernet Sauvignon, Cabernet Merlot, Pinot Noir, Sauvignon Blanc, Riesling, Chardonnay

RECENT AWARDS
Solstone Cabernet Franc Reserve 2001 – Silver: Air NZ Wine Awards 2003; Solstone Chardonnay 2001 – Bronze: International Chardonnay Challenge 2003; Solstone Pinot Noir 2001 – Bronze: Liquorland Top 100 2003

119 Solway Crescent, Masterton
Tel: (06) 377 5505
Fax: (06) 377 7504
Email: wine@solstone.co.nz
Website: www.solstone.co.nz

DIRECTIONS
At the southern end of Masterton, Solway Cres runs off the main Highway. Winery is 100m along.

OPENING HOURS Cellar door and tastings: Mon–Sun, 11am 4pm. Restaurant: Mon–Sun, 11.30am–late

WINERY SALES Cellar door, retail, mail order, Internet

PRICE RANGE $18–$42

TASTING & TOURS
Tasting fee: $5 for 3 wines, refundable on purchase. Tours Mon–Sun: 2pm or by appointment for larger groups.

RESTAURANT
Reservations: (06) 377 5522 (evening bookings essential).

PICNIC AREA Available during the summer musical events.

OTHER FACILITIES Courtesy van for motel/B&B pickups within Masterton. Celebration wine and labels: personalise your own bottle(s) of wine; contact www.celebrationwine.co.nz. Available for functions.

EVENTS & ACTIVITIES
Solstone Wine Down Days: outdoor musical events held over summer months. Wairarapa Genesis Balloon Fiesta: mass ascension from the vineyard in March.

OWNERS
Elizabeth Barrell-Hackel & Lloyd Hackel

WINEMAKER
Bernard Newman

DATE ESTABLISHED 1981

Matahiwi Estate

Matahiwi Estate is a newcomer to the Wairarapa. A family-owned business just north of Masterton, Matahiwi covers part of the Opaki Plains, an area of fine alluvial soil over old riverbeds of the Waingawa and Ruamahanga Rivers. The free-draining soils and cool climate make an excellent location for the Pinot Noir and Sauvignon Blanc planted on the 74-hectare home vineyard. Matahiwi has just finished building a stylish state-of-the-art winery that will eventually crush 1000 tonnes. The tasting area (to be built in 2005) will open onto a terrace with panoramic views over the vineyard, and a large internal window will offer viewing back through to the barrel room. This new winery will also make wine for local vineyard owners who do not have their own facilities.

WINES
Matahiwi Pinot Noir, Sauvignon Blanc, Riesling, Rosé, Chardonnay, Merlot

RECENT AWARDS
No shows have been entered to date, as 2004 is the first vintage.

48 Paierau Road, Masterton
Tel: (06) 370 1000
Email: alastair.scott@matahiwi.co.nz
Website: www.matahiwi.co.nz

DIRECTIONS
4km north of Masterton, Matahiwi is on the corner of the Masterton By-pass Rd and Loopline Rd.

OPENING HOURS
Spring, summer, autumn (and fine days in winter): 10am–3pm

PRICE RANGE $15–35

TASTING & TOURS
A small tasting fee applies, refundable on purchase. Tours by appointment.

PICNIC AREA
BYO food and enjoy Matahiwi wine amongst the ongoing development of the picnicking area.

OWNERS
Alastair and Gina Scott

WINEMAKER
Jane Cooper

DATE ESTABLISHED Planted from 1998, first vintage 2004

Dry River Rd, Martinborough
Tel: (06) 306 8345
Fax: (06) 306 8344
Email: coneywines@xtra.co.nz

DIRECTIONS
From Martinborough Village Square, follow Jellicoe St towards Lake Ferry for 6km. Turn left into Dry River Rd and continue 1km to the winery entrance.

OPENING HOURS
Open for lunch most weekends and public holidays. Mon–Fri & evenings: group bookings only.

WINERY SALES
Cellar door, retail, mail order and at the vineyard restaurant

PRICE RANGE $19+

TASTING & TOURS
Tasting is free of charge. Tours by appointment.

OTHER FACILITIES
A perfect venue for small weddings, corporate and private functions.

OWNERS
Tim & Margaret Coney

WINEMAKER
Debbie Christensen

DATE ESTABLISHED 1996

Coney Wines

Coney Wines is a family owned and operated vineyard — Pinot Noir and Riesling were planted in 1996 with Pinot Gris and Syrah added in 2003. The vines are hand-tended and 'serenaded' to capture the quintessence of each berry. The Coney signature of the treble clef logo and wine titles such as 'Pizzicato' (meaning 'plucking of the strings'), denote the happy harmony felt when drinking Coney wines. As a special treat you get a Coney poem on each label.

At the vineyard restaurant you can dine indoors in stylish surroundings or in the elegant Mediterranean-style outdoor courtyard, with its open fire and views over the vineyard to the Tararua Ranges in the distance. Here you can experience café cuisine designed to complement Coney's award-winning wines.

WINES
Coney Pinot Noir, Riesling, Rosé
(Pinot Gris & Syrah from 2006)

Margrain Vineyard

In the heart of the Martinborough vineyard area, Margrain Vineyard was born from the passion for fine wine, good food and the country lifestyle held by owners Daryl and Graham Margrain. From the outset, the company's aim has been to grow top-quality grapes and produce wines of excellence. A 4-hectare vineyard was planted in 1992 using only the most successful grape varieties and clones grown from the Martinborough region. Three years later the first wines from the estate were produced, coinciding with the opening of the Margrain Vineyard Villas. With 15 luxury accommodation units set on the edge of the picturesque terrace vineyard and close to other world-renowned Martinborough wineries, the villas offer a unique 'stay amongst the vines' experience and are particularly suitable for a distinctive executive retreat. In 2000 an adjacent vineyard was purchased where the cellar shop and The Old Winery Café are located. Modern New Zealand cuisine is the speciality, which visitors can enjoy in rustic and relaxed surroundings.

Cnr Ponatahi & Huangarua Rds
Martinborough
Tel: (03) 306 9202
Fax: (03) 306 9297
Email: margrain@xtra.co.nz
Website: www.margrainvineyard.co.nz

DIRECTIONS
Near the intersection of Huangarua Rd and Princess St, a few minutes drive from Martinborough Square.

OPENING HOURS
Cellar door: Fri/Sat/Sun & public holidays: 11am–5pm. Café: all year, lunch Fri–Sun, dinner Fri–Sat. Functions by arrangement.

WINERY SALES
Cellar door, retail, mail order, Internet

PRICE RANGE $22 $46

TASTING
Tasting fee: $4 refundable on purchase.

CAFÉ
The Old Winery Café. Reservations: (06) 306 8333

ACCOMMODATION
Margrain Vineyard Villas: deluxe accommodation tastefully decorated, each with its own individual style. Equipped with tea/coffee making facilities, TV, clock radios, en suites and private balconies.

OTHER FACILITIES
Informal conference facilities are available. 'The Woolshed' seats up to 35 people and 'The Boardroom' up to 20 people with fabulous views of the Tararuas.

OWNERS
Graham & Daryl Margrain

WINEMAKER
Strat Canning

DATE ESTABLISHED 1992

MARGRAIN
Pinot Noir
MARTINBOROUGH
2003
WINE OF NEW ZEALAND

WINES
Margrain Pinot Noir, Merlot, Chardonnay, Chenin Blanc, Gewürztraminer, Petit Pinot Noir, Pinot Gris, Riesling, Botrytis Selection Riesling

RECENT AWARDS
2001 Pinot Noir – Gold: Royal Easter Show 2002; 2000 Pinot Noir – Blue-Gold: Sydney International Wine Competition 2001; 1999 Pinot Noir – Silver: Air NZ Wine Awards 2000; 1998 Pinot Noir – Gold: Air NZ Wine Awards 1999

Princess St, Martinborough
Tel: (06) 306 9955
Fax: (06) 306 9217
Email: winery@martinborough-vineyard.co.nz
Website: www.martinborough-vineyard.co.nz

DIRECTIONS
Turn left into Princess St off the main road driving into Martinborough. Cross New York St and Martinborough Vineyard is on the left.

OPENING HOURS
7 days, 11am–5pm, or by appointment

WINERY SALES
Cellar door, retail, mail order, Internet

PRICE RANGE $20–$60

TASTING & TOURS
A small fee applies, refundable on purchase. Tours by appointment.

OWNERS
Martinborough Vineyard Estates Ltd

WINEMAKER
Claire Mulholland

DATE ESTABLISHED 1980

Martinborough Vineyard

Martinborough Vineyard was established in 1980 by a small partnership with the objective of producing world-class cool-climate wines from classical grape varieties. Located on the Martinborough Terrace appellation, the vineyard comprises 75 hectares of vines with over half planted in their flagship Pinot Noir. The portfolio also includes Chardonnay, Pinot Gris, Sauvignon Blanc and Riesling.

The appellation has free-draining soils and experiences cool-climate conditions with long summers and low rainfall, comparable with Burgundy. Vines aged up to 25 years, a diversity of clones, and emphasis on balance in the vineyard all contribute to the complexity and structure of their wines. Sustainability is actively promoted, using organic means wherever possible, in order to limit impact on the environment and with a view to the long-term future of the wine industry in New Zealand.

The Martinborough Vineyard philosophy is 'Handcrafted Excellence in Wine', and over the years they are proud to have stayed small, consistent and quality driven. Their journey has seen them produce outstanding wines, become a pioneer of Pinot Noir in New Zealand and one of the most prestigious winemakers in the New World.

Martinborough Vineyard

PINOT NOIR

2001

No. 32594

PRODUCED AND ESTATE BOTTLED BY MARTINBOROUGH VINEYARD LTD, PRINCESS STREET, MARTINBOROUGH, NEW ZEALAND.
13.5% VOL   PRODUCT OF NEW ZEALAND   750ml

WINES
Pinot Noir, Te Tera Pinot Noir, Chardonnay, Pinot Gris, Riesling, Late Harvest Riesling, Sauvignon Blanc, Rosé

AWARDS
All of the Martinborough Vineyard varieties have received numerous accolades, medals and trophies in New Zealand and internationally.

Murdoch James

Established in 1986 by Roger and Jill Fraser, Murdoch James Estate is a family owned and run boutique producer of premium award-winning wines. From their initial purchase of a 2.5-hectare vineyard, over 30 hectares have now been planted and for the last four vintages they have operated on a fully organic basis, only making wine from their Martinborough-grown grapes.

Amid beautiful surroundings on the north-facing terraces of the Dry River, visitors are offered the 'complete wine experience' with tasting, a range of tours to cater for all interests, delicious lunches, and accommodation in the beautifully restored Winemaker's Cottage. The café has a wonderful outlook across the Dry River to Lake Wairarapa and the snow-capped Tararua mountain ranges. During summer large bi-fold doors open onto an extensive outdoor eating area, while in the winter you can relax indoors in front of the fire while still enjoying the view. The kitchen team places emphasis on sourcing local produce to create a café experience to remember.

WINES
Three individual vineyard Pinot Noirs ('Blue Rock', 'Fraser' and 'River View'), Syrah, Pinot Gris, Cabernet Franc, Chardonnay (unoaked), Sauvignon Blanc, Riesling

RECENT AWARDS
Murdoch James has an outstanding record of trophies and medals (both domestically and overseas) across their full range of wines, along with many accolades from wine critics worldwide. In recent years, the Pinot Noirs (Fraser & Blue Rock) and Syrah have won four trophies and 34 medals at the Air NZ Wine Shows, the London Wine Challenge and the International Wine & Spirit Competition (UK).

ACCOMMODATION
The Winemaker's Cottage – a fully restored self-contained cottage set amongst the vineyard with beautiful views, furnished with antiques, 2 double bedrooms, $150–$200 per night.

Dry River Road, Martinborough
Tel: (06) 306 9165
Fax: (06) 306 9120
Email: info@murdoch-james.co.nz
Website: www.MurdochJames.co.nz

DIRECTIONS
From Martinborough Village Square, follow Jellicoe St towards Lake Ferry for 6km. Turn left into Dry River Rd and continue 3km to the winery entrance on the right.

OPENING HOURS
Wine tasting and sales: 7 days, 11am–5.30pm. Café: Fri, weekends & public holidays, 11.30am–3.30pm. Closed Christmas Day and New Year's Day.

WINERY SALES
Cellar door, retail, mail order, Internet

PRICE RANGE $19–$60

TASTING & TOURS
Hosted wine tasting: $3 pp, includes a 20-min talk and sampling of up to five wines. A variety of tours are available, including the tours of barrel caves and vineyards, finishing with a tasting. Fee: $15–$30 pp (depending on format). Phone for bookings.

CAFÉ
The Riverview Café.

PICNIC AREA
By the vines and lake.

OTHER FACILITIES & ACTIVITIES
Wine and Food Match dinners, blind tastings and wine appreciation classes can be organised for groups. Available for weddings and conferences. To assist with planning there is a comprehensive co-ordination service.

OWNERS
Roger & Jill Fraser

WINEMAKER
James Walker

DATE ESTABLISHED 1986

Palliser Estate Wines

Margrain Vineyard

Palliser Estate Wines

Palliser Estate is well established as one of the leading wineries in the Wairapapa. The first vineyards were planted in 1984 and there are now 84 hectares under vine on the renowned Martinborough Terrace. The philosophy of the company has always been to produce wines of quality, distinction and style — the success of this ambition is reflected in the numerous medals and trophies won worldwide since their first vintage. Wines are produced under two labels: the ultra-premium Palliser Estate range that has a well-established reputation worldwide, and the Pencarrow range offering quality varietal wines with immediate appeal. For those genuinely interested in wine, a visit to the very attractive colonial-style winery and cellar door is not to be missed.

WINES
Palliser Estate: Pinot Noir, Chardonnay, Riesling, Sauvignon Blanc, Pinot Gris, Méthode Champenoise. Pencarrow: Pinot Noir, Chardonnay, Sauvignon Blanc

RECENT AWARDS
Palliser Estate Pinot Noir – Gold: London International Wine Challenge 2001; Sauvignon Blanc of the Year 2002, *Winestate* magazine

Kitchener St, Martinborough
Tel: (06) 306 9019
Fax: (06) 306 9946
Free phone: 0800 PALLISER
(0800 7255 4737)
Email: palliser@palliser.co.nz
Website: www.palliser.co.nz

DIRECTIONS Turn right at Featherston onto SH53 and follow the signs to Martin-borough. Palliser Estate is the first vineyard on the left as you enter Martinborough.

OPENING HOURS 7 days, 10.30–4pm (6pm on weekends during daylight saving).

WINERY SALES Cellar door, retail, mail order, Internet

PRICE RANGE $17–$38

TASTING & TOURS Tasting fee for groups: $4 pp. New releases are available for tasting from the end of September until the wines sell out. Tours by appointment. Fee: $4–$10 (depending on tour format).

OWNERS
Palliser Estates Wines of Martinborough Ltd

WINEMAKER
Allan Johnson

DATE ESTABLISHED 1984

Te Kairanga Wines

Te Kairanga is a popular point of call for anyone visiting the Martinborough area. At this pretty country vineyard cellar-door sales are available year round from the historic 130-year-old farmhouse affectionately known as 'The Cottage'. Visitors are encouraged to taste the wines before buying, and the staff are more than happy to guide you through the range. The weekend tours are a great way to see what happens behind the scenes, showing how the vineyard and winery operate before finishing off with a well-structured wine tasting. Outside 'The Cottage' there is a very attractive picnic spot and visitors are welcome to bring their own picnic or choose from an interesting selection of deli foods.

Martins Rd, Martinborough
Tel: (06) 306 9122
Fax: (06) 306 9322
Email: info@tekairanga.co.nz
Website: www.tkwine.co.nz

DIRECTIONS
From Martinborough town square, drive to the end of Cambridge Rd, turn right into Puruatanga Rd and travel to the end where the road veers right into Martins Rd. Te Kairanga is located on this corner.

OPENING HOURS
7 days, 10am–5pm

WINERY SALES
Cellar door, retail, mail order

PRICE RANGE $14–$65

TASTING & TOURS
Tasting is free of charge. Casual wine tours (45min–1hr): Sat & Sun, 2pm. Fee: $5 pp (deductible from wine purchases). Large groups by prior arrangement only, $5 fee non-refundable.

FOOD OPTIONS
A range of deli items is available for picnics.

PICNIC AREA
Outside the cellar door there is a very attractive picnic area on an extensive grassy area shaded by trees and picnic tables.

EVENTS & ACTIVITIES
Annual TK Day — Wellington Anniversary Weekend Sunday: live music, plenty of food, and white wine chilled to perfection.

OWNERS
Te Kairanga Wines Limited

WINEMAKER
Peter Caldwell

DATE ESTABLISHED 1983

WINES
Labels: Reserve range: flagship wines only made when conditions are ideal; low cropping, selective handpicking, small batch fermentation and skilful oak treatment set these wines apart.
Premium range: High-quality wines at an accessible price; includes a Chardonnay and Merlot from Gisborne.
Castle Point Range: easy-drinking, soft styles ready to be enjoyed now.
Wine styles: Pinot Noir, Chardonnay, Sauvignon Blanc, Riesling, Merlot, Cabernet Sauvignon

RECENT AWARDS
Reserve Pinot Noir 2001 – Trophy & Blue-Gold: Sydney International Wine Challenge 2003, Top 100: Royal International 2003, Gold: Air New Zealand Wine Awards 2002

Nelson

Grant Stirling

NELSON lies in the north-west of the South Island, the country's eighth largest wine region with around 3 per cent of the national crop, and an area of great natural beauty including three national parks. **Nelson** city, on the seaside in Tasman Bay, is the biggest urban centre, the hub of the local horticultural and viticultural industries, and with an energetic community of craftspeople and artists. Bordered on three sides by hills, the Nelson region enjoys a warm, sunny climate, cooled by sea breezes. Most grape-growing takes place on the free-draining alluvial soils of the broad **Waimea Plains** that stretch to the coast, with a number of wineries around the town of **Richmond** and in the **Brightwater** district. A wide range of varieties is produced in chiefly fruit-driven styles. Above the north-western edge of the plains, the heavier clay and gravel soils of the **Upper Moutere** hills produce complex, minerally wines. Further north-west, new grape-growing areas are developing around **Motueka** and at **Golden Bay**.

Nelson is well known for its food, wine, arts and crafts, as well as a diverse range of adventure activities.

For more information on the Nelson region visit www.nelsonnz.com or www.nelsonwines.co.nz. Or contact Nelson Visitor Information Centre: Corner Trafalgar and Halifax Streets, Nelson, (03) 548 2304, vin@nelsonnz.com.

Woollaston Estates

HISTORY

German immigrant winemakers arrived in the region in the 1840s but moved on instead to South Australia. Nelson became dominated by horticultural crops and no serious attempts at grape-growing were made until Rod Neill planted a small vineyard at Stoke, south of Nelson, in the late 1960s, making his first wines in 1972. Austrian-born Hermann Seifried planted a couple of hectares of grapes at Upper Moutere in 1973 and he was to become an important figure in the area, advising beginning grape-growers in the late 1970s. Most of Nelson's wine companies have been centred on the Upper Moutere, but in recent times clusters of wineries have emerged on the Waimea Plains.

SOILS

Alluvial loam covers the Waimea Plains while soils in the Upper Moutere district are predominantly clay loams and gravels over hard clay subsoil.

CLIMATE

Nelson enjoys warm summers with very high sunshine hours (the country's highest) and cold, crisp winters. The proximity to the sea helps moderate temperature extremes, and frosts are extremely rare. The Waimea Plains can be windy, more so than the Moutere Hills district. Most of Nelson's rain falls in the autumn and winter.

GRAPE VARIETIES AND WINE STYLES

Nelson winemakers specialise and excel in grape varieties that respond to cooler growing conditions. Pinot Noir, Sauvignon Blanc, Chardonnay and Riesling are the major varieties. The region's temperate climate is ideal for making plummy Pinot Noir and ripe, fruit-flavoured Sauvignon Blanc. Chardonnay is produced in a wide range of rich, creamy, oaked styles and crisp, fresh unoaked styles.

SUB-REGIONS

Waimea Plains, unfurling from the surrounding ranges inland and spreading to the sea. Its alluvial soils are known for producing Chardonnay, Sauvignon Blanc, Pinot Noir and Riesling in fruit-driven styles. Most wineries are clustered around the towns of Richmond and Brightwater.

Moutere Hills, surrounding the fruit-growing town of Upper Moutere to the west of Nelson city. Its heavier clay and gravel soils produce minerally wines, principally Chardonnay, Pinot Noir and Sauvignon Blanc.

Woollaston Estates

Seifried Estate

Events

- **Taste Nelson.** A food and wine festival featuring regional specialities. Held annually in January.
- **Hooked on Seafood.** Nelson's premier wine and seafood event showcases the best of regional offerings. Held annually in March. www.hookedonseafood.co.nz.

For more information visit www.nelsonnz.com

Waimea Estate

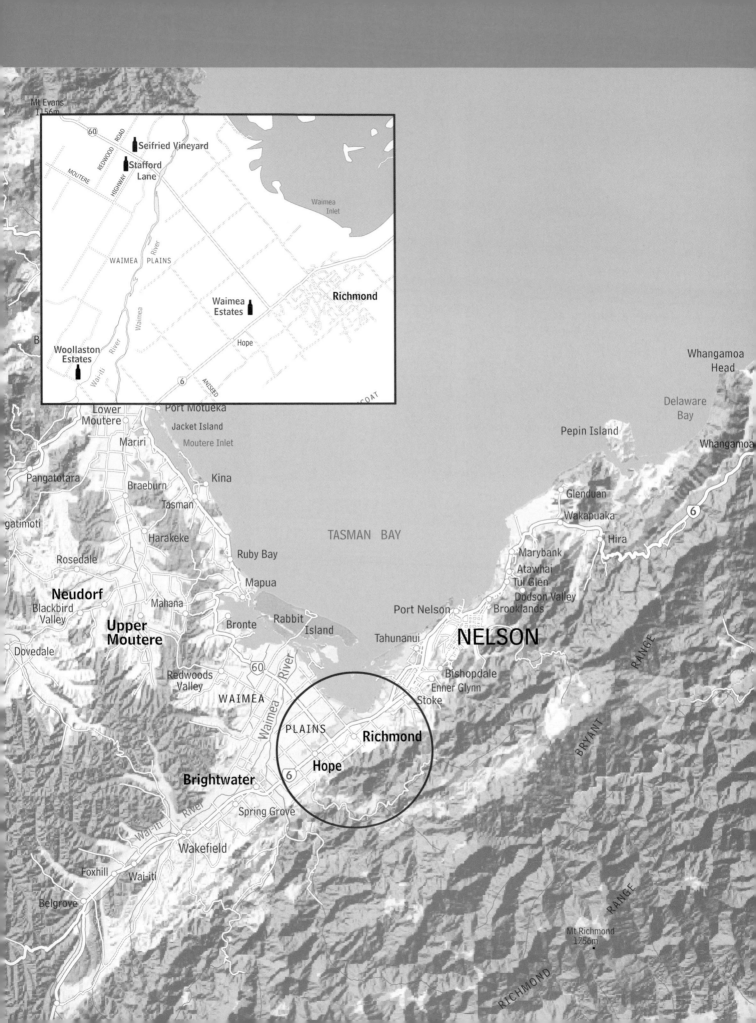

Mt Evans
1156m

60

REDWOOD ROAD

MOUTERE HIGHWAY

Seifried Vineyard

Stafford Lane

WAIMEA PLAINS

Waimea River

Waimea Estates

Richmond

Waimea Inlet

Waimea River

Hope

Wai-iti

Woollaston Estates

6

ANISEED

SCOAT

Port Motueka

Lower Moutere

Jacket Island

Moutere Inlet

Mariri

Kina

Pangatotara

Braeburn

Tasman

gatimoti

Harakeke

Rosedale

Ruby Bay

TASMAN BAY

Whangamoa Head

Delaware Bay

Pepin Island

Whangamoa

Glenduan

Wakapuaka

6

Hira

Neudorf

Blackbird Valley

Mahana

Mapua

Marybank

Atawhai

Tui Glen

Port Nelson

Dodson Valley

Brooklands

Upper Moutere

Bronte

Rabbit Island

Dovedale

Tahunanui

NELSON

RANGE

Redwoods Valley

60

Waimea River

WAIMEA

Bishopdale

Enner Glynn

Stoke

PLAINS

Richmond

Brightwater

6

Hope

River

Spring Grove

BRYANT

Wai-iti River

Wakefield

Foxhill

Wai-iti

Belgrove

RANGE

Mt Richmond
1756m

RICHMOND

Seifried Vineyard Restaurant & Winery

Seifried Estate is a family owned and operated company that has been making stylish, food-friendly wine since 1976 — all three children now work in various areas of the winery carrying on the family tradition. Success continues year after year with awards and accolades for their exquisite, intensely varietal hand-crafted wines, all made from their own estate-grown fruit.

NELSON • NEW ZEALAND

Seifried

NELSON 2002
PINOT NOIR

PRODUCE OF NEW ZEALAND

The winery complex includes a tasting area, shop and restaurant and is a great place to visit. At the cellar door, located in the Rabbit Island vineyard, the knowledgeable staff will assist you in tasting the range of wines and answer any questions. You can enjoy simply delicious food at the Vineyard Restaurant complemented by the fine food-friendly wines. Specialising in the wonderful range of fresh produce that Nelson has to offer, the restaurant provides indoor dining facilities as well as a spacious and pretty outdoor garden with a well-equipped playground to keep the children occupied while you dine at leisure.

WINES

Labels: Winemakers Collection, Seifried, Old Coach Road
Wine Styles: Sauvignon Blanc, Riesling, Chardonnay, Gewürztraminer, Pinot Gris, Pinot Noir, Cabernet Sauvignon, Merlot, Zweigelt

RECENT AWARDS

Seifried Sauvignon Blanc 2003 & Seifried Riesling 2003 – Double-Gold: 2004 San Francisco International Wine Competition; 2001 Winemakers Collection Barrique Fermented Chardonnay – Double Gold: 2003 San Francisco International Wine Competition, Blue-Gold: 2003 Sydney Top 100 Wine Awards; 2003 Winemakers Collection Gewürztraminer – Gold & Top of Class: 2003 Bragato Wine Awards; 2001 Winemakers Collection Pinot Noir – Gold: 2003 Wine Society Royal Easter Wine Show

Corner State Highway 60 &
Redwood Rd
Appleby
Tel: (03) 544 5599
Fax: (03) 544 5522
Email: wines@seifried.co.nz
Website: www.seifried.co.nz

DIRECTIONS
Located just 20 minutes from central Nelson City, on the Coastal Highway (SH60) towards Motueka. Look for the winery on the right, at the Rabbit Island intersection.

OPENING HOURS
7 days (closed Christmas Day, Boxing Day and Good Friday)
Cellar door: 10am–5pm
Restaurant: lunch and dinner

WINERY SALES
Cellar door, retail, mail order, Internet

PRICE RANGE $10–$35

WINE TASTING
A small fee, refundable on purchase, applies.

WINERY TOURS
By appointment only.

RESTAURANT
Seifried Vineyard Restaurant is open year-round. Lunch: 7 days; Evening dining: 7 days during summer, Friday and Saturdays during winter. For reservations Tel: (03) 544 1555

OTHER FACILITIES
Two beautiful function rooms are available: 1) 'Applebys' opens into an intimate garden area, with a beautiful hand-crafted fireplace to add to the cosy atmosphere. 2) 'Vines' has panoramic views over the vineyard and surrounding countryside from a spacious balcony.

OWNERS
Hermann & Agnes Seifried

WINEMAKER
Chris Seifried

DATE ESTABLISHED
1973

Stafford Lane Estate

Stafford Lane is a family-owned boutique winery, olive grove and orchard located on the beautiful Waimea Plains. Unique soil conditions and the region's favourable climate combine to produce an abundance of fruit perfect for their wide range of quality products. Their first Sauvignon Blanc produced in 2002 was a sellout and the owners have increased their planting from the original tiny 0.5-hectare site to 1.5 hectares. Gourmet preserves are made from the feijoas, apples and pears grown on the property using traditional recipes. Their olive oil is pressed from over 10 varieties of olives grown on their property and is sold as varietal extra virgin olive oil throughout New Zealand.

WINES
Stafford Lane Estate Nelson Sauvignon Blanc, Riesling, Chardonnay, Late Harvest Chardonnay, Botrytised Chardonnay

RECENT AWARDS
Sauvignon Blanc 2002 – 4 stars: *Cuisine* magazine

OTHER PRODUCTS Varietal extra virgin olive oil and olives; dukkah, gourmet preserves; paintings by local artist Paula Fitzgerald (Fitzart).

80 Moutere Highway
Richmond
Tel: (03) 544 2851
Fax: (03) 544 2051
Email:
mike.carol.mcgrath@xtra.co.nz

DIRECTIONS 800m from the intersection of the Coastal Highway (SH60) and the Moutere Highway; 8km from Richmond.

OPENING HOURS
Sept–Mar (or while stocks last): 11am–5pm, closed Mon; Dec and Jan, open 7 days.

WINERY SALES
Cellar door, retail, mail order

PRICE RANGE $13.95–$19.95

WINE TASTING Tasting fee: $3, includes five wines, two olive oils, dukkah, olives, chutney and bread; refundable on purchases over $15.

FOOD OPTIONS Tasting platters of olive oil, dukkah, olives, chutney and bread.

PICNIC AREA Picnic tables are set amongst the olives and feijoa trees.

OTHER FACILITIES Private tasting functions can be organised at the cellar door.

OWNERS
Mike & Carol McGrath

WINEMAKERS
Carol McGrath

DATE ESTABLISHED 2001

Waimea Estates

Since their first vintage in 1997, Waimea Estates have been creating award-winning Nelson wines. Their philosophy is that 'good wine is made in the vineyard' and their belief in intensive canopy management and low cropping ensures ripe and highly concentrated fruit. The three words winemaker Michael Brown uses to sum up his aims in his wines are: 'concentration, texture, balance'. At their celebrated 'Café in the Vineyard', you can sample and purchase Waimea wines including some hard-to-find back vintages. Or you can lunch or snack from the seasonal menu that features superb cuisine based on fresh Nelson-sourced ingredients. There is a mix of indoor and outdoor dining that flows out into the vines with live music in the weekends throughout the summer.

WINES
Labels: Waimea Estates & Bolitho Reserve (prestige range)
Wine Styles: Nelson Sauvignon Blanc, Riesling, Chardonnay, Gewürztraminer, Pinot Gris, Rosé, Pinot Noir, Cabernet Sauvignon/Merlot

RECENT AWARDS
Taste Nelson Awards Best Vineyard Café; Waimea Estates was nominated in 2003 by Winestate magazine as one of the 'Top 5 New Zealand Wine Companies'.

EVENTS AND ACTIVITIES
Annual Vintage Open Day (Anzac Day, 25 April), Annual Winemaker Dégustation Dinner (spring), Wine Appreciation Workshops, Changing exhibitions of local artists. Contact winery for dates and details.

Appleby Highway, Hope
Tel: (03) 544 6385
Fax: (03) 544 6385
Email: office@waimeaestates.co.nz
Website: www.waimeaestates.co.nz

DIRECTIONS
At the start of the Appleby Highway to Motueka and Golden Bay.

OPENING HOURS
7 days, 10am–5pm. Closed Christmas Day, Boxing Day, Good Friday and Queen's Birthday

WINERY SALES Cellar door, retail, mail order, Internet

PRICE RANGE $14.95–$39.95

TASTING & TOURS 50 cents per tasting, refundable up to $2. Tours by appointment only. Tour fee varies according to the size and need of a group.

CAFÉ
Café In The Vineyard.
Reservations: (03) 544 4963

OTHER FACILITIES
Evening functions and wedding receptions are a speciality of the café and cater to a wide range of tastes and budgets.

OWNERS
Trevor & Robyn Bolitho

WINEMAKER Michael Brown

DATE ESTABLISHED 1993

Woollaston Estates

The Woollaston Estates winery at Mahana in the Upper Moutere, has panoramic views across Tasman Bay from D'Urville Island to Nelson City in the east and of the majestic Mt Arthur range to the west.

Committed to producing high-quality distinctive wines, the owners of Woollaston Estates believe passionately that these are defined in the vineyard and subtly enhanced in the winery. Varieties and clones are carefully matched to their vineyards' sites and soils: Pinot Noir and Pinot Gris on the Moutere clays, Sauvignon Blanc and Riesling from the gravels of the Waimea Plains of Nelson. A unique gravity-fed, four-level winery building is partly underground and has a 'living roof' of soil and vegetation.

Fine art complements fine wine at Woollaston Estates Gallery, which features works by Toss Woollaston and contemporary New Zealand artists. Acknowledged as one of New Zealand's foremost 20th-century painters, Woollaston lived and painted nearby. A vineyard walk and sculpture park is being developed under the guidance of leading New Zealand sculptor, Andrew Drummond.

Grant Stirling

Grant Stirling

Grant Stirling

WINES
Woollaston Estates Nelson Sauvignon Blanc, Chardonnay, Riesling, Pinot Noir

OTHER FACILITIES
The Woollaston art gallery. Vineyard walk and sculpture park, scheduled to open in

2005. The winery complex has two function rooms that may be hired for conferences, weddings and social events. A 'function lawn' with sweeping vineyard, mountain and sea views is also available.

Woollaston
ESTATES

2003

Pinot Noir

NELSON

13% Alc/Vol   750ml

WINE OF NEW ZEALAND

Woollaston Estates
243 Old Coach Rd
Upper Moutere
Tel: (03) 543 2817
Fax: (03) 543 2317
Email: mail@woollastonestates.co.nz
Website: www.woollastonestates.co.nz

DIRECTIONS
The best way to get to Woollaston is on the road towards Mapua. Turn left onto Dominion Rd just after passing Nile Rd. Follow Dominion Rd 2km to the top of the hill and turn left onto Old Coach Rd. Travel for approx. 1km before turning right onto School Rd, the winery entrance is on the right a few metres into School Rd.

OPENING HOURS
By appointment only.

WINERY SALES
Retail, mail order (Cellar Club), Internet. Woollaston Estates does not have a cellar door shop but Cellar Club members or intending members are welcome to taste and purchase wines by appointment. Sales from the winery are by the case or half-case. To enquire about becoming a Cellar Club member contact: cellar@woollastonestates.co.nz or phone the winery.

PRICE RANGE $18–$45

WINE TASTING
Woollaston Estates does not have a casual tasting facility; however, Cellar Club customers and those wishing to join the club are welcome to visit and taste by appointment.

WINERY TOURS
By appointment only.

PICNIC AREA
Picnic facilities are being developed.

OWNERS
Philip & Chan Woollaston
Glenn Schaeffer

WINEMAKER
Andrew Sutherland

DATE ESTABLISHED 2000

Marlborough

MARLBOROUGH, in the north-eastern corner of the South Island, is the largest grape-growing and winemaking region in New Zealand with 65 wineries and 290 grape-growers. The region boasts three distinct landscapes: the breathtaking Marlborough Sounds, the stunning high country rolling down to the Pacific coast, and central Marlborough which is known as vineyard country. At the heart of this central area is the region's main urban centre of **Blenheim**, and the satellite wine country village of **Renwick**. Between the **Wither Hills** and the **Richmond Ranges** (made famous by the Cloudy Bay label) you'll find the heartland of Sauvignon Blanc across the **Wairau River** plains.

Wine lovers and foodies come to tour Marlborough wineries and they discover culinary paradise. Not only can you taste a variety of award-winning wines at the region's many vineyards, you can also sample fresh Sounds oysters with the world's best Sauvignon Blanc, taste local lamb or game in a first-class restaurant, or discover salmon secrets in a top cooking school.

For more information on the Marlborough region visit www.destinationmarlborough.com or contact Blenheim Visitor Information Centre: 2 High St, Blenheim, (03) 578 9904, blm_info@clear.net.nz.

Lake Chalice Wines

HISTORY

In the early 1970s, Montana Wines were looking for more land on which to expand their North Island grapegrowing and winemaking enterprise. They decided on Marlborough. When the first Marlborough vines were planted in 1973 few people predicted that the region would become New Zealand's largest and best-known winegrowing area in little more than 20 years. The distinctive qualities of the first wines captured the imagination of the country's winemakers and wine drinkers alike and sparked an unparalleled boom in vineyard development. Although Montana triggered this 20th-century boom in Marlborough, wine was in fact being produced here much earlier with the first commercial harvests in the 1870s.

SOILS

The free-draining alluvial loams over gravelly subsoils in the Wairau and Awatere River Valleys provides ideal growing conditions.

CLIMATE

Marlborough regularly claims the highest sunshine hours in New Zealand. This sunshine, coupled with cool nights and a long growing season, helps to build and maintain the vibrant fruit flavours for which Marlborough is now renowned. The region has relatively low rainfall during the ripening season which helps protect the thin-skinned and tight-clustered bunches of Sauvignon Blanc grapes from developing botrytis and other fungal diseases.

GRAPE VARIETIES AND WINE STYLES

Sauvignon Blanc is the most planted grape variety with Chardonnay in second place, followed by Pinot Noir and Riesling. Sauvignon Blanc may be the star but Marlborough has also earned an enviable reputation for Méthode Traditionelle sparkling wines as well as a wide range of both white and red table wines.

SUBREGIONS

Wairau Valley, surrounding Blenheim and predominantly south of the Wairau River, bounded by the Richmond Ranges and the Wither Hills. The heartland of Sauvignon Blanc.
Awatere Valley, south of Blenheim, stretches right along the lower Awatere River. The town of Seddon is in the centre of the region. Sauvignon Blanc, Riesling and Chardonnay are produced here.

Saint Clair Estate Wines

Domaine Georges Michel

Highfield Estate

Highfield Estate

Events

- **The BMW Wine Marlborough Festival.** A high-summer wine, food and jazz event, showcasing over 40 wineries and gourmet food producers. Wine workshops and culinary demonstrations. Second Saturday in February.
- **Seresin at Waterfall Bay.** An international guest chef prepares gourmet Marlborough cuisine matched with Seresin organic wines, set in a restored cottage in the Marlborough Sounds in February.
- **Blues, Brews & Barbecues.** Showcases boutique beers from around NZ. First Saturday in February.
- **Winter Wine Weekend.** Features workshops, blind tastings, dinners at leading restaurants with menus individually tailored to complement boutique wines. Late July/August annually
- **Sauvignon Blanc release.** Various events to celebrate the new vintage release during September and October.
- **Pinot at Cloudy Bay.** For lovers of Pinot Noir, NZ's most sophisticated wine-tasting event with over 20 Pinot Noirs from around the world, and fine food.

For more information contact the Marlborough Visitor Centre

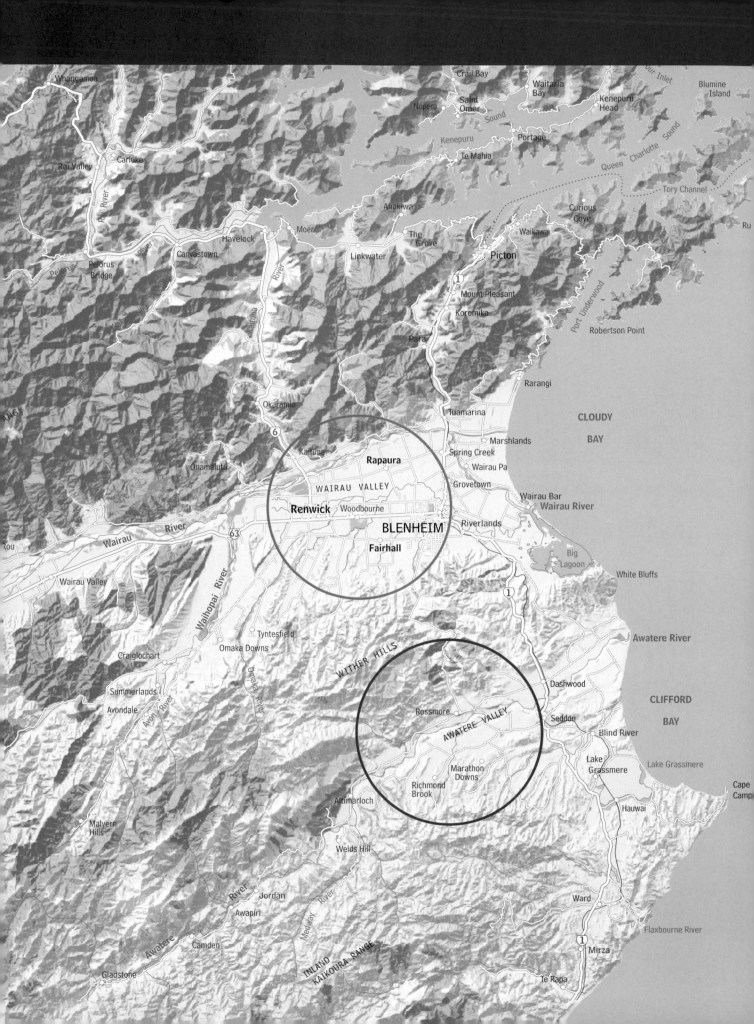

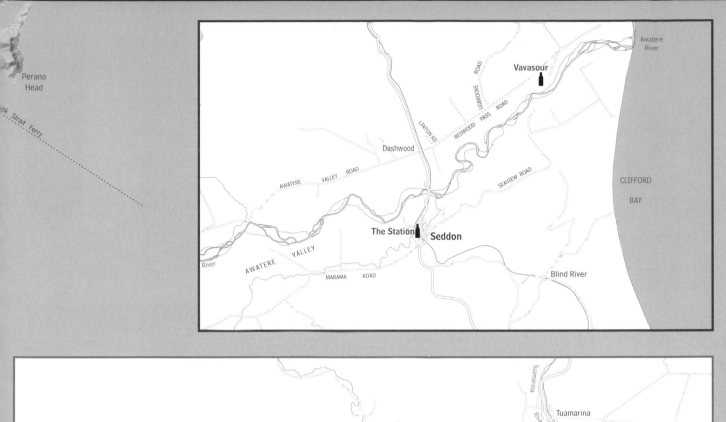

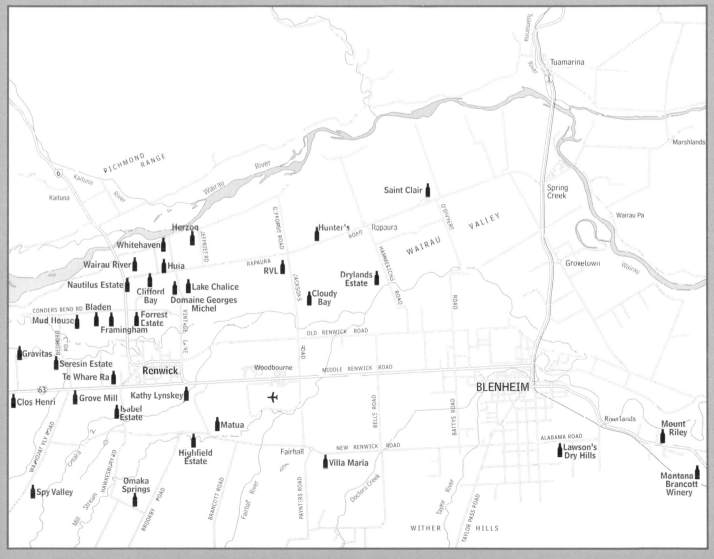

Bladen Estate

One of the smallest and friendliest tasting rooms in Marlborough, Bladen Estate is a boutique family owned and run vineyard that offers the special experience of meeting and tasting with the owners. Chris and Dave are passionate about the wines they produce and their belief that 'wine is made on the vine' ensures that quality is foremost at every step of their winemaking process. Best known for their aromatics, though Pinot Noir is their latest planting venture, the wines reflect the individuality and personality of this small vineyard. Every year these highly sought after wines that are often exclusive to the cellar door sell out very quickly.

WINES
Bladen Marlborough Gewürztraminer, Pinot Gris, Riesling, Sauvignon Blanc, Pinot Noir, Merlot/Malbec

RECENT AWARDS
Sauvignon Blanc 2003 – 5 stars: *Winestate* magazine

Bladen
MARLBOROUGH
PINOT NOIR
2002

750 ml   13.0% alc/vol
PRODUCT OF NEW ZEALAND
Produced & Bottled by Bladen Estate
Conders Bend Road, Renwick, Marlborough

Bladen Estate
Conders Bend Rd, Renwick
Tel: (03) 572 9417
Fax: (03) 572 9217
Email: info@bladen.co.nz
Website: www.bladen.co.nz

DIRECTIONS
Turn into Conders Bend Rd on the western side of SH6, 1km north of Renwick. Bladen Estate is 500m on the left.

OPENING HOURS
October (commencing Labour Weekend) to Easter: 7 days, 11am-5pm

WINERY SALES
Cellar door, retail, mail order, Internet

PRICE RANGE $18–$35

TASTING
Tasting is free of charge.

OWNERS
Dave Macdonald & Christine Lowes

WINEMAKER
Simon Waghorn

DATE ESTABLISHED 1989

Clifford Bay Estate

Growing on the terraces above the Awatere River near the coast are the sauvignon, chardonnay and riesling vines that produce the wonderful grapes for Clifford Bay Estate wines. Since their first vintage in 1997 when the Sauvignon Blanc was awarded three gold medals and numerous other credits, Clifford Bay Estate wines have continued to receive significant accolades in New Zealand and overseas. The distinctive 'Tuscan-style' cellar door is conveniently located on Rapaura Road for wine tastings and sales and includes a very popular restaurant that features fresh local produce. Diners can enjoy the Marlborough sunshine at sheltered courtyard tables set around a central water feature, or indoors beside a cosy open fire on cooler days. Private functions are also available.

WINES
Clifford Bay Sauvignon Blanc, Chardonnay, Riesling, Pinot Noir

RECENT AWARDS
2003 Sauvignon Blanc –
Gold: Sydney International Wine Competition 2004; 2002 Riesling – Gold and Trophy: NZ Wine Society Royal Easter Wine Show 2003

Clifford Bay Estate
26 Rapaura Rd, Renwick
Tel: (03) 572 7148
Fax: (03) 572 7138
Email: wine@cliffordbay.co.nz
Website: www.cliffordbay.co.nz

DIRECTIONS
Located just east of the intersection of SH6 and Rapaura Rd, next to Nautilus Estate.

OPENING HOURS
Cellar Door: 7 days, Oct–Apr: 9.30am–5pm; May–Sept: 10am–4.30pm. Restaurant: 7 days, winter from 10am, summer from 9.30am

WINERY SALES Cellar door, retail, mail order, Internet

PRICE RANGE $16–$30

TASTING Tasting fee: $2 (refundable on purchase).

RESTAURANT
Bookings recommended. Tel: (03) 572 7132

ACCOMMODATION
With Vintners Retreat, Clifford Bay offers a package for small groups in villas amongst the vines. Bookings: (03) 572 7420 or 0800 3 Vintners; website: www.TheVintnersRetreat.co.nz

OWNERS
Clifford Bay Estates Ltd

WINEMAKER
Glenn Thomas (Vavasour Wines)

DATE ESTABLISHED 1994

Clos Henri

Clos Henri, pronounced 'Klo Onrie', is an exciting new vineyard development in Marlborough's Upper Wairau Valley. It is owned by the internationally recognised winemaking family of Henri Bourgeois of Sancerre, France. For ten generations the family has crafted premium-quality Sauvignon Blanc and Pinot Noir wines and in 2000 chose 100 hectares of Marlborough land to extend their passion abroad.

The Clos Henri objective is to create top-quality Marlborough wines following the French traditions and art of Henri Bourgeois — wines that marry Old World winemaking history with New World purity of varietal character.

Tastings are held by appointment in Ste Solange, a quaint old country church complete with steeple which was moved onto the property. It may also be used as a private function and wedding venue.

WINES
Clos Henri Marlborough Sauvignon Blanc, Pinot Noir

Clos Henri
639 State Highway 63, Renwick
Tel: (03) 572 7923
Fax: (03) 572 7926
Email: closhenri@closhenri.com
Website: www.closhenri.com

DIRECTIONS
Travel 6km west of Renwick on SH63; Clos Henri (No. 639) is on the left — look for the church and head towards it.

OPENING HOURS
By appointment

WINERY SALES
Cellar door only

PRICE RANGE $20–$40

TASTING
By appointment

OTHER FACILITIES
Available for private functions and weddings.

OWNERS
Bourgeois family

WINEMAKERS
Sally & Jasper Raats

DATE ESTABLISHED 2001

Cloudy Bay Vineyards

One of the original wineries in the region, Cloudy Bay quickly became recognised internationally as a benchmark producer of Marlborough Sauvignon Blanc.

The Cloudy Bay winery and vineyards are situated in the heart of the Marlborough wine region where the Cloudy Bay team combines meticulous viticulture, modern winemaking technology and traditional vinification techniques in the commitment to produce premium-quality wines.

Flanked in the north by the Richmond Ranges, as depicted on the Cloudy Bay label, and in the south by the Wither Hills, the Wairau Valley terminates on the east coast at the bay after which the winery is named. Visitors are welcome at the cellar door and to picnic in the picturesque winery grounds.

WINES
Pelorus NV, Pelorus Vintage Cloudy Bay Sauvignon Blanc, Te Koko, Chardonnay, Gewürztraminer, Pinot Noir, Late Harvest Riesling

Jacksons Road, Blenheim
Tel: (03) 520 9140
Fax: (03) 520 9040
Email: info@cloudybay.co.nz
Website: www.cloudybay.co.nz

DIRECTIONS Jacksons Road runs between Middle Renwick Rd, across Old Renwick Rd, to Rapaura Rd; Cloudy Bay is at the Rapaura Rd end.

OPENING HOURS
7 days, 10am–4.30pm; closed Christmas Day and Good Friday.

WINERY SALES Cellar door, retail, and mail order

PRICE RANGE $26–$40

TASTING & TOURS
Tastings of all currently released wines and the occasional limited release are available. Group tours available by appointment (max. 20 persons), some charges may apply. Enquiries: info@cloudybay.co.nz.

PICNIC AREA Visitors are welcome to picnic on the winery lawns.

EVENTS/ACTIVITIES
'Pinot at Cloudy Bay' Second Saturday every June.

OWNERS
Moët Hennessy Wine Estates

WINEMAKERS
Chief Winemaker: Kevin Judd
Winemaker: Eveline Fraser

DATE ESTABLISHED 1985

Domaine Georges Michel

Georges Michel is no stranger to the wine industry — he already owns France's prestigious Chateau de Grandmont Beaujolais vineyard and winery estate in southern Burgundy. Consultant winemaker Guy Brac de la Perrière, from one of France's oldest winemaking dynasties and vice-president of the Beaujolais Winemakers' Association, oversees production — his aim is to blend his years of French winemaking with the fresh flavours of Marlborough. Domaine Georges Michel operates a stunning cellar door that also sells giftware and artwork by Georges' wife Huguette and fine French gourmet products. Set amongst the vines, the winery restaurant, La Veranda is a perfect place for an afternoon of great food and wine.

WINES
Golden Mile Sauvignon Blanc, Chardonnay, Pinot Noir; La Reserve Chardonnay, Pinot Noir; Petit Pinot Noir; Marc of Marlborough grape spirit made in traditional French style

RECENT AWARDS
Winners of numerous medals and awards including: Liquorland Top 100, Air NZ Wine Awards, Royal Easter Wine Show, *Cuisine* recommendations and many international awards.

56 Vintage Lane
Rapaura, Blenheim
Tel: (03) 572 7230
Fax: (03) 572 7231
Email: georgesmichel@xtra.co.nz
Website: www.georgesmichel.co.nz

DIRECTIONS Vintage Lane is off Rapaura Rd at the Renwick end. The vineyard is on the right.

OPENING HOURS
Cellar Door: Mid-Oct–mid-Apr: 7 days, 10.30am–4.30pm; Mid-Apr–mid-Oct: Wed–Sun, 11am–4pm.
Restaurant: Summer, 7 days, 12–4pm; Fri & Sat night for dinner. Winter: phone for details.

WINERY SALES
Cellar door, retail, mail order

PRICE RANGE $16–$49

TASTING & TOURS
Tasting is free of charge. Tours by appointment.

RESTAURANT La Veranda: indoor and outdoor dining, serving modern à la carte cuisine. Res: (03) 572 9177.

OTHER PRODUCTS
Gourmet French products, fine French imported wines including Georges' own and those made by Guy Brac de la Perrière.

OWNER Georges Michel

WINEMAKERS
Guy Brac de la Perrière and Peter Saunders

DATE ESTABLISHED 1997

Drylands Marlborough

Nestled in the picturesque sun-drenched area of the renowned Marlborough winegrowing region, Drylands produces wines of the finest quality and individual character. The cellar door is looked after by knowledgeable, friendly staff, and visitors can taste and purchase Drylands' extensive selection of varietals, all exclusively from Marlborough. And as part of the Nobilo Wine Group, they also offer an extensive range of Nobilo, Selaks and other imported brands. The Drylands philosophy is 'Searching for the Best' — resulting in the finest wines, sourced from only their best vineyards. This endeavour for quality was recently acknowledged at the prestigious 2003 International Wine & Spirit Competition in London, when Nobilo Wine Group was awarded Best New Zealand Wine Producer of the Year.

WINES
Labels: White Cloud, Fernleaf, Fall Harvest, Station Road, House of Nobilo, Nobilo Icon, Selaks Premium Selection, Selaks Founders Reserve, Drylands
Wine styles: Sauvignon Blanc, Chardonnay, Riesling, Pinot Gris, Pinot Noir, Syrah, Merlot, Cabernet Sauvignon, Sparkling, Dessert Wines, Port

RECENT AWARDS
Best New Zealand Wine Producer of the Year Trophy: International Wine & Spirit Competition London 2003; Highest Awarded Winery Trophy: International Chardonnay Challenge 2003; Champion of Champions Winemaker Trophy: Hawke's Bay A&P Mercedes-Benz Wine Show 2003

Hammerichs Rd, Blenheim
Tel: (03) 570 5252
Fax: (03) 570 5272
Email: drylands@nobilo.co.nz
Website: www.drylands.co.nz

DIRECTIONS
Less than 5 minutes from Blenheim and the airport, Hammerichs Road runs between Rapaura and Old Renwick Roads.

OPENING HOURS
7 days, 10am–5pm

WINERY SALES
Cellar door, retail and mail order

PRICE RANGE $8–$100

TASTING & TOURS
Tasting is free of charge. Tours by appointment.

OTHER PRODUCTS
Comprehensive range of imported wines from Australia, as well as South Africa and Italy.

OWNERS
Constellation Brands Inc.

WINEMAKER
Chief winemaker: Darryl Woolley

DATE ESTABLISHED
Vineyards 1980
Winery 1995

Forrest Estate

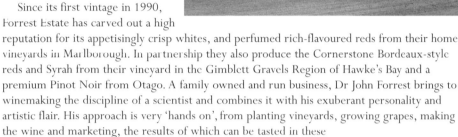

Forrest Estate is a pleasure to visit — from the stone wall that greets you at the State Highway 6 entrance, to the two hectares of shady parkland in which to picnic and the relaxing garden wine bar and tasting rooms. It's also special for the warm, friendly and informative wine service you'll receive, and if you have time and make prior arrangements the staff can take you through the vineyard and winery.

Since its first vintage in 1990, Forrest Estate has carved out a high reputation for its appetisingly crisp whites, and perfumed rich-flavoured reds from their home vineyards in Marlborough. In partnership they also produce the Cornerstone Bordeaux-style reds and Syrah from their vineyard in the Gimblett Gravels Region of Hawke's Bay and a premium Pinot Noir from Otago. A family owned and run business, Dr John Forrest brings to winemaking the discipline of a scientist and combines it with his exuberant personality and artistic flair. His approach is very 'hands on', from planting vineyards, growing grapes, making the wine and marketing, the results of which can be tasted in these world-acclaimed wines.

WINES
Labels: Forrest Estate, Newton Forrest Estate Cornerstone
Wine Styles: Sauvignon Blanc, Riesling (several styles), Chardonnay, Gewürztraminer, Pinot Gris, Chenin Blanc, Merlot/Malbec, Rosé, Pinot Noir, Cabernet Sauvignon, Merlot, Syrah

RECENT AWARDS
Winemaker of the Year: Royal Easter Show 2000; Sauvignon Blanc – Wine of the Show: Royal Easter Show 2001; Newton Forrest Cornerstone Cabernet Sauvignon 1998 – Wine of the Show: Bragato Wine Awards 2001.

MARLBOROUGH
Wairau Valley

Blicks Rd, Renwick
Tel: (03) 572 9084
Fax: (03) 572 9086
Email: forrestwines@xtra.co.nz
Website: www.forrest.co.nz

DIRECTIONS
1km north of Renwick on SH6 towards Nelson, turn right at the Forrest Estate stone wall and follow the signs.

OPENING HOURS
7 days, 10am–4.30pm (closed Christmas Day, Boxing Day, Good Friday, New Year's Day)

WINERY SALES
Cellar door, retail, mail order, Internet

PRICE RANGE $15–$80

TASTING & TOURS
Tasting fee: $2 for six wines. Tutored tasting can be arranged on request. Tours by appointment only.

FOOD OPTIONS
A picnic fridge is stocked with a selection of deli items — cheeses, cold meats and crackers for purchase.

PICNIC AREA
In beautiful park-like setting that includes a lake, picnic tables, pétanque, tennis and badminton courts.

OWNERS
Drs John & Brigid Forrest

WINEMAKERS
Dr John Forrest & Dave Knappstein

DATE ESTABLISHED 1990

Framingham Wine Company

Drylands Marlborough

FRAMINGHAM

MARLBOROUGH
2002
Dry Riesling

Wine of New Zealand

Framingham has become one of the most regularly recommended 'must-see' wineries on the Marlborough wine trail and it certainly lives up to its promise to deliver the best, not only with their much awarded aromatic wines but also with their facilities. Through the gatehouse entranceway, the rose-planted walled courtyard leads to an elegant tasting room with native timber panels and a marble fireplace for cold winter days. A staircase leads to underground cellars where vintages past and present are aged in perfect conditions and there is a museum of wine-related memorabilia. You will be given a warm welcome to taste and purchase these wines at the cellar door year round.

WINES
Framingham Sauvignon Blanc, Gewurztraminer, Riesling (several styles), Pinot Gris, Pinot Noir, Chardonnay and a Merlot/Malbec blend. Occasionally wines of special interest are released through the cellar door.

RECENT AWARDS
2003 Sauvignon Blanc – Blue-Gold: Sydney International Wine Challenge 2004; 2002 Classic Riesling – Gold: 2003 Air New Zealand Wine Awards, Blue-Gold: Sydney International Wine Challenge 2004

Framingham Wine Company
Conders Bend Rd, Renwick
Tel: (03) 572 8884
Fax: (03) 572 9884
Email: sales@framingham.co.nz
Website: www.framingham.co.nz

DIRECTIONS
Turn into Conders Bend Rd on the west side of SH6, 1km north of Renwick. Framingham is immediately on the left.

OPENING HOURS
Oct–Apr: 7 days, 10am–5pm;
May–Sept: 7 days, 11am–4pm

WINERY SALES Cellar door, retail, mail order, Internet

PRICE RANGE $18.50–$35

TASTING & TOURS
Tasting is free of charge. Tours by appointment only.

OTHER ACTIVITIES
Underground wine cellar, native gardens and courtyard

OWNERS
Orlando Wyndham

WINEMAKER
Andrew Hedley

DATE ESTABLISHED 1994

Mount Riley

Seresin Estate

Gravitas Wines

1. Vineyard Manager & Viticulturalist:
Peter Kerdemelidis
45 Lanark Lane, Renwick
Tel: (03) 572 2531
Fax: (03) 572 2531
Email: vineyard@new-zealand-wines.com
2. CEO & Proprietor: Martyn Nicholls
Tel: +44 (0)1732 460 685
Fax: +44 (0)1732 461 598
Email: ceo@new-zealand-wines.com
Website: www.new-zealand-wines.com

DIRECTIONS
7km west of Renwick on SH63, turn right into Lanark Lane, the vineyard is on the left.

OPENING HOURS
Dec–Apr: by appointment only

WINERY SALES
Cellar door, retail (Cellar Select chain), mail order, Internet

PRICE RANGE $16–$30

TASTING & TOURS
Tasting fee: $3 per wine (refundable on purchase). Tours by appointment only.

ACCOMMODATION
A guesthouse located in the vineyards, with four bedrooms and a swimming pool, will be available from January 2005.

CAFÉ
Opening December 2004, serving vineyard platters, light snacks and deli items for picnics.
Reservations: 03 572 2731.

PICNIC AREA
Situated under the shade of two rows of great fir trees with picnic tables, a gas barbecue and a pétanque court. A spectacular viewing site is located nearby at a height of about 400 feet where the view extends right down both the Wairau and Waihopai Valleys and, on a clear day, as far as the North Island.

OWNERS
Pam & Martyn Nicholls and their three children, Garth, Bryony & Hugo

WINEMAKER
Brian Bicknell

DATE ESTABLISHED 1994

The Gravitas name comes from the Latin word denoting something of great stature, quality and elegance — words that summarise the company's philosophy and practice. Their impressive rise to global fame in a few short years is one of the great stories of the New Zealand wine industry. Gravitas has recently been described as 'setting the standard for the antipodean wine industry, the most exciting wine producer in New Zealand' by *Swig* (UK). Its Chardonnay has been rated as one of the world's top 25 white wines (Burgundy/aromatic) by Jancis Robinson MW, Europe's foremost wine writer and judge; its Sauvignon Blanc the best in New Zealand by Bob Campbell MW.

Gravitas has been described as being 'on the lunatic fringe end of the quality control spectrum', with all wines meticulously crafted and made only from estate-grown grapes. Each vine has its own computer record and the grapes are picked by hand over a one-month period, at extremely low yields. This, along with the cooler climate in the lower Wairau Valley, gives Gravitas wines their legendary concentration.

While Gravitas has traditionally exported 100 percent of its wines, their new vineyard tasting facilities open in December 2004. Set in the higher reaches of the Wairau Valley, bordered by mountains, it has one of the most spectacular views of any vineyard in Australasia.

WINES
Gravitas Oaked and Unoaked Chardonnay, Sauvignon Blanc, Pinot Noir, Sparkling and two Dessert wines

RECENT AWARDS
In 2003 Gravitas wines won an average of seven medals per wine in competitions in New Zealand, the USA, UK and Japan. Michael Cooper, author of the *Wine Atlas of New Zealand* , rated all Gravitas wines 5/5.

13 Waihopai Valley Rd, Renwick
Tel: (03) 572 8200
Fax: (03) 572 8211
Email: info@grovemill.co.nz
Website: www.grovemill.co.nz

DIRECTIONS
Situated on the corner of Waihopai Valley Road and SH63 just south of Renwick, approximately 14km west of Blenheim.

OPENING HOURS
7 days, 11am–5pm (closed on Christmas Day, Boxing Day, New Year's Day, Anzac Day and Easter Sunday)

WINERY SALES
Cellar door, retail, mail order

PRICE RANGE $15–$40

TASTING & TOURS
Tasting is free of charge. For pre-booked groups the unique aroma demonstration is a fun learning experience. Other options for groups include blind tasting, wine & food matching or gourmet platters. Tours by appointment only.

PICNIC AREA
Includes picnic tables, pétanque

OWNERS
The New Zealand Wine Company

WINEMAKER
David Pearce

DATE ESTABLISHED 1988

Grove Mill

The striking Grove Mill winery is situated in the heart of their home vineyard, in the magnificent Waihopai Valley. Its airy cellar door commands spectacular mountain views and here you can taste a mix of current releases, limited edition and previous vintage wines and enjoy a Sauvignon Blanc aroma demonstration. Grove Mill Sauvignon Blanc has been described as an icon Marlborough wine. First released in 1990 it has become a Marlborough classic with devotees around the world.

The cellar door also houses the Diversion Art Gallery that features regular exhibitions from leading New Zealand artists and sculptors. Adjacent to the cellar door is a unique Vine Library that allows you to view different grape varieties and compare leaf and grape shape size and colour. Around harvest visitors are encouraged to wander through the vines and taste the grapes alongside the finished wine. A short stroll from the cellar door are well-established native gardens and a wetland sanctuary, home to a growing population of wildlife including native ducks, shags and other birds as well as the Southern Bell frog that features on the Grove Mill label.

GROVE MILL
2003
SAUVIGNON BLANC
MARLBOROUGH
e750ml   WINE OF NEW ZEALAND   12.5% Vol

WINES
Labels: Grove Mill, Sanctuary, Frog Haven, Landsdown, Blackbirch
Wine Styles: Sauvignon Blanc, Chardonnay, Riesling, Gewürztraminer, Pinot Gris, Pinot Noir, Pinot Blanc

RECENT AWARDS
With 352 (comprising 53 gold, 118 silver and 181 bronze) medals gained in national and international shows since 1991, all wines have earned a deserved reputation for consistent exceptional quality.

OTHER ACTIVITIES
The Diversion Art Gallery featuring regular exhibitions from NZ's leading artists; vine library, native gardens, wetland sanctuary

Herzog Winery & Luxury Restaurant

Hans and Therese Herzog come from a winegrowing family that dates back to 1482. They moved their winery and Michelin-starred restaurant from their native Switzerland to Marlborough where they run one of New Zealand's leading boutique estates. The vineyard's unique microclimate and extremely low yields allow Hans to create rare and precious wines of extraordinary depth and structure. The restaurant was built out of pure passion, giving locals and visitors to New Zealand the opportunity to experience the Herzog wines with world-class food as they were intended. This is destination dining at its best in a stunning secluded location, overlooking the estate's 11-hectare vineyard and mountains beyond.

WINES
Herzog Marlborough Merlot/Cabernet Sauvignon — 'Spirit of Marlborough', Pinot Noir, Montepulciano, Pinot Gris, Chardonnay, Viognier, FeatherWhite

RECENT AWARDS
Herzog Malborough do not enter competitions; recent accolades include: 'No one is making better wine in New Zealand than Hans Herzog': Malcolm Gluck, UK *Guardian*; Herzog Montepulciano — one of the top 50 Reds: UK *Decanter*

OTHER PRODUCTS
Exclusive range of gourmet deli items from the restaurant kitchen — available in the 'Emporium Gourmand' in the tasting room.

81 Jeffries Rd, Blenheim
Tel: (03) 572 8770
Fax: (03) 572 8730
Email: info@herzog.co.nz
Website: www.herzog.co.nz

DIRECTIONS Turn into Jeffries Rd, off Rapaura Rd. Herzog is at the end of the road

OPENING HOURS Tasting: 7 days, Mon–Fri, 11am–3pm; weekends, 11am–4pm.

WINERY SALES
Cellar door, retail, mail order and from the restaurant

PRICE RANGE $29–$59

TASTING & TOURS Tasting fee: $10 for 3 wines (refundable on purchase of 3 bottles). Tours by appointment only.

RESTAURANT Oct–May; dinner: Tues–Sun from 7pm, lunch: Sun only, 1 Dec–28 Feb 12pm–4pm. Reservations: (03) 572 8770.

EVENT & ACTIVITIES
Cooking classes, kitchen tours and themed degustation dinners.

OWNERS
Hans & Therese Herzog

WINEMAKER Hans Herzog

DATE ESTABLISHED 1994

Highfield Estate

To form a lasting impression of Marlborough as a unique winemaking region Highfield Estate is a must-see. With unsurpassed views across the Wairau Valley vineyards from their dramatic viewing tower this is one of Marlborough's most visited sites. Enjoy winetasting at the cellar door, dine at the restaurant or play pétanque. Offering indoor and outdoor dining the restaurant specialises in matching fresh local cuisine with their food-friendly wines to give you one of the best culinary experiences in the Wairau Valley. Highfield's Tuscan-inspired winery specialises in making wines using only Marlborough grapes grown on their chosen vineyards. Sold in seven countries these award-winning wines, made only when vintage quality permits, are emerging as an ultra-premium New World wine brand.

WINES
Highfield Marlborough Sauvignon Blanc, Pinot Noir, Chardonnay, Riesling, Elstree Cuvée Brut

RECENT AWARDS
Sauvignon Blanc 2003 – Gold: Air New Zealand Wine Awards 2003, Trophy: Champion Commercial White Wine Air NZ Wine Awards 2003, Gold: Royal Easter Wine Show 2004; Pinot Noir 2002 – Gold: Royal Hobart Wine Show 2003

OTHER PRODUCTS
Art exhibitions (art for sale), local craft

Brookby Rd, Blenheim
Tel: (03) 572 9244
Fax: (03) 572 9257
Email: winery@highfield.co.nz
Website: www.highfield.co.nz

DIRECTIONS
Turn off SH6 onto Godfrey Rd, turn right into Dog Point Road then left into Brookby Rd.

OPENING HOURS
Cellar Door: 7 days, 10am–5pm
Restaurant: 7 days, 11.30am–3.30pm

WINERY SALES Cellar door, retail, mail order, Internet

PRICE RANGE $22–$44

TASTING Tasting is free of charge. Tours by appointment only.

RESTAURANT Highfield Restaurant. Reservations: (03) 572 9244 ext 3

ACCOMMODATION Luxury, single-bedroom, self-contained apartment with unsurpassed views of the Wairau Valley. $200 per night.

OWNERS
Shin Yokoi & Tom Tenuwera

WINEMAKERS
Alistair Soper & Samuel Bennett

DATE ESTABLISHED 1987

Huia Vineyards
22 Boyces Rd, Blenheim
Tel: (03) 572 8326
Fax: (03) 572 8331
Email: wine@huia.net.nz
Website: www.huia.net.nz

DIRECTIONS
Turn off Raparua Rd into Boyces Rd;
100m along turn right to the winery.

OPENING HOURS
7 days, 10am–4.30pm

WINERY SALES
Cellar door, retail, mail order

PRICE RANGE $20–$36

TASTING
Tasting free of charge.

OTHER PRODUCTS
Huia-branded wine knives, sparkling
stoppers, T-shirts, caps & hats, wine
glasses

OWNERS
Mike & Claire Allen

WINEMAKERS
Mike & Claire Allen

DATE ESTABLISHED 1990

Huia Vineyards

After studying wine at Roseworthy College in Australia, Claire and Mike Allan were drawn to Marlborough by the intense fruit flavours in the wines. Here they established Huia, a boutique-sized private company committed to the production of premium and classical Marlborough wines that are aromatic, elegant and food-friendly. Huia wines are now in demand worldwide — currently 85 per cent of their wines are exported.

The owners chose the name Huia to reflect the feel of the South Pacific and their focus on crafting unique wines. The Huia was an indigenous New Zealand bird that inhabited the dense forest canopy and whose tail feathers were highly prized by both Maori and Europeans. The Huia symbolism is also reflected in the design of the cellar door with its distinct Pacific look and feel including an impressive display of Pacific artefacts along with New Zealand artwork. Here you are welcome to taste and purchase these special wines that fully express the richness of their Marlborough grapes.

WINES
Huia Marlborough Sauvignon Blanc, Riesling, Pinot Gris, Gewürztraminer, Chardonnay, Pinot Noir, Vintage Brut

RECENT AWARDS
Huia do not enter competitions although some recent accolades include: 2002 Sauvignon Blanc — *Wine Spectator*: 91/100 points; 2003 Riesling — *Wine Enthusiast Magazine*: 89/100 points; 2002 Pinot Gris — 4 stars: *Restaurant Wine* (USA); 1999 Huia Brut — *Decanter* (Jun): Best Sparkling Wine

Steven Spurrier, consultant editor at *Decanter* magazine, writes: 'A classic "Champagne" blend of 38 percent Chardonnay, 33 percent Pinot Noir and 29 percent Pinot Meunier, barrel-fermented with full malolactic, followed by 42 months on the yeast, this is brioche-y and lively, with ripe, pure fruit and a smooth, dry finish. It will show more complexity as it matures.'

Hunter's Wines

It was the late Ernie Hunter and his wife Jane who put Marlborough on the world map when their Sauvignon Blanc was voted Best White Wine by the London Sunday Times Vintage Festival in 1986. Now one of New Zealand's most established wineries, Jane continues to build on the company's formidable reputation producing award-winning wines based on the intense fruit flavours of the region. Recent expansion has seen the vineyard increase by two and a half times and production grow to around 60,000 cases, nearly half of which is exported. Jane Hunter has been awarded an OBE and an honorary doctorate for services to the wine industry, and recently received the inaugural 'Women in Wine Award' at the International Wine & Spirit Competition (UK).

The winery is set amongst native gardens where a vine-covered trellised walkway links the restaurant, wine shop and gallery where the artist in residence has his studio. Set in the vineyard, Hunter's Restaurant is renowned for its gourmet fare and is a winner of numerous culinary awards. The outdoor dining area includes a pool and children's play area or during winter relax indoors by the open fire in the farmhouse-style dining room.

WINES
Hunter's Marlborough Sauvignon Blanc, Chardonnay, Pinot Noir, Riesling, Gewürztraminer, Brut and Miru Miru (a Methode Champenoise; Maori for 'bubbles')

WINE MEDALS
Over the past 20 years Hunter's Wines have won numerous international awards and medals including the Marquis de Goulaine Trophy for 'Best Sauvignon Blanc in the World' at the 1992 International Wine & Spirit Competition and a Black Diamond award (3 golds in one year) in 1995 at Intervin New York.

EVENTS & ACTIVITIES
Hunter's Garden Marlborough: A programme of garden workshops, tours and social events held each November. Website: www.garden-marlborough.co.nz
Artist in residence: Visit Clarry Neame in his studio.
Sculpture exhibitions in the gardens.

MARLBOROUGH
Wairau Valley

Hunter's Wines
Rapaura Rd, Blenheim
Tel: (03) 572 8489
Fax: (03) 572 8457
Email: wine@hunters.co.nz
Website: www.hunters.co.nz

DIRECTIONS
Located on the north side of Rapaura Rd between Jacksons and Hammerichs Rds.

OPENING HOURS
Cellar Door: 7 days, 9am–4.40pm
Restaurant: lunch 7 days, 12pm–3pm; dinner Thurs–Sun from 6pm

WINERY SALES
Cellar door, retail, mail order, Internet

PRICE RANGE $12–$28

TASTING
Wine tasting available 7 days, 9am–4.30pm

OTHER PRODUCTS
Marlborough olive oils

RESTAURANT
Hunter's Garden Restaurant. Open all year. Bookings are advised for dinner. Reservations: (03) 572 8803.

PICNIC AREA
Set amongst an extensive native garden.

OWNER
Jane Hunter

WINEMAKER
Gary Duke

DATE ESTABLISHED 1979

Isabel Estate
72 Hawkesbury Rd
Renwick
Tel: (03) 572 8300
Fax: (03) 572 8383
Email: info@isabelestate.com
Website: www.isabelestate.com

DIRECTIONS
Turn into Hawkesbury Rd, off West
Coast Highway 63 near Renwick
and the winery is 500m on the right
(signposted).

OPENING HOURS
By appointment.

WINERY SALES
Cellar door and retail

PRICE RANGE $20–$49

TASTING & TOURS
Tasting and tours by appointment.
Please note: during busy periods the
cellar may be unavailable to visit.

OTHER PRODUCTS
Isabel estate-grown olive oil, Isabel
shirts, aprons and wine accessories

OWNERS
Michael & Robyn Tiller

WINEMAKERS
Michael Tiller & Anthony Moore

DATE ESTABLISHED 1982

Isabel Estate

Set on the elevated Omaka Terrace, Isabel Estate is one of the largest privately owned estates in Marlborough, containing some of the oldest vines in the region. Producing grapes of exceptional quality, yields are restricted by pruning to low bud numbers and, where necessary, shoot and bunch thinning. Isabel Estate's terroir combines deep free-draining gravel with a narrow layer of calcium-rich clay. The modern winery situated in the middle of the vineyard combines the very best of high- and low-tech equipment to maximise vineyard flavours.

Recognised internationally as a producer of fine wines, most of the estate's production is destined for export markets. However, a small amount of wine is retained at the winery where visitors can enjoy a tasting in the stylish and purpose-built tasting salon that has superb views of the vineyards. Currently, tasting is by appointment only although there are plans to extend opening hours. For the complete vineyard experience you can stay on the estate in their cosy and rustic self-contained lodge.

WINES
Isabel Marlborough Sauvignon Blanc,
Chardonnay, Dry Riesling, Pinot Gris, Pinot
Noir, Noble Sauvage

RECENT AWARDS
Highest score in tasting of 80 NZ Sauvignon
Blancs, UK *Wine* magazine, March 2002;
Sauvignon Blanc 2001 – Best 100 wines
worldwide 2002: *Wine Spectator* (USA);
Sauvignon Blanc 2002 – 5 stars: *Winestate*
magazine; 2001 Pinot Noir – 5 stars: *Winestate*
magazine; Isabel Chardonnay 2002 – Gold:
International Wine Challenge 2004

ACCOMMODATION
Located on the estate, Isabel Lodge has a
spacious, rustic feel with a large stone
fireplace, a well-equipped kitchen and private
access. With views of the Richmond ranges, it
accommodates couples or a small group
comfortably. Marlborough Airport is 5
minutes away by car and the village of
Renwick is just 2 minutes away. For details
and bookings visit: www.isabelestate.com or
Tel: (03) 572 8300.

Kathy Lynskey Wines

Kathy Lynskey Wines is a privately owned boutique Marlborough wine company producing only 5000 cases of limited release, hand-crafted wines annually. The company's estate vineyard comprises nine hectares planted on old riverbed soils adjoining the Omaka River.

Owners Kathy Lynskey and Kent Casto live on the vineyard, which allows them to adopt a 'hands-on' approach to vineyard management. Vines are cropped at levels that maximise the intense fruit flavours and all grapes with the exception of Sauvignon Blanc are hand-picked. Since releasing its first Sauvignon Blanc in 1998 the company has achieved excellent recognition in New Zealand and the United States, winning awards in major competitions and receiving regular 4- and 5-Star ratings.

Their tasting room is located on the vineyard. You may sample all available varietals, providing they have not sold out, as well as their estate-grown, hand-picked extra virgin olive oil. If you are a passionate gardener, you may ask to walk through the private cottage garden behind the tasting room.

KATHY LYNSKEY WINES

MARLBOROUGH

Block 36 Reserve
PINOT NOIR
2002
PRODUCT OF NEW ZEALAND

WINES
Kathy Lynskey Wines Marlborough Vineyard Select Sauvignon Blanc, Single Vineyard Gewürztraminer, Single Vineyard Pinot Gris, Godfrey Reserve Chardonnay, Block 36 Reserve Pinot Noir, 15 Rows Reserve Merlot

RECENT AWARDS
15 Rows Reserve Merlot 2002 – Gold: Air NZ Wine Awards 2003;
Godfrey Reserve Chardonnay 2002 –

91/100 points and one of top NZ wines for the year: *Wine Spectator* (USA);
Pinot Noir 2001 – Winner of 3 gold medals, represented Marlborough in International Pinot Noir 2004 Conference

Kathy Lynskey Wines
36 Godfrey Rd, Blenheim
Tel: (03) 572 7180
Fax: (03) 572 7181
Email: lynskeys.wines@xtra.co.nz
Website: www.kathylynskeywines.co.nz

DIRECTIONS
On the corner of Godfrey and Middle Renwick Rd, near Renwick.

OPENING HOURS
Summer: 7 days, 10.30am–4pm;
Winter: Reduced hours

WINERY SALES
Cellar door, retail, mail order, Internet

PRICE RANGE $20–$55

TASTING
Tasting is free of charge.

OTHER PRODUCTS
Estate-grown extra virgin olive oil

OWNERS
Kathy Lynskey & Kent Casto

WINEMAKERS
Marlborough Vintners Ltd
Consulting winemaker: Alan McCorkindale

DATE ESTABLISHED 1998

Lake Chalice Wines
93 Vintage Lane, Renwick
Tel: (03) 572 9327
Fax: (03) 572 9327
Email:wine@lakechalice.com
Website: www.lakechalice.com

DIRECTIONS
Near the Renwick end of Rapaura Rd.
Turn south into Vintage Lane, proceed
for 1km and look for the two blue
towers.

OPENING HOURS
October (commencing Labour Day) to
Easter: 7 days, 11am–4pm
Rest of the year: by appointment

WINERY SALES
Cellar door, retail, mail order, Internet

PRICE RANGE $17–$150

TASTING
Tasting is free of charge.

PICNIC AREA
BYO picnic and enjoy the quiet sheltered
and shady dell.

OWNERS
Phil Binnie, Chris Gambitsis (Gambo) &
Matt Thomson

WINEMAKER
Matt Thomson

DATE ESTABLISHED 1989

Lake Chalice Wines

Lake Chalice Wines is a proud sponsor of the Wingspan Birds of Prey Charitable Trust, which is dedicated to the preservation of New Zealand's endangered raptors. Their emblem, proudly displayed on every bottle, is the native New Zealand falcon — the karearea. In a country without land-based mammals before the arrival of man, the karearea was the top predator. Fearless and flying high, the karearea signifies how the owners, Chris and Phil, feel about their wines.

Chris and Phil bought and named the Falcon Vineyard in 1989. This was an existing but derelict vineyard that they completely replanted. They later rehabilitated the adjacent quarry block turning this eyesore wasteland into valuable vineyards, winning a Ministry of the Environment Green Ribbon Award for their efforts. Visitors are amazed that vines are able to survive let alone flourish in the extremely stony ground, which produces low crop yields with intense flavours. Lake Chalice may not be the prettiest vineyard in Marlborough but no one can deny the quality of the wines produced.

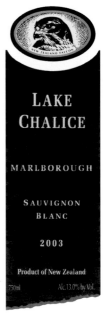

LAKE CHALICE

MARLBOROUGH

SAUVIGNON BLANC

2003

Product of New Zealand
750ml   Alc.13.0% by Vol.

WINES
Lake Chalice Platinum (Reserve) Chardonnay, Merlot, Cabernet Sauvignon; The Raptor Oak-Aged Sauvignon Blanc; Black Label Sauvignon Blanc, Chardonnay, Unoaked Chardonnay, Merlot, Rosé, Pinot Noir, Botrytised Late Harvest Riesling

RECENT AWARDS
Marlborough Riesling 2000 – Reserve Wine of the Show, Champion Riesling &Gold: Air NZ Wine Awards 2000; Sauvignon Blanc 2002 – Gold: Royal Easter Wine Show 2003; Platinum (Reserve) Chardonnay 1999 – Gold: Royal Easter Wine Show 2001

OTHER PRODUCTS
Wingspan Birds of Prey Trust merchandise includes traditional falcon hoods, posters and ceramics

Lawson's Dry Hills

Lawson's Dry Hills is committed to the production of premium Marlborough wines and has received many accolades and show successes. Grapes are harvested from right across the spectrum of soil types, ranging from light stony soils to heavy loams, including clay-based. As one of the pioneers in the New Zealand screwcap initiative they are committed to ensuring the quality and integrity of all their wines by using screwcap closures. The winery has a modern cellar door and there is an attractive picnic area. You can meet Tomi, the owners' Golden Labrador who in 2002 achieved international celebrity status for being able to pick when the harvest should start just by sniffing the grapes.

WINES

Lawson's Dry Hills Marlborough Sauvignon Blanc, Riesling, Gewürztraminer, Pinot Gris, Chardonnay, Pinot Noir, Pinot Rosé, Late Harvest Sémillon

RECENT AWARDS

2003 Pinot Gris – Trophy: Air NZ Wine Awards; 2003 Gewürztraminer – Trophy: Liquorland Top 100

Lawson's Dry Hills
Alabama Rd, Blenheim
Tel: (03) 578 7674
Fax: (03) 578 7603
Email: wine@lawsonsdryhills.co.nz
Website: www.lawsonsdryhills.co.nz

DIRECTIONS From Blenheim any of the roads to the Wither Hills. Turn left into Alabama Rd. The winery is on the right, 1km from Redwood St intersection.

OPENING HOURS
7 days, 10am–5pm

WINERY SALES
Cellar door, retail, mail order

PRICE RANGE $16.50–$28

TASTING & TOURS Tasting is free of charge. Tours can be arranged.

FOOD OPTIONS
Cheese platters can be organised to accompany tastings.

PICNIC AREA
Vine-enclosed courtyard adjacent to the cellar door.

OTHER PRODUCTS
Clothing from Merino Mink, Snowy Peak & Lawson's Dry Hills, locally made gold & silver jewellery, Gewürztraminer brandy, brandy truffles

OWNERS
Barbara & Ross Lawson

WINEMAKERS
Mike Just & Marcus Wright

DATE ESTABLISHED 1992

Matua Marlborough

Matua is the Maori word for 'main stem' or 'head of the family', which is very appropriate as this is the winery credited with producing New Zealand's first Sauvignon Blanc. With vineyards in all of New Zealand's major winegrowing regions, Matua focuses on taking advantage of unique regional qualities to create innovative and distinctive wines. They have been associated with Marlborough since the late 1980s with the highly regarded Shingle Peak range. At the cellar door you can taste an extensive range of Matua wines from around New Zealand.

WINES

Labels: Shingle Peak, Estate Series, Ararimu
Wine styles: Riesling, Sauvignon Blanc, Pinot Noir, Pinot Gris, Chardonnay, Gewürztraminer, Botrytis Riesling, Pinot Noir, Merlot, Merlot Cabernet

RECENT AWARDS

Air NZ Wine Awards 2003 – Gold: Paretai Sauvignon Blanc 2003, Gold: Judd Chardonnay 2003, Gold: Shingle Peak Botrytis Riesling; International Wine Challenge 2003 – Gold: Ararimu Chardonnay 2001

Matua Marlborough
New Renwick Rd, Blenheim
Tel: (03) 572 8642
Fax: (03) 572 9034
Email: matua.marlborough@xtra.co.nz
Website: www.matua.co.nz

DIRECTIONS Turn into Godfrey Rd off Middle Renwick Rd and travel 2km into New Renwick Rd, the vineyard is on the left.

OPENING HOURS
Oct–Apr: 7 days, 9am–5pm
May–Sept: 7 days, 10am–4.30pm

WINERY SALES Cellar door, retail, mail order

PRICE RANGE $11.95–$39.95

TASTING Tasting is free of charge along with tasting of olive oil and other gourmet food items. Wine & food matching is available at a negotiated charge.

FOOD OPTIONS A selection of gourmet items for sale to accompany your wine.

PICNIC AREA Under trees in the vineyard or in covered areas with picnic tables and gas BBQ.

OTHER PRODUCTS
NZ-grown olive oils, gourmet food items, art & craft

OWNERS
Beringer Blass Wine Estates

WINEMAKERS
Corey Hall & Joanne Gear

DATE ESTABLISHED 1985

Montana Brancott Winery
State Highway 1
Riverlands, Blenheim
Tel: (03) 578 2099
Fax (03) 578 0463
Email: information@montanawines.com
Website: www.montanawines.co.nz

DIRECTIONS
Five minutes south of Blenheim on SH1.

OPENING HOURS
Cellar door: 7 days, 9am–5pm
Restaurant: 9am–5pm

WINERY SALES
Cellar door, retail, and mail order
(through subscription to the winery
newsletter 'Brancott Brio')

PRICE RANGE $13–$99

TASTING & TOURS
Tasting trays available for $5 and $7.
Daily tours, 10am–3pm. Bookings are
advisable. Tour fee: $7.50, with a
discount for group bookings.

RESTAURANT
Brancott Winery Restaurant is one of
the region's leading winery
restaurant/cafés offering premium
Marlborough fare. Bookings advisable:
(03) 577 5776

OTHER FACILITIES
Conference and private function
facilities. With its unique ambience,
award-winning wines, fabulous cuisine
and picture-perfect setting this is one of
Marlborough's premier wedding venues.

OWNER
Montana Wines Ltd

SENIOR WINEMAKER
Patrick Materman

DATE ESTABLISHED 2000

Montana Brancott Winery

The Montana Brancott Winery is home to some of New Zealand's finest wines and is one of Marlborough's top tourist attractions. This building is designed for the celebration of life and what's best about it — food and wine, music and crafts. Visitors can pop in for a quick coffee, a meal with a distinct Marlborough flavour or a winery tour and tasting. Its spacious downstairs restaurant and outdoor area can cater for large groups, and the exclusive Tower Room is perfect for more intimate gatherings.

A tour of the winery is de rigueur. Montana planted the first vineyards in Marlborough in 1973 and this is the oldest working winery in the region. The giant grape-tipping tanks are the first of their kind in the world, the French Coquard grape press the first in the southern hemisphere, and the large traditional wooden cuves remain a rarity in New Zealand. This winery makes some of New Zealand's best — including the Montana Reserve range and the Montana Terraces, Brancott, Fairhall and Renwick Estate wines.

WINES
Montana Marlborough Sauvignon Blanc,
Riesling, Pinot Noir
Montana Reserve Sauvignon Blanc,
Chardonnay, Pinot Noir, Merlot, Riesling
Montana Estate Terraces Pinot Noir, Brancott
Sauvignon Blanc, Fairhall Cabernet Sauvignon,
Renwick Chardonnay

RECENT AWARDS
Montana Reserve Marlborough Chardonnay
2002 – Gold: Japan Wine Challenge 2003,
4 stars: Michael Cooper 2003, 4 stars: *Cuisine*
magazine (Jul 2003); Montana Reserve
Marlborough Riesling 2001 – Gold:

2003 Liquorland Top 100; Montana Reserve
Marlborough Sauvignon Blanc 2002 – Gold:
Hong Kong International Wine Challenge
2003, Silver: Japan Wine Challenge 2003, 4½
stars: Michael Cooper 2003, 4½ stars:
Winestate June 2003

Mount Riley Wines

Mount Riley is the predominant peak in the Richmond range of mountains that overlooks the vineyards of Mount Riley Wines and the Wairau Valley. Its distinctive crag is instantly recognisable to wine lovers — photographs of Mount Riley and the Richmond Hills often appear in articles on the Marlborough region. Five vineyards, totalling 102 hectares in the Wairau and Seventeen Valley areas, are owned by Mount Riley

Wines — each site carefully chosen for its unique attributes and ability to produce grapes of outstanding quality. The stylish new glass-and-concrete winery and cellar door cleverly incorporates the company logo making it instantly recognisable to visitors, and the glass frontage allows views of the wine tanks. As well as wine-tasting, visitors are welcome to picnic in the grounds.

MOUNT RILEY
marlborough

SAUVIGNON BLANC
MARLBOROUGH
NEW ZEALAND

2003

WINES
Mount Riley Sauvignon Blanc, Riesling, Chardonnay, Pinot Noir, Merlot/Malbec; Seventeen Valley (flagship range) Chardonnay, Pinot Noir, Sauvignon Blanc; Savee (Sparkling Sauvignon Blanc)

RECENT AWARDS
Seventeen Valley 1998 Chardonnay – NZ's only Chardonnay Gold Medal: London International Wine & Spirit Competition. The wines have since continued to receive medals for each vintage from a variety of shows.

Mount Riley Wines
Cnr Malthouse Lane & State Highway 1, Riverlands, Blenheim
Tel: 0800 494 632
Fax: 0800 494 633
Email: sherlye@mountriley.co.nz
Website: www.mountriley.co.nz

DIRECTIONS
Five minutes south of Blenheim on the corner of Malthouse Rd and SH1 opposite Cobb Cottage.

OPENING HOURS
Oct–March: 7 days, 10am–4pm
Rest of the year: by appointment

WINERY SALES
Cellar door, retail

PRICE RANGE $15–$34

TASTING & TOURS
Tasting is free of charge. Tours by appointment only.

FOOD OPTIONS Tasting platters containing a selection of local Marlborough produce (e.g. salmon, cheeses, olives).

PICNIC AREA
Situated in the vineyard with picnic tables and umbrellas.

OWNER John Buchanan

WINEMAKER Bill Hennessy

DATE ESTABLISHED 1991

Omaka Springs Estates

Located on 71 hectares in the heart of the picturesque Omaka Valley, Omaka Springs Estates specialises in producing premium cool-climate varietal grapes. Owners Geoff and Robina Jensen and winemaker Ian Marchant produce their entirely estate grown, classic medal-winning wines at the on-site winery, where their aim and philosophy is to produce only 'high quality wines at affordable prices'. As a result, the Omaka Springs Estates label is growing in reputation and demand all over the world. Included on the estate is one of the country's largest commercial olive groves with over 3500 trees, including 23 different varieties. These trees produce high-quality olives that are processed on the estate into fine extra virgin olive oil.

OMAKA SPRINGS
ESTATES
MARLBOROUGH
2003
Winemaker's Selection
Pinot Noir
PRODUCE OF NEW ZEALAND

WINES
Omaka Springs Sauvignon Blanc, Riesling, Chardonnay, Pinot Gris, Pinot Noir, Merlot, Dog Rock Red, Jaime (Sparkling)

RECENT AWARDS
Sauvignon Blanc 2003, Pinot Gris 2003, Winemakers

Selection Chardonnay 2002 – Bronze: Royal Easter Wine Show 2004; Chardonnay 2002 – Bronze: International Chardonnay Challenge 2002

OTHER PRODUCTS
Omaka Springs Extra Virgin Olive Oil, walnuts

Omaka Springs Estates
Kennedys Rd, Renwick
Tel: (03) 572 9933
Fax: (03) 572 9934
Email: wine@omaka.co.nz
Website: www.omaka.co.nz

DIRECTIONS
Turn into Brookby Rd off Dog Point Rd. Travel 3km then turn right into Kennedys Rd. The vineyard is 500m on the right.

OPENING HOURS
October (commencing Labour Weekend) to end of February: Mon–Fri, 10am–4pm

WINERY SALES
Cellar door, retail, Internet

PRICE RANGE $17–$50

TASTING
Tasting by appointment, free of charge. Tours by appointment.

OWNERS
Geoff Jensen & Robina Jensen

WINEMAKER
Ian Marchant

DATE ESTABLISHED 1992

The Mud House Village

Situated in the heart of the Rapaura wine district, the Mud House Village has become a 'must visit' for locals and tourists alike offering a wide variety of activities on site. Visitors to the mud-brick cellar door have the opportunity to taste all the Mud House wines, the main label in New Zealand, and the highly sought after Le Grys range, only available here or by mail order as most is exported. Lovers of bubbles can taste the Family Estate No. 1 and No. 8 Méthode Traditionelle owned and produced by Daniel and Adele.

Adjoining the cellar door is the Village Café, which offers seasonal home-made cuisine with excellent coffee and treats to tempt anyone. Sometimes during the summer there are BBQ lunches with live music. With a lake and landscaped native garden this forms the perfect setting for alfresco dining, enjoying a glass of wine or friendly game of pétanque. Or you can be deciding what gifts or special mementoes to purchase from the various shops on site — a magnificent quilt or perhaps some special olive oil.

WINES

Mud House Sauvignon Blanc, Chardonnay, Riesling, Pinot Gris, Late Harvest Riesling, Merlot, Vineyard Selection Pinot Noir, Black Swan Reserve Pinot Noir
Le Grys Sauvignon Blanc, Chardonnay, Merlot, Home Vineyard Pinot Noir

RECENT AWARDS

2000 Mud House Sauvignon Blanc – Silverado trophy for best Sauvignon Blanc: International Wine & Spirits Competition (UK) 2001; 2003 Mud House Sauvignon Blanc – Gold: NZ Wine Society Royal Easter Wine Show 2004; 2002 Mud House Black Swan Pinot Noir – Gold: Hong Kong International Wine Challenge 2003, Blue-Gold: Sydney International Wine Challenege, five years running from 1999–2003; 2003 Le Grys Sauvignon Blanc – Gold: NZ Wine Society Royal Easter Wine Show 2004, Blue Gold: Sydney International Wine Challenege 2003

OTHER ATTRACTIONS

The Olive Shop has a range of award-winning local olive oils that you can taste to help make your choice, plus a wide variety of gifts including a selection of locally made silver jewellery and gourmet foods.

The Quilter's Barn is a national attraction and people come from far and wide for quilting lessons and to buy materials. They have an impressive range of interesting handcrafts imported giftware, Janome sewing machines and Chinese furniture. Day and evening workshops are available.

The Mud House Village
193 Rapaura Road, Blenheim
Tel: (03) 572 9170   Fax: (03) 572 9170
Email: mudhousevillage@xtra.co.nz
Website: www.mudhouse.co.nz

DIRECTIONS
On Rapaura Road. Turn right off SH1 at Spring
Creek if coming from Picton, or left off SH6 just
over the Waihopai River Bridge if coming from
the Nelson direction.

OPENING HOURS
7 days, 10am–5pm (closed Christmas Day)

WINERY SALES
Cellar door, retail, mail order, Internet

PRICE RANGE $18.50–$40

TASTING
Tasting is free of charge but there may be a
small fee for large groups (this is refundable on
purchase). Large groups by appointment only.

CAFÉ
The Mud House Village Café offers indoor and
outdoor dining. The seasonal menu features
freshly prepared soups, salads, platters, quiche,
panini, delicious cakes and gateaux for an
afternoon treat and Rush Monroe ice creams.

ACCOMMODATION
On site: Self-contained lodge; sleeps two and
contains bedroom/lounge/dining, bathroom, fully
equipped kitchen with gas BBQ and use of
laundry. Wide decks overlooking the lake,
vineyards and mountains provide the perfect spot
to relax. Full breakfast provisions are provided
daily. Price: $135 per night. Bookings: (03) 572
9791 or 021 567 440/021 567 441
Off site: Waterfall Lodge is a luxury, self-
contained mud brick cottage set amongst the
vines at the Le Grys vineyard with stunning views
over the vineyard and the Richmond Ranges.
Contains two bedrooms, separate bathroom,
dining/lounge/kitchen area, verandah with gas
BBQ and access to an indoor swimming pool.
Guests are greeted with a glass of wine and
nibbles on arrival and in the morning a breakfast
hamper to start the day. Price: $225 double +
$45 pp extra — max. 4 persons. For bookings
phone: (03) 572 9490 or 021 313 208 or
email: stay@legrys.co.nz

OWNERS
Mud House Wine Company:
John & Jennifer Joslin
Mud House Village: Andy & Adele Joslin

WINEMAKERS
Allan Hedgeman & Matt Thomson (consultant)

Nautilus Estate
12 Rapaura Rd, Renwick
Tel: (03) 572 9364
Fax: (03) 572 9374
Email: sales@nautilusestate.com
Website: www.nautilusestate.com

DIRECTIONS
Located at 12 Rapaura Rd,
approximately 100m east of the
intersection of SH6 and Rapaura Rd.

OPENING HOURS
7 days, 10am–4.30pm

WINERY SALES
Cellar door, retail, mail order

PRICE RANGE $14.50–$35.90

TASTING & TOURS
Tasting is free of charge. Tours by
appointment only.

OTHER PRODUCTS
Speciality South Island cheeses

OWNERS
The Hill Smith family

WINEMAKER
Clive Jones

DATE ESTABLISHED 1985

Nautilus Estate

Nautilus Estate is named after the beautiful *Nautilus pompillius*, a native of the South Pacific Ocean, the shell of which is their brand emblem and appears on every label. The stylish cellar door makes extensive use of the natural curves found in the shape of the Nautilus shell, with the tones and colours reflecting the local environment — the river gravels of the Wairau River and the natural timbers. The winery incorporates an underground library cellar and by appointment you can tour the specialised Pinot Noir winery — a unique facility designed specifically for small-batch winemaking.

All wines are produced exclusively from Marlborough fruit with approximately 60 per cent of the production exported to 28 countries. Winemaker Clive Jones produces stylish, concentrated wines that cellar well and go nicely with food. Premium wines are available to taste and for sale under the Nautilus brand and a range of fruit-driven easy-drinking wines that are good value for money under the Twin Islands label. As well, a wide variety of speciality South Island cheeses are available for sale.

WINES
Nautilus Estate Cuvée Marlborough
Brut NV, Sauvignon Blanc,
Chardonnay, Pinot Gris, Pinot Noir
Twin Islands Sauvignon Blanc,
Chardonnay, Pinot Noir,
Merlot/Cabernet

RECENT AWARDS
An array of awards and gold medals
including the International Wine
Challenge 'Sparking Wine of the Year'
and 'Sauvignon Blanc of the Year'.

Kathy Lynskey Wines

Gravitas Wines

Lake Chalice Wines

Grove Mill

Saint Clair Estate Wines Cellar Door
13 Selmes Rd
Rapaura, RD3, Blenheim
Tel: (03) 570 5280
Fax: (03) 570 5280
Email: cellardoor@saintclair.co.nz
Website: www.saintclair.co.nz

DIRECTIONS
Just off Rapaura Rd in Selmes Rd, approximately 5 minutes drive from Blenheim — look for the sign on the corner.

OPENING HOURS
7 days, 9am–5pm

WINERY SALES
Cellar door, retail, mail order, Internet (delivery free within NZ — overseas service available)

PRICE RANGE $14.95–$26.95

TASTING
Tasting fee: $2 (refundable on any purchase).

ACCOMMODATION
Springvale Vineyard Cottage: a modern, fully self-contained cottage in a quiet garden setting; sleeps 4. Bookings: (03) 570 5449 or email: cellardoor@saintclair.co.nz

OTHER FACILITIES
Pétanque. Private function and wedding enquiries welcome.

EVENTS
Halo Nights at the Cellar Door: a series of Saturday-night winter dinners where it is mandatory to wear the pink and white fluffy halos supplied.

OTHER PRODUCTS
Halos, monks' habits, full range of branded merchandise including clothing, imported glassware and decanters. The adjacent Traditional Country Preserves stocks gourmet pickles, sauces and chutneys, and includes a gallery and gift shop.

OWNERS
Saint Clair Estate Wines: Neal & Judy Ibbotson
Saint Clair Cellar Door and Café: Bruce and Bridget Crawford

WINEMAKER
Matt Thomson

DATE ESTABLISHED
Winery: 1994, Cellar Door: 2000

Saint Clair Estate Wines Cellar Door & Café

Set right in the middle of a vineyard, the Saint Clair cellar door truly captures the essence of Marlborough with its fine wines, relaxed dining and reputation for friendliness: 'Every wine a medal-winning wine' is the catch-cry of Saint Clair Wines and reflects the care and experience invested from the vines to the cellar door and beyond — their wines are now exported to over 35 countries.

The welcoming and knowledgeable cellar-door team will be happy to spend time taking you through a wine tasting, and an affordable tasty blackboard menu offers all-day food, wine, coffee and tea. It's easy to while away the hours over a long lazy lunch; the light airy café has vineyard views from every table and a cosy open fire in winter, or you can dine in the garden courtyard under shady umbrellas. A full-sized pétanque court is adjacent to the cellar door for guests to try out their skills. And if you are looking for a special place to stay, Springvale Cottage offers a private haven in the vineyard.

WINES
Premium range: Saint Clair Rosé, Riesling, Sauvignon Blanc, Chardonnay, Unoaked Chardonnay, Merlot
Limited edition: Doctor's Creek Pinot Noir, Vicar's Choice Pinot Noir, Godfrey's Creek Pinot Gris
Reserve: Saint Clair Wairau Sauvignon Blanc, Omaka Chardonnay, Rapaura Merlot, Fairhall Riesling, Doctor's Creek Noble Riesling, Omaka Pinot Noir

RECENT AWARDS
Saint Clair has an outstanding record of trophies and medals (both domestically and overseas) across the full range of wines. Saint Clair Wairau Sauvignon Blanc has won eight trophies over three successive vintages.

Seresin Estate

Seresin Estate is a Marlborough wine producer committed to creating premium wine and extra virgin olive oil. Michael Seresin, a New Zealand-born film-maker based in London, established the estate in 1992.

The image of the hand is a symbol of strength, gateway to the heart, tiller of the soil, the mark of the artisan and embodies their philosophy to elicit a true Marlborough character in their wines and extra virgin olive oils.

Seresin Estate believes in working in harmony with nature: grapes are organically and biodynamically grown, hand tended, and fermented predominantly with wild yeasts.

Olive trees imported from Tuscany provide the perfect companion culture of evergreen foliage amongst the bare grapevines in winter. Each June, Seresin Estate cold-press the olives selecting the blend to create a rich and peppery extra virgin olive oil.

WINES

Seresin Estate Sauvignon Blanc, Mārama Sauvignon Blanc, Estate Chardonnay, Chardonnay Reserve, Pinot Gris, Riesling, Pinot Noir, Mōana Sparkling Wine. Future wine styles include Gewürztraminer and Viognier.

OTHER PRODUCTS

Seresin Estate olive oils and honey

Seresin.
2003
SAUVIGNON BLANC
MARLBOROUGH
NEW ZEALAND

Seresin Estate
Bedford Road, Renwick
Tel: (03) 572 9408
Fax: (03) 572 9850
Email: info@seresin.co.nz
Website: www.seresin.co.nz

DIRECTIONS
Follow SH63 for about 3km past Renwick. Bedford Road is on the right. A rock featuring the hand logo points the way. The winery entrance is approximately 800m along Bedford Road on the left-hand side.

OPENING HOURS
7 days, 10.am–4.30pm

WINERY SALES
Cellar door, retail, mail order, Internet

PRICE RANGE $24–$50

TASTING & TOURS
Tasting is free of charge. Guided tours by appointment.

PICNIC AREA
A grassy area in the dell is available for picnics.

EVENTS
Waterfall Bay Dinners. International guest chefs prepare gourmet Marlborough cuisine matched with Seresin organic wines, set in a restored cottage in the Marlborough Sounds. Enquiries: info@seresin.co.nz

OWNER
Michael Seresin

WINEMAKERS
Brian Bicknell & Rachel Jackson

DATE ESTABLISHED 1992

Spy Valley Wines

Spy Valley is the local nickname for the Waihopai Valley where a satellite communications monitoring base is located. Situated amongst the rolling hills of the valley, 125 hectares of estate vineyards planted with eight varieties of grapes producing premium-quality fruit surround the Spy Valley winery. Owning their vineyards ensures total control of the winemaking process and true single-vineyard estate production. Adorning the landscape considered too hard for grapes are 3000-plus olive trees, which produce impressive yields of olive oil. A striking new state-of-the-art winery designed in sympathy with the landscape incorporates a stunning tasting room with picnic tables outside. Marvellous views extend over the vineyards and olive groves to the nearby hills.

RECENT AWARDS
Sydney International Wine Challenge 2004 – Blue-Gold & Top 100: 2003 Gewürztraminer, Blue-Gold: 2002 Chardonnay; Air New Zealand Wine Awards 2003 – Gold, Best Gewürztraminer Trophy: 2003 Gewürztraminer, Gold, Best Commercial Red

Wine Trophy: 2002 Pinot Noir, Gold: 2002 Chardonnay.

ACCOMMODATION
Luxurious and private Timara Lodge is situated on 600 acres of land with 25 acres of beautiful gardens. 4 rooms available (8 guests max.), www.timara.co.nz

37 Lake Timara Road
Blenheim
Tel: (03) 572 9840
Fax: (03) 572 9830
Email: info@spyvalley.co.nz
Website: www.spyvalleywine.co.nz

DIRECTIONS
Turn into Waihopai Valley Road off SH63 just south of Renwick. The winery is 2 km on the left.

OPENING HOURS
Summer: 7 days, Mon to Friday, 10am–4pm

WINERY SALES Cellar door, retail, mail order, Internet

PRICE RANGE $16.95–$28.95

TASTING & TOURS
Tasting fee: $3 for groups of 10 or more (refundable on purchase). Groups are advised to make an appointment. Tours by appointment only.

PICNIC AREA Picnic tables are situated outside the tasting room, commanding views and maximising sunshine.

OWNER Family owned

WINEMAKERS
Ant Mackenzie & Jayne Cosgrove

DATE ESTABLISHED 1991

Wairau River Wines

The Wairau River cellar door with its distinctive mud-brick construction, wide verandahs and stunning views is a perfect place to visit year-round. You can relax on the sun-drenched lawns under shady umbrellas or inside next to the roaring open fire. Their innovative seasonal menu utilises the freshest local produce matched with their superb wines. Wairau River is one of the oldest and largest family-owned estate wineries in Marlborough. All wines are made on site in their state-of-the-art 1000-tonne winery from 100 per cent estate-grown grapes planted on the alluvial banks of the Wairau River. Their philosophy is one of elegance, fruit power and small-batch vintning to produce award-winning, classical styles of wines.

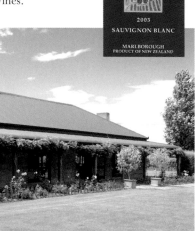

WINES
Labels: Wairau River, Stump Creek, Richmond Ridge, Sunshine Bay
Wine styles: Sauvignon Blanc, Riesling, Chardonnay, Pinot Gris, Gewürztraminer, Pinot Noir

RECENT AWARDS
Consistent high performer in all media tastings, numerous domestic and international awards & medals.

Cnr Rapaura Road & State Highway 6
Renwick
Tel: (03) 572 9800
Fax: (03) 572 9885
Email: office@wairauriverwines.com
Website: www.wairauriverwines.com

DIRECTIONS
On the corner of SH6 and Raparua Road.

OPENING HOURS
7 days, except Christmas Day and Good Friday. Cellar door: 10am–5pm. Restaurant: 12pm–3pm

WINERY SALES
Cellar door (includes exclusive wine specials), retail, mail order

PRICE RANGE $17–$40

TASTING
Tasting available 7 days, 10am–5pm. Tasting fee: $2 for groups of more than 10 (refundable on purchase).

CAFÉ Open for lunch 7 days, 12pm–3pm. Bookings recommended.

OTHER PRODUCTS
Home-made relishes and jams

OWNERS
Phil & Chris Rose

WINEMAKER
John Belsham

DATE ESTABLISHED 1978

56 Anglesea St
Renwick
Tel: (03) 572 8581
Fax: (03) 572 8518
Email: tewharera@xtra.co.nz
Website: www.te-whare-ra.co.nz

DIRECTIONS
Located in Anglesea St, Renwick near
the corner of SH63.

OPENING HOURS
Summer & public holidays:
7 days, 10am–5pm
Winter & public holidays:
Thurs–Sun, 10am–4pm
Other times by appointment.

WINERY SALES
Cellar door, retail, mail order, Internet

PRICE RANGE $18–$25

TASTING & TOURS
Tasting is free of charge and is available
by appointment outside of normal
opening hours. Tutored tastings can be
arranged for groups. Tours by
appointment.

OWNERS
Flowerday family

WINEMAKERS
Jason & Anna Flowerday

DATE ESTABLISHED 1979

Te Whare Ra Wines

Founded in 1979, Te Whare Ra is the oldest boutique winery in Marlborough. The name that translates from Maori to mean 'The House in the Sun' reflects its sunny Renwick location. The owners and winemakers Jason and Anna Flowerday both come from extensive family involvement in the Australian and New Zealand wine industries, and their winemaking philosophy is centred on producing premium estate-grown, handcrafted wines which express a 'somewhere-ness rather than a same-ness'.

Early plantings in this vineyard are some of the oldest in Marlborough, which together with long summer sunlight hours, free-draining river shingle soils and cool winters contribute to Te Whare Ra's winemaking successes. They have won many awards over the past few years, in particular with the Gewürztraminer sourced from a 25-year-old block of vines.

The winery at Te Whare Ra is constructed from mud-bricks. The cellar door is above the winery tanks so that you can see the vintage in progress, and the view from the balcony is magnificent — right over the vineyards to the surrounding Wairau and Richmond ranges.

WINES
Te Whare Ra Sauvignon Blanc, Riesling, Gewürztraminer, Chardonnay, Pinot Noir, and a Merlot blend from current plantings. There are plans to introduce Pinot Gris and Syrah in the next few years.

RECENT AWARDS
Te Whare Ra Duke of Marlborough Gewürztraminer 2002 – Gold & P&O Nedlloyd Trophy for Champion Gewürztraminer: 2002 Air NZ Wine Awards, rated a Potential Classic by Michael Cooper in 2004 *Buyer's Guide to NZ Wines*, rated one of the top 5 Gewürztraminers produced in New Zealand by Bob Campbell in *Cuisine* magazine (100th issue); Te Whare Ra Sarah Jennings Cabernet Franc/Malbec/Merlot 2002 – Silver: 2003 Air NZ Wine Awards

Whitehaven Winery & Restaurant

Whitehaven Wine Company is a family-owned business, which from modest beginnings has rapidly achieved a reputation for producing quality wines that are now exported to six countries. The cellar door and café is located in a historic 142-year-old building on the outskirts of Blenheim. Here you can taste a range of wines crafted by a winemaker focused on quality rather than quantity. Popular for lunches and dinners, you can enjoy the cosy ambience of the log fire or bask in the sunshine in the secluded cottage garden. The fabulous wines can be enjoyed with the well-priced menu that includes a tempting array of Marlborough cuisine — this is a very pleasurable place to idle away the hours.

WINES
Whitehaven Sauvignon Blanc, Chardonnay, Reserve Chardonnay, Riesling, Pinot Noir; Pinot Gris; Single Vineyard Reserve Pinot Gris & Gewürztraminer

RECENT AWARDS
2003 Sauvignon Blanc – Gold: Liquorland Top 100 2003, Blue-Gold: Sydney International Wine Challenge 2003

Whitehaven Winery & Restaurant
1 Dodson Street, Blenheim
Tel: (03) 577 6634
Fax: (03) 577 6634
Email: café@whitehaven.co.nz
Website: www.whitehaven.co.nz

DIRECTIONS On the northern outskirts of Blenheim. Travelling south on SH1 turn right just over the bridge into Dodson Street.

OPENING HOURS
Cellar door and café: 7 days. Lunch: 11.30am–3pm; dinner: from 6pm

WINERY SALES Cellar door, retail, mail order, Internet and at the Whitehaven Restaurant

PRICE RANGE $17–$29

TASTING Tasting is free of charge for up to three wines.

CAFÉ
Lunch & dinner. Booking advisable: (03) 577 6634.

OTHER ACTIVITIES
Exhibitions of up-and-coming local artists; children's play area; pétanque

OTHER FACILITIES
Available for private functions.

OWNERS Whitehaven Wine Company: Greg & Sue White Whitehaven Café: Nikki Andrews & Helen Winstanley

WINEMAKER Simon Waghorn

DATE ESTABLISHED 1994

Koura Bay Wines @ The Station

Home to the Smith family for five generations, Koura Bay is named after the Kaikoura area on Marlborough's Pacific coast. Koura is the Maori word for crayfish, and all their wines complement this seafood perfectly. The vineyard is on the banks of the Awatere River beneath Mt Tapuae-o-Uenuku, the highest peak in the Kaikoura ranges. Koura Bay consistently produces award-winning wines with over 90 per cent being exported. Tastings and sales are available nearby at The Station, the original railway station that closed in the 1980s. Since renovated, The Station is now a wine bar for tastings and sales of wines from the Awatere Valley, a café and art gallery.

WINES
Koura Bay Whalesback Sauvignon Blanc, Sharkstooth Pinot Gris, Barney's Rock Riesling, Mt Fyffe Chardonnay, Blue Duck Pinot Noir

RECENT AWARDS
Sharkstooth Pinot Gris 2003 – Best Buy: *Cuisine* magazine; Blue Duck Pinot Noir 2000 – Gold: Bragato Awards; Whalesback Sauvignon Blanc 1999 – Gold: Bragato Awards

Koura Bay Wines
7 Nursery Rd, Seddon
Tel: (03) 575 7688
Fax: (03) 575 3771
Email: info@kourabaywines.co.nz
The Station
Main Rd, Seddon
Tel: (03) 575 7902
Fax: (03) 575 7903

DIRECTIONS Situated on SH1 in the middle of Seddon, 24km south of Blenheim.

OPENING HOURS
7 days, 10am–5pm. Closed Christmas Day and Good Friday.

WINERY SALES
Retail, mail order and at The Station, SH1, Seddon

PRICE RANGE $17.95–$34.95

TASTING Tasting is free of charge.

CAFÉ The Station features platters of locally produced products. Light lunches and all-day breakfasts.

EVENTS & ACTIVITIES
The Art Gallery at The Station features exhibitions of up-and-coming local artists. Exhibitions change bi-monthly, all works for sale.

OWNERS
Koura Bay Wines: Geoff & Diane Smith
The Station: Irene Ross

WINEMAKERS
Simon Waghorn & Sam Smail

DATE ESTABLISHED 1997

Redwood Pass Rd
Awatere Valley
Tel: (03) 575 7481
Fax: (03) 575 7240
Email: vavasour@vavasour.com
Website: www.vavasour.com

DIRECTIONS
Turn off SH1 into Redwood Pass Rd just
north of Seddon. The winery is 4km on
the right.

OPENING HOURS
Oct–Apr: 7 days, 10am–5pm
May–Oct: Sun–Fri, 10am–5pm

WINERY SALES
Cellar door, retail, mail order, Internet

PRICE RANGE $16–$30

TASTING & TOURS
Tasting is free of charge. Tours by
appointment.

PICNIC AREA
Next to the winery in the garden with
picnic tables.

OWNERS
New Zealand Wine Fund

WINEMAKER
Glenn Thomas

DATE ESTABLISHED 1986

Vavasour Wines

You will find Vavasour Wines on the banks of the magnificent Awatere River, south of
Blenheim — it was here in 1986 that they became the pioneers of winemaking in the
Awatere Valley. A harsh and dramatic environment — Mt Tapuae-o-Uenuku's 2900-metre peak
rises to the south, and to the north lies the ocean reducing the risk of frosts — the rainfall is
lower, the soil less fertile and the wind helps reduce the risk of diseases.

The terraced banks of the Awatere River provide an ideal soil structure for the vineyard.
Wines are produced from low-yielding vines, which ensure the highest possible concentration of
flavours. This is a very hands-on vineyard — they often hand-pick to ensure only the best fruit
makes it into the bottle, and whole-bunch press. Extra grapes are sourced from contract
growers based in both the Wairau and Awatere Valleys.

The winery is located in the vineyard and offers an authentic cellar-door experience, the
tasting table set on a couple of wine barrels is inside the winery. Visitors are also welcome to
picnic in the sunny and sheltered garden out front.

WINES
Vavasour Sauvignon Blanc,
Chardonnay, Pinot Gris,
Riesling, Pinot Noir
Dashwood Sauvignon Blanc,
Chardonnay, Pinot Noir
The premium Vavasour range
is made predominantly from
estate-grown Awatere grapes
creating elegant finely
textured wines designed to
improve with age. The
Dashwood range, a lighter,
more approachable style
designed for early drinking, is
made from blended fruit
from the Wairau and Awatere
Valleys.

RECENT AWARDS
Vavasour Sauvignon Blanc
2002 – Gold: International
Wine and Spirit Competition,
London

DASHWOOD

MARLBOROUGH
SAUVIGNON BLANC
2 0 0 3

PRODUCT OF NEW ZEALAND

Villa Maria Estate Marlborough
Corner Paynters & New Renwick Rds
Phone: (03) 577 9530
Email: enquiries@villamaria.co.nz
Website: www.villamaria.co.nz

DIRECTIONS
Corner of New Renwick and Paynters Rd, beside the Marlborough Golf Club.

OPENING HOURS
7 days, 10am–5pm

WINERY SALES
Cellar door, retail, mail order

PRICE RANGE Starting at $14

TASTING & TOURS
Tasting is free of charge. Tours by appointment only (contact the cellar door).

OWNER
George Fistonich

WINEMAKERS
Alastair Maling MW — Group Winemaker
George Geris — Marlborough Winemaker

DATE ESTABLISHED 1961

Villa Maria Estate Marlborough

Founded in 1961 by owner and Managing Director George Fistonich, Villa Maria is New Zealand's largest privately owned winery and produces New Zealand's most awarded wines.

At the picturesque Villa Maria Marlborough winery you can taste some of the superb wines derived from this region. The Marlborough winery is state-of-the-art and has received awards for its architectural design. Built to cope with an increased grape tonnage, the winery now crushes the majority of Villa Maria's Marlborough harvest from its vineyards and contract growers throughout the region.

The winery and cellar shop were designed to blend into the surrounding landscape, set amongst the vines with the Wither Hills providing a stunning backdrop with views over the Wairau Valley towards the Richmond Ranges.

VILLA MARIA

NEW ZEALAND
Reserve

PINOT NOIR
2002
MARLBOROUGH
NEW ZEALAND WINE
BOTTLED BY VILLA MARIA ESTATE LTD
5 KIRKBRIDE ROAD AUCKLAND
e75cl 14% vol

WINES
Villa Maria produces four distinctive ranges of wine:

Private Bin A popular selection of varietal wines, which are well structured and display true varietal characteristics.

Cellar Selection An emphasis on fruit quality and minimal handling results in intensely flavoured, elegant, food-friendly wines.

Reserve Only produced from the best vineyards in New Zealand's top wine-growing areas to ensure they exhibit the finest regional characteristics possible. Wines must be of exceptional quality to justify the 'Reserve' marque.

Single Vineyard: The creation of a Single Vineyard range has been a long-term vision of the Villa Maria winemaking and viticulture team. These wines are sourced from vineyards of exceptional quality and only when vintage conditions allow the sites to fully express their individual characteristics. Wines across the ranges: Chardonnay, Sauvignon Blanc, Riesling, Pinot Gris, Gewürztraminer, Late Harvest Riesling, Late Harvest Gewürztraminer, Noble Riesling, Pinot Noir, Merlot, Merlot/Cabernet Sauvignon

RECENT AWARDS
Trophy for Most Successful Exhibitor: New Zealand Wine Society Royal Easter Wine Show 2004; two trophies, 12 gold medals and four silver medals: Air New Zealand Wine Awards 2003; Villa Maria Cellar Selection Marlborough Sauvignon Blanc 2003 – Trophy for Best Sauvignon Blanc: Cool Climate Wine Show 2004; Villa Maria Reserve Pinot Noir 2002 – Gold & Trophy for Best Pinot Noir: Royal Hobart Wine Show 2003

Kaikoura Winery

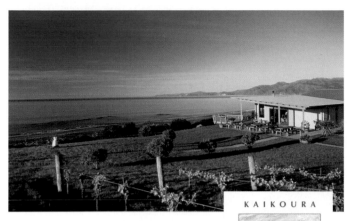

KAIKOURA

MARLBOROUGH
SAUVIGNON BLANC
2002

Kaikoura Winery is Marlborough's southernmost vineyard and arguably the most scenic in New Zealand. Situated on the limestone bluff just south of Kaikoura township, the tasting area offers magnificent views of snow-capped mountain ranges and the vast expanse of the Pacific Ocean where whales and dolphins can often be seen. Four hectares of vineyard surrounding the winery and sales area will be harvested in 2004 with most of the other grapes being sourced from contract growers in Marlborough. When visiting, one shouldn't miss the opportunity to take a tour through the facilities which takes in the vineyard, winery and underground cellar.

WINES
Kaikoura Wine Company Gewürztraminer, Sauvignon Blanc, Chardonnay, Riesling, Pinot Noir, Méthode Champenoise and Noble Riesling

RECENT AWARDS
First Green Globe Benchmarked vineyard in the world; 2002 Gewürztraminer – 4 Stars and Wine of the Month: *Cuisine* magazine (Jun 03); 2002 Sauvignon Blanc – 4 Stars: *Cuisine* magazine

140 State Highway 1
P O Box 11, Kaikoura
Tel: (03) 319 7966
Fax: (03) 319 7967
Email: Kaikoura.Wines@xtra.co.nz
Website: www.kaikourawines.co.nz

DIRECTIONS Situated 2km south of Kaikoura, follow the signposted road up the Bluff.

OPENING HOURS
7 days, 10am–5.30pm

WINERY SALES Cellar door, retail, mail order, Internet

PRICE RANGE $16.00–$24.95

TASTING & TOURS Tasting fee: $3.00 (refundable on purchase of 3 wines). Guided tours. Fee: $8.50.

CAFÉ A deli bar and gourmet platters are available.

PICNIC AREA Picnickers welcome all day. A BBQ is available for hire.

OTHER FACILITIES The cellar is available for weddings and private functions.

EVENTS/ACTIVITIES
Art exhibitions, stone carving symposium, live concerts, weddings, private functions

OWNER
Kaikoura Wine Company

WINEMAKER Mike Just

DATE ESTABLISHED 1998

Te Whare Ra Wines

Spy Valley Wines

The Mud House Village

125

Canterbury

CANTERBURY has two major wine areas: the vast **Canterbury Plains** around the South Island city of **Christchurch**, and the smaller, sheltered **Waipara Valley**, 65 kilometres north of Christchurch. This is New Zealand's fourth largest wine region, producing some 4.5 per cent of the national crop. The Canterbury Plains were first planted commercially in the 1970s, and vineyards are now scattered from **Amberley** in the north to **Timaru** in the south. Soils consist of mainly alluvial silt loams over gravel subsoils and produce generally lighter-bodied, elegant styles of chiefly Pinot Noir and Chardonnay. The more recently developed Waipara Valley, with vineyards around the towns of **Waipara** and **Omihi**, is warmer than the plains, and has predominantly chalky loam soils that can be rich in limestone. Its wines, which often display rich, ripe fruit flavours, include Pinot Noir, Chardonnay and Riesling, with Merlots and Cabernet Sauvignons in warmer vintages.

Christchurch has a reputation for its 'Englishness', with its old stone buildings and punts gliding on the tree-lined Avon River. It is the gateway to the rivers of the Canterbury Plains and the mountains and skifields of the Southern Alps.

For more information on the Canterbury region visit www.canterburyfare.co.nz or www.christchurchnz.net or contact Christchurch Visitor Information Centre: Old Chief Post Office, Cathedral Square West, Christchurch, (03) 379 9629, info@christchurchnz.net.

Pegasus Bay

Pegasus Bay

HISTORY

French immigrants brought grapes to Akaroa on Banks Peninsula in 1840 but its modern winemaking era began much later after trials at Lincoln University in the 1970s showed which varieties best suited Canterbury's cool-climate conditions. The region's first commercial winery was St Helena, planted by Robin and Norman Mundy at Belfast, just north of Christchurch in 1978. Their success inspired other pioneering producers.

SOILS

The Canterbury Plains has variable soils, mostly free-draining silty loams overlying river gravels as well as moderately fertile soils with good water-holding ability. The Waipara Valley includes stony soils, gravelly loams over alluvial subsoils, as well as chalky limestone-derived clays and loams.

CLIMATE

Abundant sunshine, warm, dry summers followed by long, dry autumns, along with relatively cool growing conditions are a feature in both the Waipara Valley and the Canterbury Plains. Waipara, however, being sheltered from the coast by a low range of hills, can be significantly warmer although late spring frosts can be a danger in both sub-regions. The hot summer days followed by cool nights help preserve the grapes' acidity, while the favourably dry autumns minimise fungal infections.

GRAPE VARIETIES AND WINE STYLES

The major variety is Pinot Noir, usually full-bodied wines rich in fruit characters. The region has a wide range of Chardonnay styles, from cool, crisp fruity wines to full-bodied ones. Pinot Noir and Chardonnay make up some 60 per cent of the crop. The third most planted variety is Riesling, made in dry, elegant styles or richer and fruitier examples. Late-harvest and botrytised wines are also popular. Other varieties include riper styles of Sauvignon Blanc, and Pinot Gris.

SUB-REGIONS

Canterbury Plains, from Amberley in the north to Timaru in the south. The scattered vineyards on the plains produce mostly lighter-bodied, elegant styles of chiefly Pinot Noir and Chardonnay.

Waipara Valley, some 65km north of Christchurch, is the scene of much recent development. Its wines show rich, ripe fruit flavours.

Banks Peninsula, east of Christchurch, was the birthplace of Canterbury's wine industry, and now produces small quantities of mainly Pinot Noir and Chardonnay from boutique wineries.

Morworth Estate

Morworth Estate

Events

- **Waipara Wine and Food Celebration**. The region's wine and food producers gather to show their wares in a festival held in the historic Glenmark Church grounds. Held annually in March.
- **Jade Wine and Food Festival of Canterbury.** All the offerings of the region. Held in Christchurch annually on the third Sunday in February.
- **New Zealand Organic Food and Wine Festival.** The country's premier organic produce festival, held in Oamaru annually in March.

For more information contact the Christchurch Visitor Information Centre.

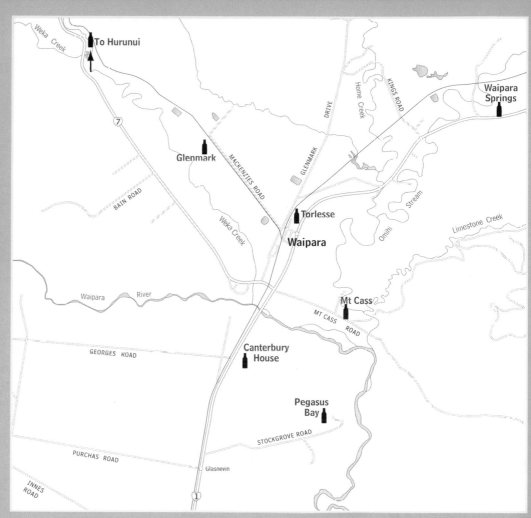

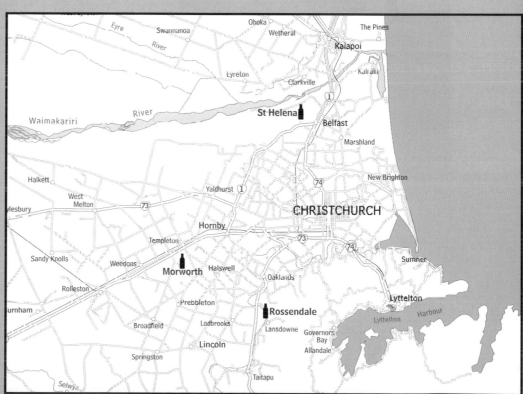

Motunau Beach

BANKS
  PENINSULA

Torlesse Wines

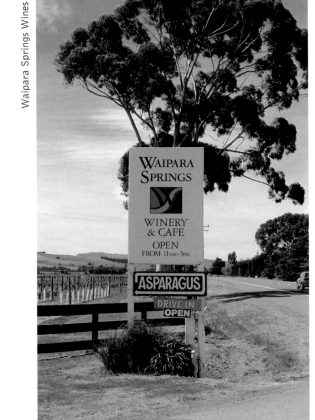

Waipara Springs Wines

Pegasus Bay

Hurunui River Wines

Hurunui River Wines come from a 2-hectare vineyard on the terraces of the braided river of that name in North Canterbury. Family owned and managed, the vineyard is part of a larger sheep and cattle farm. In this unique environment of hot dry summers, regular droughts and strong nor'west winds, the river provides life-giving water and the stony river terraces good drainage and valuable heat for vine ripening. Set amongst beautiful countryside, the cellar door, café and gift shop is a great place to spend a lazy afternoon. Along with their excellent wines, the café features platters, great coffee and delicious cakes. Or you can picnic in the picturesque grounds.

WINES
Hurunui River Sauvignon Blanc, Chardonnay, Riesling, Cabernet Sauvignon

RECENT AWARDS
Huruni River has not yet entered their wines in competitons.

OTHER PRODUCTS
Athena marinated olives, arts and crafts, Amberley Lavender Farm products

110 Costellos Rd, Hawarden
Tel: (03) 314 4495
Fax: (03) 314 4496
Email: hanley@ihug.co.nz

DIRECTIONS Travelling north on SH7, turn left into Medbury Rd, 1km before the Hurunui Hotel. Continue for 8km and veer right into The Peaks Rd (a shingle road). Continue until you reach three forks: Costellos Rd is the left-hand fork and Hurunui River Wines is first on the right.

OPENING HOURS
All year: Sat & Sun, 1pm–5pm; other times by arrangement.

WINERY SALES
Cellar door, retail, mail order

PRICE RANGE $16.50–$22

TASTING & TOURS Tasting is free of charge. Vineyard tours by appointment. Hanmer Air will fly people from Hanmer Springs for a combination scenic flight and wine-tasting.

CAFÉ Part of the cellar door and tasting facility. Reservations: (03) 314 4495.

PICNIC AREA Outside the café, includes picnic tables, pétanque and a children's playground.

OWNERS
Wendy Alabaster & Mark Hassall

WINEMAKER Belinda Gould

DATE ESTABLISHED 1993

Canterbury House

CANTERBURY HOUSE

2003
PINOT GRIS
WAIPARA
PRODUCT OF NEW ZEALAND

The impressive Canterbury House building incorporates a restaurant, tasting room and state-of-the-art winery built to handle a planned annual production of 125,000 cases of premium estate-grown wines. Surrounded by beautifully landscaped gardens and vineyards, the building with its vaulted ceiling, large fireplace, antique furniture and tapestries evokes images of the fine baronial halls and wine chateaux of Europe. The gourmet menu takes advantage of the season's freshest fare and includes a selection of dishes to suit every appetite and budget. During harvest in April there is a unique opportunity to taste fresh grape juice from the varieties grown in the Canterbury House vineyard before it completes its fermentation into wine.

WINES
Canterbury House Riesling, Noble Riesling, Sauvignon Blanc, Chardonnay, Pinot Gris, Late Harvest Pinot Gris, Pinot Noir, Merlot, Méthode Traditionnelle

Gold: Bragato Wine Awards 2003; 2003 Pinot Gris – Gold: NZ Wine Society Royal Easter Wine Show 2004; 2002 Riesling – Gold: Liquorland Top 100 2003; 2002 Noble Riesling – Gold & Trophy for Best Sweet Wine: Liquorland Top 100 2003

RECENT AWARDS
Chardonnay Reserve 2002 –

780 Glasnevin Rd, SH1 Amberley
Tel: (03) 314 6900
Fax: (03) 314 6905
Email: canterburyhouse@attglobal.net
Website: www.canterburyhouse.com

DIRECTIONS 50km north of Christchurch on SH1.

OPENING HOURS
Cellar door, wine tasting and snacks: 7 days, 10am–5pm
Lunch: 7 days, 11.30am–3pm,
Dinner: group bookings and by reservation only.

WINERY SALES Cellar door, retail, mail order, Internet

PRICE RANGE $14.90–$28.90

TASTING & TOURS
Group bookings: $3 per person, otherwise free of charge. Tours by appointment only.

RESTAURANT
Daily à la carte lunch menu, morning and late afternoon snacks and special blended coffees. Reservations: (03) 314 6900.

OTHER FACILITIES
Available for weddings and functions, to suit personal requirements.

OWNER Dr Michael Reid

WINEMAKER
Alan McCorkindale

DATE ESTABLISHED 1994

Glenmark Wines

Glenmark's owner John McCaskey started the wine industry in Waipara, planting the valley's first vineyard in 1981 and opening the first winery in a converted hay barn in 1986. His very popular wine garden is relocating just up the road for the 2004/5 season to the 'House o' Hill' site that looks across the Waipara Valley. 'House o' Hill' is named after an inn on the road between Dumfries and Ayr, Scotland, once owned by the McCaskey forebears. From this peaceful and elevated woodland park, one can relax, enjoy fine wines and food, play pétanque, giant chess or test your golfing skills with a game of GolfCross®. An animal park with deer, sheep and alpacas will entertain the children.

Shar Devine

GLENMARK
2000
WAIPARA
WEKA PLAINS
Riesling
MEDIUM
750ml℮   12% Vol.

WINES
Glenmark Riesling, Gewürztraminer, Chardonnay, Müller-Thurgau, Pinot Noir, Waipara Red (blend of Cabernet Sauvignon, Cabernet Franc, Merlot and Malbec)

RECENT AWARDS
An impressive list of wine awards over the years includes gold medal Rieslings and Chardonnays and a NZ champion Waipara Red.

330 MacKenzies Rd (previously 169), Waipara
Tel: (03) 314 6828
Fax: (03) 314 6828
Email: jsjmcc@xtra.co.nz
Website: www.glenmarkwines.com

DIRECTIONS
Take Mackenzies Rd just out of Waipara township and continue to the end; the road follows the Weka Pass Railway.

OPENING HOURS Labour Weekend–Easter: Weekends: 11am–5pm, 7 days during holidays. Rest of year: by appointment.

WINERY SALES Cellar door, retail, mail order, Internet 027 431 0272

PRICE RANGE $11–$27

TASTING & TOURS Tasting fee: $5 refundable on purchase. Tours by appointment only.

CAFÉ
House o' Hill wine garden. Reservations: (03) 314 6828.

PICNIC AREA Picnic tables and gas BBQ available.

OTHER ACTIVITIES
GolfCross®: golf with goals instead of holes and played with an oval ball instead of a round one, giant chess, pétanque, animal farm

OWNER John McCaskey

WINEMAKERS
John McCaskey & Kym Rayner (consultant)

DATE ESTABLISHED 1986

Mount Cass Vineyards

The vineyards on Mt Cass Road, established in 1982, are some of the earliest plantings in the Waipara district. The terroir of the area is not too different from Marlborough, but has the added benefit of the surrounding Teviotdale Hills and Mount Cass (the predominant peak), in protecting the vineyards from the cool easterly sea breezes. This family-owned business produces wine under two brands: Mount Cass, emphasising the location of the vineyards on Mt Cass Rd; and The Hanmer Junction, which associates the company with the tourist resort at Hanmer Springs. Both are available on the domestic and export markets. A recently opened cellar door allows visitors to sample a range of wines while overlooking the vineyard.

WINES
Mount Cass Sauvignon Blanc, Pinot Noir, Riesling, Chardonnay, Cabernet Sauvignon, Late Harvest Chardonnay
Hanmer Junction Sauvignon Blanc, Pinot Gris, Riesling, Cabernet Merlot, Cabernet Sauvignon, Unwooded and Lightly Oaked Chardonnay

RECENT AWARDS
2001 Hanmer Junction Waipara Pinot Gris – Gold & Trophy: NZ Wine Society Royal Easter Show 2002; 2002 Mount Cass Waipara Valley Late Harvest Selection – Silver: Air New Zealand Awards 2003; Mount Cass Waipara Valley Riesling – Silver: Air New Zealand Awards 2003

133 Mt Cass Rd, Waipara
Tel: (03) 314 6853
Fax: (03) 314 6894
Email: admin@alpacwines.co.nz

DIRECTIONS
Travelling North on SH1 turn right into Mt Cass Rd, opposite the SH7 turnoff to Hanmer Springs. The vineyard is 1km down Mt Cass Rd.

OPENING HOURS
Thurs–Sun: 11am–5pm. Other times by appointment.

WINERY SALES
Cellar door, retail, mail order

PRICE RANGE $15–$60

TASTING
Tasting is free of charge.

OWNERS
Chris & Carol Parker

WINEMAKER
Petter Evans

DATE ESTABLISHED 1982

Pegasus Bay

Pegasus Bay is a small family owned and operated winery whose aim is to produce wines of the highest quality that fully express the features of their vineyard. In a picturesque setting with an extensive outdoor dining area among lakes and beautiful gardens, Pegasus Bay offers a memorable experience to wine & food enthusiasts, whether it be tasting their highly regarded estate-grown wines, viewing the barrel hall and wine cellars or indulging the appetite with delectable local produce in the winery restaurant. The menu has an emphasis on freshness and simplicity and is designed to complement the wines. The atmosphere inside is warm, with a large open fire, and contemporary works from some of New Zealand's leading artists hang on the recycled native timber walls.

WINES
Pegasus Bay: Riesling, Sauvignon/Semillon, Chardonnay, Pinot Noir, Cabernet/Merlot. Reserve Wines (produced only in exceptional vintages): Aria — late-picked Riesling, Maestro — Merlot/Malbec, Prima Donna — Pinot Noir, Finale — Noble Chardonnay (barrique-fermented)

RECENT AWARDS
Pegasus Bay does not enter shows but recent accolades include: Aria 2002 – Top Sweet Wine: 2004 Tri-nations Wine Challenge

Stockgrove Road
RD 2 Amberley, Waipara
Tel: (03) 314 6869
Fax: (03) 314 6861
Email: info@pegasusbay.com
Website: www.pegasusbay.com

DIRECTIONS 45 minutes north of Christchurch. Turn right down Stockgrove Rd which is about 5 minutes past Amberley.

OPENING HOURS Wine tasting & sales: 7 days, 10.30am–5pm. Restaurant: 7 days, 12 noon–4pm

WINERY SALES
Cellar door, winery restaurant, retail, mail order, Internet

PRICE RANGE
$21.50–$70

TASTING & TOURS
Tasting fee: $2, refundable on purchase. Tours by appointment.

RESTAURANT
Bookings recommended: (03) 314 6869.

OWNERS
The Donaldson family

WINEMAKERS
Matthew Donaldson & Lynette Hudson

DATE ESTABLISHED 1985

Torlesse Wines

Torlesse Wines is named after the Torlesse mountain range that circles part of the Canterbury Plains. Interestingly the name Torlesse is also given to the underlying bedrock from which most New Zealand soils are derived — the terroir. At the on-site winery Kym Rayner, the winemaker, handcrafts a range of stylish wines that portray the character of the distinctive soil types and locations of their vineyards that are spread throughout Waipara and Canterbury. Wine-tasting facilities are available at the cellar door that also features a range of older vintages and a great selection of local arts and crafts. Maggie Rayner is the hostess and you will normally be greeted by Chloe, the Rayner's big friendly Newfoundland dog.

WINES
Waipara Riesling, Gewürztraminer, Sauvignon Blanc, Cabernet/Merlot, Merlot, Pinot Gris, Late Harvest Riesling, Reserve Port Canterbury Chardonnay (Lightly Oaked), Riesling, Pinot Noir Waipara Reserve Chardonnay, Pinot Noir

Loffhagen Drive, Waipara
Tel: (03) 314 6929
Fax: (03) 414 6867
Email: krayner@xtra.co.nz
Website: www.torlesse.co.nz

DIRECTIONS
Located near the Waipara School, adjacent to SH1 and 2km past the turnoff to Hanmer Springs (SH7).

OPENING HOURS
Fri–Sun & public holidays: 11am–5pm, or by appointment.

WINERY SALES
Cellar door, retail, mail order, Internet

PRICE RANGE $14.50–$30

TASTING & TOURS
Tasting is free of charge except for groups when a fee of $3 pp applies and includes an extensive personalised tasting. Tours by appointment only.

OTHER PRODUCTS
Local arts and crafts, clothing and wine accessories

OWNERS
The Tomlin, Rayner, Blowers, Pharis and Fabris families

WINEMAKER
Kym Rayner

DATE ESTABLISHED 1991

Waipara Springs Wines

Waipara Springs is a boutique vineyard and winery producing premium-quality wines that have received acclaim in New Zealand and internationally since opening in 1990. Originally planted with 4 hectares of grapes, this has now been expanded to 20 hectares. The café and winery are housed in attractive old farm buildings originally built as stables and a grain shed. Visitors can enjoy tasting at the wine bar with an informative and friendly commentary or dine at the café, now one of the most popular in the region. With indoor and outdoor seating, the eclectic menu features a wonderful array of tempting dishes using as many local ingredients as possible, including salmon, lamb, cheeses, asparagus and other seasonal produce.

WINES
Waipara Springs Barrique Chardonnay, Lightly Oaked Chardonnay, Sauvignon Blanc, Riesling, Pinot Blush, Botrytised Riesling, Pinot Noir, Reserve Pinot Noir, Cabernet Sauvignon

RECENT AWARDS
Waipara Springs is dedicated to quality and has received numerous accolades with Gold, Silver and Bronze medals won in competitions worldwide.

409 Omihi Rd, SH1, Waipara
Tel: (03) 314 6777
Fax: (03) 314 6777
Email: wine@waiparasprings.co.nz
Website: www.waiparasprings.co.nz

DIRECTIONS
On SH1, a 50-minute drive north of Christchurch and 4km past the turnoff to Hanmer Springs (SH7).

OPENING HOURS
Wine tasting, sales & cafe: 7 days, 11am–5pm (closed 24/25/26 December & 1 Jan). Café closed June, July & August

WINERY SALES Cellar door, retail, mail order, Internet

PRICE RANGE $16–$36

TASTING Tasting fee $3, refundable on purchase.

CAFÉ
Waipara Springs Café. Reservations: (03) 314 6777.

ACTIVITIES
Clydesdale Wagon Tours with Colonial Horse Treks. Bookings: 025 227 6120.

OTHER PRODUCTS
Local Athena olive oil, pottery and paintings

OWNERS
Grant & Moore families

WINEMAKER
Stephanie Henderson Grant

DATE ESTABLISHED 1990

Morworth Estate

Stephen Goodenough

Set in the heart of the Canterbury Plains with panoramic views to the Southern Alps and Port Hills is Morworth Estate's stylish café restaurant, wine-tasting facility and state-of-the-art winery. Family-owned and committed to fine wine and dining, the elegant restaurant offers a seasonal menu best described as antipodean fusion — simple clean flavours from local fresh produce — to complement their wines. Morworth Estate has vineyards in both the Canterbury Plains and Marlborough and has quickly established a reputation for the production of superior quality wines that reflect the character of both sites. Currently around 85 per cent of production goes to overseas markets. The Morkane family's crest — *fidus et audex*, 'faithful and bold' — is a reflection of the excellent wine, food and service they offer.

WINES
Morworth Estate Canterbury Pinot Noir, Pinot Gris, Gewürztraminer, Riesling, Marlborough Sauvignon Blanc, Chardonnay

EVENTS & ACTIVITIES
The restaurant hosts regular exhibitions from local and visiting artists.

Block Road, Broadfield
Christchurch
Tel: (03) 349 5014
Fax: (03) 349 5017
Email: info@morworth.com
Website: www.morworth.com

DIRECTIONS Just 20 mins south of Christchurch City, take Shands Rd from Hornby, follow for 5km. Turn right into Hamptons Road; after 1km turn left into Block Rd. The winery is at the end.

OPENING HOURS Cellar door: Wed–Sun: 10am–5pm.
Café: Wed–Sun, 11am–3pm

WINERY SALES Cellar door, Morworth Estate Restaurant, retail, mail order, Internet

PRICE RANGE $18.50–$30

TASTING & TOURS Tasting by appointment. Fee: $5 per person, refundable on purchase of two bottles of wine. Tours available but appointment necessary outside of restaurant hours.

RESTAURANT & CAFÉ
Reservations: (03) 349 5014. Wines available at cellar-door prices.

OWNERS
Chris and Leonie Morkane

WINEMAKER
Sarah Morkane Deans

DATE ESTABLISHED 1993

St Helena Wine Estate

Sitting just north of Christchurch in the Canterbury Plains is St Helena Wine Estate, Canterbury's oldest commercial winery and acknowledged as the pioneer in establishing premium Pinot Noir in New Zealand. Founded in 1978 by the Mundy family, the vineyard takes advantage of the region's long warm summers and dry autumns to grow some of the best grapes in New Zealand. A stunning collection of wines is produced from their 20-hectare vineyard next to the winery and from another 50-hectare vineyard in Marlborough. Currently over 90 per cent of the winery's production is destined for export markets. Owners Robin and Bernice Mundy and award-winning winemaker Alan McCorkindale are passionate in their dedication to producing exceptional-quality fruit and wine and the development of Canterbury as one of New Zealand's finest wine-producing regions.

WINES
St Helena Pinot Noir, Riesling, Pinot Gris, Sauvignon Blanc, Chardonnay, Pinot Blanc, Gewürztraminer, Late Harvest, Merlot

RECENT AWARDS
St Helena 2003 Reserve Pinot Gris — Gold & Trophy for Best Pinot Gris in Show, St Helena 2002 Reserve Pinot Noir — Bronze, St Helena 2003 Sauvignon Blanc — Bronze: Red Hill Cool Climate Show 2004

259 Coutts Island Rd, Belfast
Tel: (03) 323 8202
Fax: (03) 323 8252
Email: sthelena@xtra.co.nz

DIRECTIONS
A 20-minute drive north of Christchurch, Coutts Island Rd is just north of Belfast off the main road (SH1) to Waipara.

OPENING HOURS
7 days, 10am–4.30pm

WINERY SALES
Cellar door, retail, mail order

PRICE RANGE
$12–$28 (cellar door)

TASTING & TOURS
Tasting is free of charge. Tours by appointment.

OWNERS
Robin & Bernice Mundy

WINEMAKER
Alan McCorkindale

DATE ESTABLISHED 1978

168 Old Tai Tapu Rd
Halswell, Christchurch
Tel: (03) 322 9684 or 322 7780
Fax: (03) 322 9272
Email: office@rossendale.co.nz
Website: www.rossendale.co.nz

DIRECTIONS
Clearly signposted, turn left off Halswell Rd (SH75 and the main Akaroa Highway) into Old Tai Tapu Rd, just south of Halswell. Rossendale is 1.5km on the right.

OPENING HOURS
Lunch & dinner: 7 days, 10am–10pm (closed Christmas Day)

WINERY SALES
Cellar door, retail, mail order, Internet

PRICE RANGE $17–$20

TASTING
Tasting free of charge for diners and casual small groups. For large groups there is a tasting fee of $6 pp for six wines (by appointment).

RESTAURANT
Reservations: (03) 322 9684 or 322 7780

OTHER PRODUCTS
Full range of branded merchandise including clothing and wine accessories

EVENTS & ACTIVITIES
Rossendale road race/walk is an annual event held in May.

OWNERS
Brent & Shirley Rawston

WINEMAKER
Alan McCorkindale

DATE ESTABLISHED 1994

Rossendale Winery & Restaurant

Rossendale is a family-owned beef farm, vineyard, winery and restaurant, just 15 minutes from the centre of Christchurch. The vineyard restaurant is in the exquisitely restored gatekeeper's lodge of the historic Lansdowne homestead and gardens — originally the residence of Edward Stafford, twice Premier of New Zealand between 1856–1869.

Delicious country-style fare can be enjoyed in the beautiful sheltered garden or indoors where you can relax in old-world ambience. The restaurant is also the cellar door and wine-tasting facility for the premium Rossendale wines, all of which are estate-grown and made at the on-site winery.

The home 4.5 hectare vineyard is in nearby Halswell and is planted with Chardonnay, Pinot Noir and Gewürztraminer, and in Marlborough they have 33 hectares planted in Sauvignon Blanc. Since the first vintage in 1993 all wines have received numerous accolades and awards, while currently around 80 per cent of the wine is exported, mainly to the UK with most of the balance being consumed at the restaurant.

WINES
Rossendale Canterbury Riesling, Pinot Noir, Chardonnay Gewürztraminer; Rossendale Marlborough Sauvignon Blanc; Rossendale Hawke's Bay Merlot

RECENT AWARDS
Rossendale Riesling 2002 – Bronze: Royal Easter Show 2004; Stafford Lodge Marlborough Sauvignon Blanc 2003 (English label for Marlborough Sauvignon Blanc 2003) – 2004 New Zealand Meat Board's NZ Hallmark of Excellence

OTHER FACILITIES
Lansdowne is a fully restored homestead set in 2.5 acres of beautiful gardens. The setting is ideal for weddings, private functions and corporate meetings. Catering is done by Rossendale Restaurant. Enquiries phone: (03) 322 7780.

Central Otago

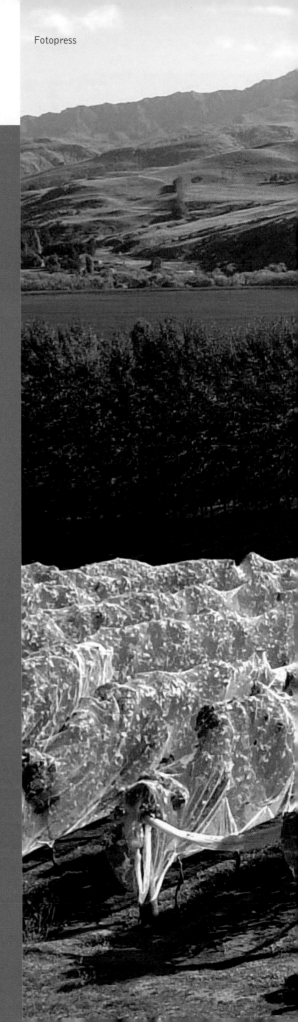

CENTRAL OTAGO, comprising the South Island area around the glacial lakes of **Wakatipu**, **Wanaka** and **Dunstan**, is New Zealand's seventh largest wine region, producing some 4.7 per cent of the national crop. This is New Zealand's highest (200-450 metres above sea level) and the world's most southerly (45°S) wine region. It enjoys a magical setting, with vines planted among spectacular alpine scenery. Mountains and gorges separate its four distinct sub-regions. Cromwell Basin has the bulk of the region's vineyards around the towns of **Bannockburn** and **Cromwell**, and north alongside Lake Dunstan to **Lowburn** and **Bendigo**. The next largest sub-region is the Gibbston area, between **Cromwell** and **Queenstown**, where most vineyards sit on steep sites above the dramatic **Kawarau River** gorge. In the south-west, vineyards occupy a dry basin around the towns of **Clyde** and **Alexandra**. There is also a small, high-altitude area around the town of Wanaka overlooking **Lake Wanaka**. Apart from sheep farming, Central Otago is at the heart of the South Island's tourism industry, centred on Queenstown, and offers innumerable adventure and adrenalin activities.

For more information on the Central Otago region visit www.centralotago.net.nz, www.queenstown-nz.co.nz or www.wanaka.co.nz. Or contact the Queenstown Visitors Information Centre, Clocktower Building, Queenstown, (03) 442 4100, info@qvc.co.nz.

Chard Farm Winery

The Big Picture Wine Adventure

HISTORY

Frenchman John Desiré Feraud, attracted by the Dunstan gold rush of 1862, is said to have planted the region's first vines near Clyde in 1864, and won a prize for his Burgundy-style wine in Sydney in 1881. Trial plantings in the 1950s were followed by the first commercial ventures in the modern winemaking era in the 1970s and 1980s. Bill Grant, of William Hill Vineyard, planted vines at Alexandra in 1973, and in 1976 Rolfe Mills planted the Rippon Vineyard at Wanaka. The first commercial wines flowed after 1987, under the Rippon, Taramea and Gibbston Valley labels.

SOILS

Soils in the region vary dramatically, ranging from wind-blown sands to silt loams and broken schist and mica rock. Most soils are derived from loess or alluvial deposits, often with gravel subsoils that allow free drainage. In the west around Wanaka some soils are based on glacial moraine. Each soil type has a distinct effect on plant growth and grape flavours.

CLIMATE

The region has New Zealand's most continental climate, with marked seasonal extremes of hot summers and cold winters, and a large day/night temperature variation that gives flavour intensity and depth of colour to the grapes. Cold winters mean heavy frosts can occur anytime between March and October. Hot and dry summers are followed by extremely dry, cool autumns, which allow an extended ripening period. A relatively low rainfall, spread evenly throughout the year, results in low risk of fungal diseases.

GRAPE VARIETIES AND WINE STYLES

Pinot Noir is the major grape variety, and one that has won it many accolades. Styles range from perfumed and spicy wines to more fruity, plummier wines grown on warmer sites. Styles of Pinot Gris, the second most planted variety, range from crisp and spicy to rich and oily. Chardonnay, Riesling and Sauvignon Blanc are the other key wines. The region is picked to excel at sparkling wines in the future.

SUB-REGIONS

Cromwell Basin, around the towns of Bannockburn and Cromwell, and north alongside Lake Dunstan to Lowburn and Bendigo, is the warmest subregion, producing powerful, concentrated Pinot Noirs, limey Rieslings and fresh Pinot Gris.

Gibbston, between Cromwell and Queenstown, with sites at 350-420 metres altitude is the coolest subregion, producing concentrated Pinot Noirs, appley Rieslings and crisp Pinot Gris.

Clyde and Alexandra, in the south of the region, can produce elegant, perfumed Pinot Noirs from its hot, north-facing sites as well as aromatic Gewürztraminers.

Wanaka, another high-altitude subregion, has a slightly more temperate climate due to its proximity to the lake. It produces elegant Pinot Noirs, limey Rieslings and flinty Chardonnays.

Packspur Vineyard

View to Chard Farm Winery

Packspur Vineyard

Olss ens Garden Vineyard

Events

- **Central Otago Wine and Food Festival.** Held in the picturesque Queenstown Gardens annually in late January/early February.
- **Clyde Harvest Festival.** A wine and food festival held in Clyde township every Easter.
- **Pinot Noir Celebration.** An event to celebrate the region's hallmark variety, Pinot Noir, which includes seminars, tastings and international speakers. Held at the end of January/early February annually.
- **Feraud Dinner.** Named in honour of pioneer winemaker John Desiré Feraud, this dinner is attended by grape-growers and winemakers. Held at the end of May/June annually.

For more information visit www.centralotago.net.nz

Black Ridge Winery

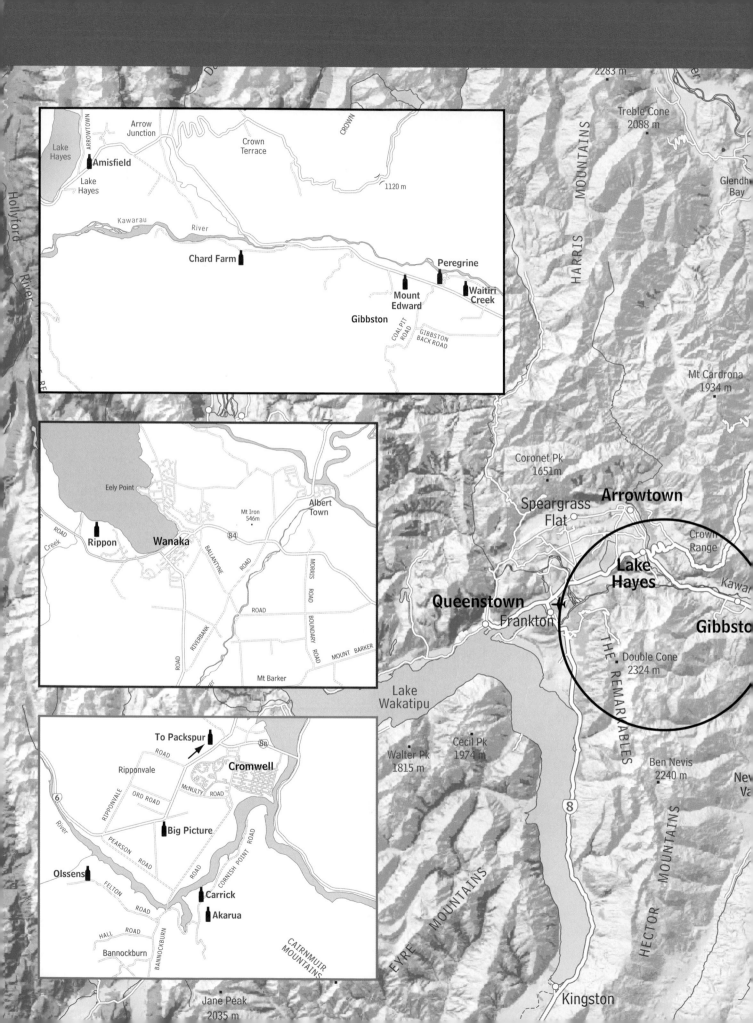

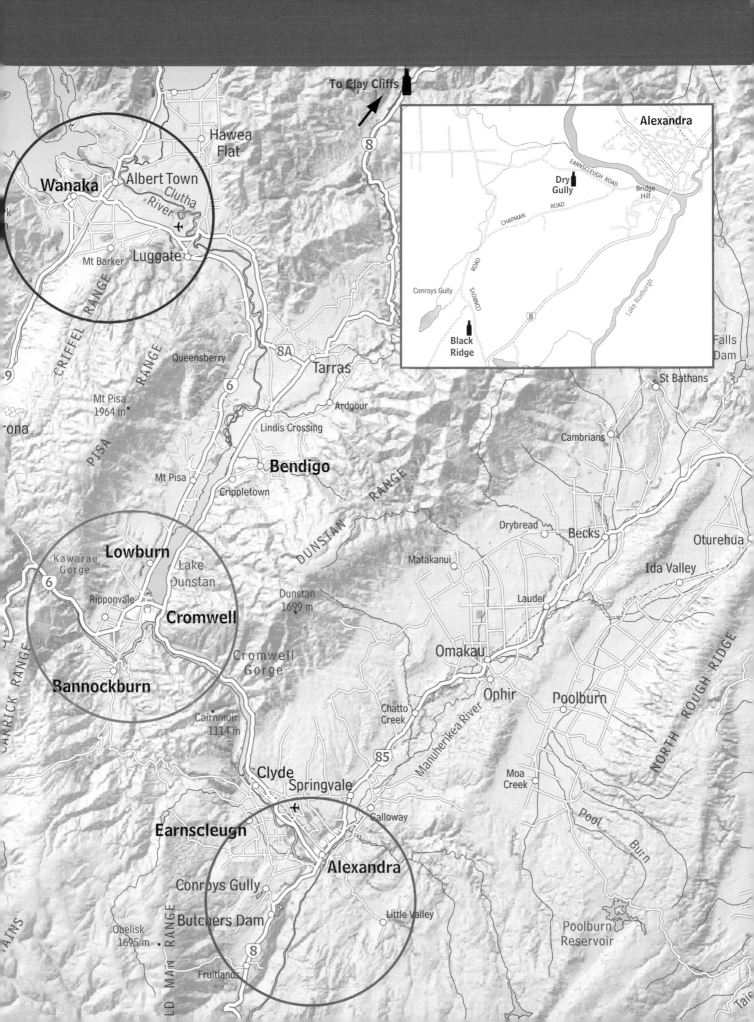

Rippon Vineyard & Winery
Mount Aspiring Rd (Rural no. 246)
Lake Wanaka
Tel: (03) 443 8084
Fax: (03) 443 8034
Email: info@rippon.co.nz
Website: www.rippon.co.nz

DIRECTIONS
4km from the township on Mount Aspiring Road towards Glendhu Bay.

OPENING HOURS
Dec–Apr: 7 days, 11am-5pm
May–Jun: closed (appointment only)
Jul–Nov: 7 days, 1.30pm–4.30pm

WINERY SALES
Cellar door, retail, mail order, Internet

PRICE RANGE $15–$50

TASTING
Tasting is free of charge.

FOOD OPTIONS
A gourmet barbeque lunch accompanied by a selection of Rippon's fine wines is available on the property during the summer months.

OTHER PRODUCTS
Verjus (available in Pinot Noir or Riesling); Sirop de vin (a slightly sweetened wine syrup for vinaigrettes and dessert sauces). Only available from the tasting room.

PICNIC AREA
BYO picnic and enjoy the marvellous scenery on the lawn outside the cellar door; tables provided.

OWNER
Lois Mills

WINEMAKER
Nick Mills

DATE ESTABLISHED 1988

Rippon Vineyard & Winery

The stunningly beautiful Rippon Vineyard is situated on the shores of Lake Wanaka, with views across the lake to Ruby Island and the magnificent snow-capped peaks of the Buchannan Mountains. One of Central Otago's oldest vineyards, it is also one of the highest at 330 metres above sea level with an 1800-metre mountain as a backdrop. The 15-hectare vineyard runs down north-facing schist slopes to the shores of Lake Wanaka. The family-run property is cared for as a diverse and biodynamic whole, fostering wines that mirror their dreamscape surrounds.

Pinot Noir makes up 40 per cent of the vineyard plantings; other varietals are Chardonnay, Sauvignon Blanc, Gewürztraminer, Riesling, Osteiner, Gamay and a small amount of Shiraz and Merlot. The cellar door lies by the lakeshore, providing picnic spots on the lawn for a relaxing afternoon. Or you can test your golfing skills with a game of GolfCross® — Rippon has the distinction of being the birthplace of this game.

ACTIVITIES & EVENTS
GolfCross®: golf with goals instead of holes and played with an oval ball instead of a round one. The challenging course is a rare combination of the best elements of links, woodland and parkland all set against a magnificent mountain and lake backdrop.

Rippon Music Festival is one of New Zealand's best contemporary music events. Held at Rippon Vineyard in February every second year, it is an eclectic mix of well-known and new Kiwi music.

WINES
Rippon Ricsling, Sauvignon Blanc, Hotere White (Unoaked Chardonnay), Osteiner, Gewürztraminer, Pinot Noir, Chardonnay, Merlot Syrah, Gamay Rosé, Jeunesse (young vines Pinot Noir)

Amisfield Lake Hayes Winery

Dry Gully

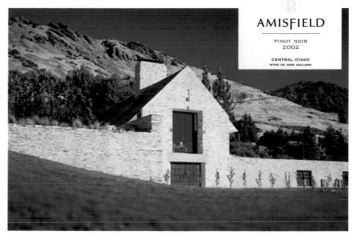

Located 10 minutes from Queenstown with spectacular views over Lake Hayes, the Amisfield tasting facility and underground barrel hall celebrates excellence not only in its wines but also in its impressive architectural style. The building was constructed from local schist and recycled ironwood timbers capable of withstanding the extremes of the Central Otago climate.

Grapes are sourced from their vineyard at Amisfield Farm near Lake Dunstan. Originally a high-country merino stud, it now consists of 38 hectares of vines close-planted on alluvial and glacial schist soils. Yields are kept low to provide concentrated fruit flavour with complexity derived from the range of sites — lakeside to high altitude — within the vineyard.

WINES

Amisfield Pinot Noir, Pinot Gris, Sauvignon Blanc, Dry Riesling, Noble Riesling, Rocky Knoll Riesling, Rosé Arcadia Central Otago Cuvée, Non Vintage Brut

Amisfield Lake Hayes Winery
10 Lake Hayes Rd
Queenstown
Tel: (03) 442 0556
Fax: (03) 442 0553
Email: admin@amisfield.co.nz
Website: www.amisfield.co.nz

DIRECTIONS
Leaving Queenstown via Frankton continue on SH6 until you reach the Arrowtown turnoff; Amisfield Winery is located at this junction.

OPENING HOURS October
(Labour weekend) to Easter:
7 days, 10am–6pm; May–Oct:
7 days, 11am–6pm

WINERY SALES Cellar door,
retail, mail order, Internet

PRICE RANGE $19–$40

TASTING & TOURS
Tastings available.
Tours by appointment.

PICNIC AREA
Picnic tables and a pétanque court are situated in the courtyard and lawns extending out from the building.

WINEMAKER
Jeff Sinnott

DATE ESTABLISHED
Vineyard: 1999
Winery: 2002

State Highway 6
Gibbston, Queenstown
Tel: (03) 442 6110
Fax: (03) 441 8400
Email: sales@chardfarm.co.nz
Website: www.chardfarm.co.nz

DIRECTIONS
From Queenstown drive along SH6 towards Cromwell for 20km; 100m past the famous 'Bungy Bridge' turn right onto Chard Rd, which takes you up to the winery.

OPENING HOURS
Mon–Fri: 10am–5pm; Sat & Sun: 11am–5pm

WINERY SALES
Cellar door, retail, mail order & Internet

PRICE RANGE $18–$57

TASTING
Tasting is free of charge.

PICNIC AREA
BYO picnic and enjoy the grassy bank under trees or the large stone table in front of the winery, with views to the vines and surrounding mountains.

OTHER FACILITIES
Subterranean purpose-built Pinot Noir barrel cellar.

OWNERS
Rob Hay & Gerda Schumann

WINEMAKER
John Wallace & Rob Hay

DATE ESTABLISHED 1987

Chard Farm Winery

Chard Farm is a small family-owned winery located at the confluence of the Kawarau and Arrow Rivers, just 20km from Queenstown. The winery was named after the Chard family who came from England in 1862, settling and farming the land that the winery and vineyard now occupies. One of Central Otago's largest producers, the location of the north-facing vineyard with its unique continental climate (latitude 45° South) delivers concentrated fruit from low-yielding vines. Dramatically aspected, Chard Farm is worth the visit for the trip alone. Located at the end of a precipitous road that winds above the Kawarau River, there are magnificent views across the gorge to the snow-capped Cardrona Range and Coronet Peak. At the cellar door the knowledgeable staff will not only enhance your winery visit but also make it a memorable experience. Recently opened is a subterranean purpose-built Pinot Noir barrel cellar. This large room provides a great ambience for wine-tasting, as well as an inside look at the winemaking process. You are welcome to BYO picnic and enjoy the views. Chard Farm has received numerous accolades, both nationally and internationally.

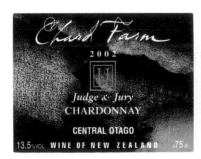

WINES
Chard Farm Finla Mor Pinot Noir, River Run Pinot Noir, Red Gate Pinot Noir, Pinot Gris, Riesling, Sauvignon Blanc, Closeburn Chardonnay, Judge and Jury Chardonnay, Gewürztraminer

Mount Edward Wines

Peregrine Wines

Mount Edward Wines is a small specialist Pinot Noir producer situated in the heart of the Gibbston grape growing district. Owner and winemaker Alan Brady was the first to plant grapes in this valley in 1981, and he has helped to put Central Otago on the map as one of the world's most exciting new winemaking regions. He founded and managed Gibbston Valley Wines Ltd, which developed into a company with an international reputation for its Pinot Noir.

His new project (first vintage 1998) overlooks some of the big new vineyards that have been planted since his pioneering efforts of 20 years ago. Mount Edward is dedicated almost exclusively to Alan's passion for Pinot Noir, and the only other wine produced is a small amount of very good Riesling made from grapes grown on a steep hillside behind the winery. An export-driven enterprise, the Pinot Noir is very highly rated in the UK, which gets the majority of the production.

WINES
Mount Edward Central Otago Pinot Noir, Riesling

The Peregrine Winery is located in the valley of Gibbston, perched above the Kawarau River. The new state-of-the-art winery and cellar door is designed to be both functional and a piece of art in harmony with the landscape. Whilst the winery itself is built underground, the free-floating roof depicts the wing of the Peregrine falcon and mimics the schist rock reefs which rise out of the ground throughout the Gibbston area. Already chosen as one of the 80 most architecturally important wineries in the world, it will hopefully stimulate people's perception as to what is possible yet unobtrusive in the Central Otago landscape. Founded and co-owned by Greg Hay, Peregrine's primary focus is growing premium Pinot Noir, Pinot Gris and Riesling from their estate-managed vineyards.

WINES
Peregrine Pinot Noir, Sauvignon Blanc, Chardonnay, Riesling, Pinot Gris, Gewürztraminer, Wentworth Pinot Noir (the Wentworth label only appears when vintages are exceptional)

RECENT AWARDS
Peregrine Pinot Noir 2002 – Pinot Noir Trophy: Top 100 Wine Awards Sydney 2004, Gold: du Mondial Switzerland; voted one of the Top 10 Pinots of 2003: *Cuisine* magazine

Mount Edward Wines Ltd
32 Coal Pit Rd, Gibbston
Queenstown
Tel: (03) 442 6113
Fax: (03) 442 9119
Email: wines@mountedward.co.nz
Websit: www.mountedward.co.nz

DIRECTIONS Situated in Coal Pit Rd, off SH6 in the middle of the Gibbston winegrowing district between Queenstown (25km) and Cromwell (30km).

OPENING HOURS By arrangement only. Wines sell out quickly, so it is important to call in advance if you intend to visit.

WINERY SALES
Cellar door (by appointment), retail, mail order

PRICE RANGE $20–$45

TASTING
There is no charge for tasting.

EVENTS & ACTIVITIES
Occasionally art exhibitions are held featuring local artists.

MANAGING DIRECTOR
Alan Brady

WINEMAKER
Alan Brady

DATE ESTABLISHED
Vineyard: 1995; Winery: 1997

Peregrine Wines
Kawarau Gorge, Gibbston
Tel: (03) 442 4000
Fax: (03) 442 4048
Email: info@peregrinewines.co.nz
Website: www.peregrinewines.co.nz

DIRECTIONS In Gibbston Valley on the main route into Queenstown (25km away). It is prominently signposted.

OPENING HOURS
7–days, 10am–5pm

WINERY SALES Cellar door, retail, mail order, Internet

PRICE RANGE $19–$35

TASTING & TOURS
Tasting is free of charge. Tours by appointment.

PICNIC AREA
Beside the winery and pond.

ACCOMMODATION
Soon to be available in a rustic old stone cottage.

OTHER FACILITIES
The Wentworth Estate woolshed, next door to the winery, with romantic vineyard views and breathtaking mountain vistas is a rustic functions venue that allows you to 'do it yourself'.

OWNER Greg Hay

WINEMAKER
Michelle Richardson

Waitiri Creek
Church Lane, Gibbston Valley
Queenstown
Tel: (03) 441 3315
Fax: (03) 441 3316
Email: mark@waitiricreek.co.nz
Website: www.waitiricreek.co.nz

DIRECTIONS
30km from Queenstown on State
Highway 6 towards Cromwell, turn left
into Church Lane. Winery is well
signposted.

OPENING HOURS
Oct–Apr: 7 days, 10am–5pm
May–Sept: 7 days, 11am–4pm

WINERY SALES
Cellar door, retail, mail order, Internet

PRICE RANGE $20–$40

TASTING & TOURS
Tasting fee: $1 per wine (refundable on
purchase). Tours by appointment. $5
tour fee.

OTHER FACILITIES
The winery provides a stunning
backdrop for special occasions from
private dinner parties to weddings.
Packages can be tailored to suit
requirements.

OWNERS
Alistair Ward & Paula Ramage

WINEMAKER
Steve Bird

DATE ESTABLISHED 1994

Waitiri Creek

Established in 1994 amongst the magnificent landscape of the Gibbston Valley, Waitiri Creek is a family-owned vineyard with eight hectares planted in Pinot Noir, Chardonnay and a small parcel of Gewürtztraminer vines. The picturesque tasting facility and café was originally the Wangaloa Presbyterian Church, built in the early 1890s, before being moved to its current location in 2000. Set amongst the vines and now beautifully restored, it is a unique place to taste the much-awarded Waitiri Creek wines and a relaxing dining experience where you can choose to dine al fresco or inside the tasting room. The seasonally changing menu showcases the best regional produce that is matched to complement the wines.

WINES
Waitiri Creek Central Otago
Chardonnay, Pinot Gris, Pinot Noir,
Gewürtztraminer

RECENT AWARDS
Waitiri Creek Pinot Noir has
consistently achieved bronze medal
status in the Air New Zealand, Royal
Easter Show and Bragato Awards.

Cairnmuir Road
Rapid Number 210, Bannockburn
Tel: (03) 445 0897
Fax: (03) 445 0898
Email: warren@akarua.co.nz
Website: www.akarua.com

DIRECTIONS
Travelling from Cromwell towards Bannockburn, turn left at the Bannockburn Bridge onto Cairnmuir Rd; continue for 2km and Akarua is on the right.

OPENING HOURS
Cellar door: 7 days, 10am 5pm
Restaurant: 7 days, lunch: 11.30am–3pm, dinner from 6pm

WINERY SALES
Cellar door, retail, Internet

PRICE RANGE
$21.95–$39.95

TASTING & TOURS
Tasting is free of charge. Tours by appointment only.

RESTAURANT
Alice's Restaurant, Reservations: (03) 445 3211

OTHER PRODUCTS
Wines can be purchased in wooden gift boxes containing Akarua glasses.

PICNIC AREA
The Bannockburn Bay reserve, a popular picnic spot, is nearby.

OWNER
Sir Clifford Skeggs

WINEMAKER
Carol Bunn

DATE ESTABLISHED 1996

Akarua

AKARUA

BANNOCKBURN · CENTRAL OTAGO

2002 Pinot Noir

750ML · WINE OF NEW ZEALAND · Alc 14.5% Vol

Located amongst the dramatic scenery of the Bannockburn area — also known as 'the heart of the desert' — and with its great reputation for warm and friendly hospitality, the Akarua winery and cellar door is a must to visit. Committed to a philosophy of perfection since their first vintage in 1999, they have rapidly developed a reputation for producing quality wines. The 2000 Pinot Noir received an outstanding accolade as the only gold medal awarded at the 2001 International Wine and Spirit Competition in London, while their most recent success, the Akarua Pinot Noir 2002, won the Pinot Noir Trophy and was judged Wine of the Show at the 2003 Air New Zealand Wine Awards.

The cellar door is surrounded by a 50-hectare vineyard planted with 70 per cent Pinot Noir, Pinot Gris and Chardonnay. Here you can taste and buy the full range of Akarua wines. Next door is Alice's Restaurant, winner of the 2003 NZ Supreme Lamb Award. Offering indoor and outdoor dining in a sheltered courtyard, the cuisine ranges from a casual Mediterranean style at lunch to gourmet fare for dinner.

OTHER FACILITIES
The winery complex includes a microbrewery — BannockBrew — producing a range of craft beers branded 'Wild Spaniard' available for tasting and purchase at the cellar door.

WINES
Akarua Pinot Noir, 'The Gullies' Pinot Noir, Chardonnay, Unoaked Chardonnay, Pinot Gris

RECENT AWARDS
Akarua Pinot Noir 2002 – Champion Wine of Show and Pinot Trophy: 2003 Air New Zealand Wine Awards, Gold: 2004 Royal Easter Show, Gold: 2003 Liquorland Top 100; both Pinot Noirs were rated 1st and 2nd by *Cuisine* magazine in 2003; Akarua Chardonnay 2003 – Gold: 2004 Royal Easter Show

Cairnmuir Rd, Bannockburn
Tel: (03) 445 3480
Fax: (03) 445 3481
Email: wines@carrick.co.nz
Website: www.carrick.co.nz

DIRECTIONS
Travelling from Cromwell towards Bannockburn, turn left at the Bannockburn Bridge onto Cairnmuir Rd. Continue for 2.5km: Carrick is on the left.

OPENING HOURS
Cellar Door: 7 days, 11am–5pm
Restaurant: 7 days, 12pm–3pm

WINERY SALES
Cellar door, retail, mail order, Internet

PRICE RANGE $18–$38

TASTING
Tasting fee: $4, refundable on purchase.

RESTAURANT
Lunch and platters are available. The innovative and interesting menu changes regularly. Reservations: (03) 445 3480.

EVENTS & ACTIVITIES
Degustation dinners to celebrate the new-release wines. Contact winery for details.

GENERAL MANAGER
Steve Green

WINEMAKER
Steve Davies

DATE ESTABLISHED 1999

Carrick

Overlooking the beautiful Bannockburn inlet of Lake Dunstan out to the rugged Carrick mountain range in the west, the Carrick Winery is a stunning place to taste wine and share a lunch with friends. The stylish winery building with its cellar door and tasting room incorporates a much-acclaimed restaurant. The blackboard menu features innovative regional cuisine and there is inside-and-outside dining to maximise the spectacular views.

The interesting architectural design of the winery reflects the Carrick philosophy that the primary function must be to facilitate quality winemaking. Everything else follows on from this belief — the winery looks like a winery, and the tasting room and restaurant enable visitors to be part of this experience (the underground barrel cellar can be viewed through glass panels in the restaurant floor). Very much a working winery, the wine can be tasted where it is made, in view of the surrounding vineyards from which the grapes are picked.

All wines are made from Carrick's 25 hectares of vines planted on the Cairnmuir terraces. Pinot Noir is their premium variety, although all the wines exhibit the grace, taste and distinctive style of Central Otago.

WINES
Carrick Pinot Noir, Pinot Gris, Chardonnay, Sauvignon Blanc, Riesling

RECENT AWARDS
Carrick Pinot Noir 2002 – Trophy for Best 2002 Pinot Noir: International Cool Climate Wine Show 2004, Top 100 & Blue-Gold award: Sydney International Wine Challenge 2004, Gold: New Zealand Wine Society Royal Easter Wine Show 2004

OTHER ACTIVITIES
Regular art exhibitions by leading New Zealand artists – all works are for sale.

Olssens Garden Vineyard

As pioneer winemakers in the Cromwell Basin, John Olssen and Heather McPherson have created a rural oasis amongst the dry, thyme-covered hills of Bannockburn. Here the essence of nature is captured by vines deeply rooted in the rocky, gold-bearing schist soils. They produce a range of wines, all made from 100 per cent estate-grown fruit, many of which are sold exclusively to cellar-door visitors and mail-order customers. In addition to the 10 hectares of vines, thousands of trees, shrubs and bulbs have been planted around sweeping glades of grass and a number of mountain-reflecting ponds. Visitors are encouraged to walk amongst the trees, picnic by a pond, sit under an umbrella or a tree, enjoy the garden art, play pétanque or quoits with a glass of wine to hand, partake of a vineyard platter or cheese board, or simply taste the wines. The vineyard caters for young children and baskets of toys are available.

2002
PINOT NOIR
JACKSON BARRY
CENTRAL OTAGO

750 ml   WINE OF NEW ZEALAND   14% Alc/Vol

WINES
Olssens (flagship) Slapjack Creek plus the Jackson Barry Pinot Noir, Charcoal Joe Chardonnay and Bannockburn Club Unoaked Chardonnay, Riesling, Sauvignon Blanc, Gewürztraminer, Robert the Bruce (blend of Pinotage/Shiraz/Cabernet Sauvignon), Desert Gold Late Harvest Riesling, Autumn Gold Late Harvest Chardonnay and Summer Dreaming (a Pinot Noir Rosé)

AWARDS
Every Olssens wine label has won critical acclaim at the national wine industry Air New Zealand Wine Awards and/or the national grape-grower's Bragato Awards. They have twice taken the 'Mike Wolter Trophy' for best Pinot Noir at Bragato.

EVENTS
The Olssens have developed a number of vineyard events offering visitors the opportunity to enjoy themselves. Music in the Vines: A midsummer event in which artists entertain guests while they picnic and relax. The Scarecrow Gathering: Held on the last Sunday in November; schools, businesses and individuals compete for prizes and have a fun day out. The Barrel Party: A fun event, held periodically, in which a bus brings guests from Cromwell to the vineyard where they enjoy a meal, music and Pinot Noir and Chardonnay from the barrel.

Olssen's Garden Vineyard
306 Felton Rd, Bannockburn
Tel: (03) 445 1716
Fax: (03) 445 0050
Email: wine@olssens.co.nz
Website: www.olssens.co.nz

DIRECTIONS
Travelling from Cromwell towards Bannockburn, turn right just after the Bannockburn Bridge onto Felton Rd; continue for 3km, the vineyard is on the right.

OPENING HOURS
Cellar Door: 7 days, summer 10am–5pm, winter 11am–4pm; Café: Boxing Day–end March

WINERY SALES
Cellar door, retail, mail order, Bannockburn Club, Internet. Members of the Bannockburn Club automatically receive a single bottle of each new wine (in 3-bottle lots, four times per year) at a 5 percent discount and receive a 10 percent discount on all other purchases subsequently made. Email winery for details.

PRICE RANGE $17–$50

TASTING & TOURS
Tasting fee: $4 for 5 wines, refundable on purchase of 2 bottles. Tours by appointment.

CAFÉ
Specialises in café-style food, vineyard platters and open sandwiches.

PICNIC AREA
In the expansive rural gardens, barbecue, tables, pétanque and quoits. Visitors are welcome to BYO food.

OTHER FACILITIES
Available for private functions — enjoy the ambience of the vineyard for a wedding or anniversary celebration.

OWNERS
John Olssen & Heather McPherson

WINEMAKER
Peter Bartle

DATE ESTABLISHED 1989

The Big Picture
Cnr Sandflat Rd & State Highway 6
Cromwell
Tel: (03) 445 4052
Fax: (03) 445 4053
Email: info@wineadventure.co.nz
Website: www.wineadventure.co.nz

DIRECTIONS

On the corner of Sandflat Rd and SH6,
The Big Picture is 40km from
Queenstown and 5km from Cromwell.

OPENING HOURS

7 days, 9am–8pm

CHARGES

Aroma Room: complimentary with a
meal or Virtual Flight.
Virtual Flight: $15. Includes a tasting
of five wines.

SHOP

This shop has the largest selection of
Central Otago wines in New Zealand at
cellar-door prices. There is also a
selection of wine-related merchandise
including glassware, aroma kits, wine
tools, books and clothing.

OWNERS

Phil & Cath Parker

DATE ESTABLISHED 2003

The Big Picture Wine Adventure

The Big Picture is a one-stop 'essential wine adventure' to take you on a journey of discovery. Here you can uncover the fine wines of Central Otago, meeting the winemakers and viewing the stunning scenery that makes the region so geographically unique. Enjoy the Mediterranean flavours of the restaurant, the awe-inspiring aromas of the aroma room, the interactive wine film and tasting in the auditorium.

A world first in wine presentation, the concept was developed by Phil and Cath Parker after realising many visitors passing through the Central Otago region did not visit wineries or know anything about wine. This experience has been designed to satisfy the interactive traveller whether experienced in wine or a 'first-time naïve inquirer'.

THE AROMA ROOM

Whether experienced in wine tasting or not, you can loose your senses here and discover the aromas that are used to describe wine varieties and styles.

THE FLIGHT

A wine-tasting auditorium takes the viewer on an 18-minute 'virtual flight' across the spectacular landscape and vineyards that are unique to Central Otago and outlines the area's history. There is a winetasting lesson and a 'virtual meeting' with five Central Otago winemakers who lead you through a personalised tasting when you 'land' at each vineyard.

RESTAURANT AND CAFÉ

Taste a wide range of Central Otago wines while you snack or dine from the seasonal menu that features superb Mediterranean and local-style cuisine. There is a mix of indoor and outdoor dining that flows out onto a sunny courtyard overlooking the Pinot Noir vineyard surrounding the building.

Packspur Vineyard

Carrick

Rippon Vineyard

Olssens Garden Vineyard

Packspur vineyard and winery is a small family owned and operated vineyard. Located in the secluded Lowburn Valley it has magnificent views of the Pisa Range, the Dunstans and the St Bathans. It takes its name from the track that was used to pack supplies over the Pisa Range from the Lowburn Valley to the goldfields of Cardrona. Their water right for irrigation is a miners' right dating from 1863 and they are continuing on the tradition of independence and enterprise that characterised those who worked the land before.

Packspur's philosophy as members of Sustainable Winegrowers of New Zealand is to use viticulture techniques that enhance the soil and minimise chemical use. They believe that healthy vines produce bright individual wines that reflect the potential of the terroir. All wines are made from their four hectares of vines planted on the hillside surrounding the winery.

WINES
Packspur Pinot Noir, Pinot Gris, Riesling, Sauvignon Blanc (barrel-fermented)

PACKSPUR
CENTRAL OTAGO
Basket Press
PINOT NOIR
750ml   2002   Alc. 13.5% vol

RECENT AWARDS
Bragato Wine Awards 2003: Packspur Pinot Noir 2002 – Gold; Packspur Riesling 2001 – Bronze; Packspur Sauvignon Blanc 2001 – Bronze

Heaney Rd, Cromwell
Tel: (03) 445 1638
Fax: (03) 445 1639
Email: annelaurie@packspur.co.nz
Website: www.packspur.co.nz

DIRECTIONS
Turn off at Burn Cottage Road on the Queenstown Wanaka Highway (SH6) 1km north of the Cromwell intersection. Continue until you see Packspur on the left. The sign is on top of the mailbox.

OPENING HOURS
By appointment only.

WINERY SALES Cellar door, retail, mail order, Internet

PRICE RANGE $16.95–$30.95

TASTING & TOURS
Tasting fee: $5 pp, refundable on the purchase of three or more bottles of wine. Tours by appointment only.

OWNERS
Anne & Laurie McAuley

WINEMAKERS
Anne & Laurie McAuley

DATE ESTABLISHED 1992

Dry Gully

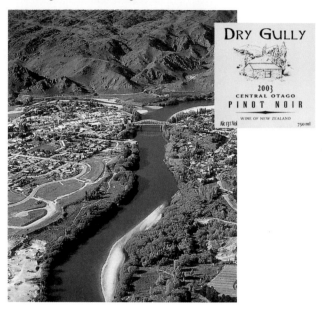

Dry Gully is a small family-run vineyard and specialist Pinot Noir producer situated in the heart of the Alexandra grapegrowing region of Central Otago. In the late 1970s, Bill and Sibylla Moffit bought a small, 100-year-old apricot orchard and in 1992 — encouraged by their sons, Stephen and James, both viticulturalists and who also own vineyards nearby — they planted 1.5 hectares of Pinot Noir grapes. Situated on river silt over alluvial gravels, the vines are surrounded by old thyme-covered gold dredging tailings. The single wine Pinot Noir that Dry Gully produces has enjoyed remarkable success in competitions and is in high demand with a large portion of production exported to the UK and USA.

WINES
Dry Gully Pinot Noir

RECENT AWARDS
Five Stars: *Cuisine* magazine 2003

Earnscleugh Road, Alexandra
Tel: (03) 449 2030
Fax: (03) 449 2030
Email: s.moffitt@xtra.co.nz

DIRECTIONS
Turn into Earnscleugh Rd from SH8 near the Alexandra Bridge. Continue for 1km and the vineyard is on the right opposite Chapman Rd.

OPENING HOURS
By appointment only.

WINERY SALES
Cellar door (by appointment), retail, mail order

PRICE $29

WINE TASTING
By appointment only.

OWNERS
William & Sybilla Moffitt

WINEMAKER
Dean Shaw
(Central Otago Wine Company)

DATE ESTABLISHED 1992

Black Ridge Winery & Vineyard

One of the southernmost vineyards in the world, Black Ridge was established on the outskirts of Alexandra in 1981 through the pioneering vision and determination of Verdun Burgess and Sue Edwards. The vineyard setting is dramatic, carved out of steep rugged outcrops of schist that rise starkly above the vines creating many different microclimates. Pockets of vines cling to the hillside in between, in vivid green contrast to the barren rock.

All wines, made exclusively from their own hand-picked grapes, reflect this unique terroir. Pinot Noir is the flagship wine with eight different clones planted to provide complexity and greater depth. The winery, built out of schist rock in the style of an early Central Otago barn, has an attractive tasting room leading to an outdoor picnic area.

WINES
Black Ridge Pinot Noir, Chardonnay, Gewürztraminer, Riesling, Cabernet Sauvignon, Otago Gold (blended white)

AWARDS
1997 & 1998 Black Ridge Pinot Noir – Gold: Royal Easter Show

Conroy's Rd, Alexandra
Tel: (03) 449 2059
Fax: (03) 449 2597
Email: blackridge@clear.net.nz
Website: www.blackridge.co.nz

DIRECTIONS
Turn into Earnscleugh Rd from SH8 near the Alexandra Bridge. Continue for 4km and turn left onto Conroys Rd. The vineyard is 700m on the right.

OPENING HOURS
7 days, 10am–5pm

WINERY SALES Cellar door, retail, mail order, Internet

PRICE RANGE $12.50–$45

TASTING Tasting fee: $1 per wine, refundable in proportion to wine purchased.

FOOD OPTIONS
Gourmet barbecues available for lunch over the Christmas/New Year period.

PICNIC AREA
Just outside the tasting room with tables with umbrellas and a pétanque court.

OTHER PRODUCTS
Paintings of the vineyard by local artist, Janet de Waght

OWNERS
Sue Edwards & Verdun Burgess

WINEMAKER
Kevin Clark

DATE ESTABLISHED 1981

Clay Cliffs Estate

At 440 metres above sea level Clay Cliffs boasts the title of being New Zealand's highest-altitude vineyard as well as being the only one in North Otago. Named after the nearby Clay Cliffs with their dramatic sharp pinnacles and deep, narrow ravines, Clay Cliffs Estate has one of Otago's earliest plantings of Pinot Gris, Muscat and Pinot Blanc. Recent plantings of Pinot Noir and more Pinot Gris have brought the total area under grapes from the original 0.5 hectares to 4 hectares. For their second label, Mount Cook, they buy in other varieties — Chardonnay, Riesling and Sauvignon Blanc — from contract growers.

The winery features a Tuscan-styled restaurant offering an extensive range of local fare. You can choose to dine inside the restaurant or outside where you can relax by the tranquil ponds, soaking up the sun or under the shade of willows enjoying a wine from the extensive Clay Cliffs cellar. Then take the opportunity to feed the large tame trout that habitate the ponds. A trip to Clay Cliffs is an opportunity not only to taste and buy these wines that are only sold through their restaurant but also to experience the spectacular McKenzie country scenery.

WINES
Clay Cliffs: Pinot Noir, Pinot Gris, Muscat, Pinot Blanc.
Mount Cook: Chardonnay, Riesling, Pinot Noir, Sauvignon Blanc.

Clay Cliffs Estate
State Highway 8, Omarama
Tel: (03) 438 9654
Fax: (03) 438 9656
Email: claycliffs@xtra.co.nz
Website: www.claycliffs.co.nz

DIRECTIONS
Omarama is 150km from Queenstown and 20km south of Twizel. Clay Cliffs is located on a slope fronting onto SH8 at the southern end of the Omarama township.

OPENING HOURS
Restaurant and cellar door: 7 days, 11am–midnight. Winter hours: June (Queen's Birthday Monday) to end July, 11am–4pm, unless bookings are made for evening dining.

WINERY SALES
Cellar door and mail order

PRICE RANGE $16.50–$31.50

WINE TASTING
Tasting fee: $5 refundable on purchase.

OTHER FACILITIES
The winery is the perfect location for weddings and other functions.

OWNERS
Brian (The Sheriff) & Judy Gilbert

WINEMAKER
Dean Shaw (Central Otago Wine Company)

DATE ESTABLISHED 1999

Index
of Wineries & Vineyards

Index
of Place Names

Tasting Notes

Date . . . .

Vineyard/Winery . . . .

Region . . . .

Name of wine tasted/purchased . . . .

. . . .

Vintage . . . .

Grape variety . . . .

Notes . . . .

. . . .

Date . . . .

Vineyard/Winery . . . .

Region . . . .

Name of wine tasted/purchased . . . .

. . . .

Vintage . . . .

Grape variety . . . .

Notes . . . .

. . . .

Date . . . .

Vineyard/Winery . . . .

Region . . . .

Name of wine tasted/purchased . . . .

. . . .

Vintage . . . .

Grape variety . . . .

Notes . . . .

. . . .

Date . . . .

Vineyard/Winery . . . .

Region . . . .

Name of wine tasted/purchased . . . .

. . . .

Vintage . . . .

Grape variety . . . .

Notes . . . .

. . . .

Date . . . .

Vineyard/Winery . . . .

Region . . . .

Name of wine tasted/purchased . . . .

. . . .

Vintage . . . .

Grape variety . . . .

Notes . . . .

. . . .

Date . . . .

Vineyard/Winery . . . .

Region . . . .

Name of wine tasted/purchased . . . .

. . . .

Vintage . . . .

Grape variety . . . .

Notes . . . .

. . . .

Date . . . .

Vineyard/Winery . . . .

Region . . . .

Name of wine tasted/purchased . . . .

. . . .

Vintage . . . .

Grape variety . . . .

Notes . . . .

. . . .

Date . . . .

Vineyard/Winery . . . .

Region . . . .

Name of wine tasted/purchased . . . .

. . . .

Vintage . . . .

Grape variety . . . .

Notes . . . .

. . . .

Date . . . .

Vineyard/Winery . . . .

Region . . . .

Name of wine tasted/purchased . . . .

. . . .

Vintage . . . .

Grape variety . . . .

Notes . . . .

. . . .

Date . . . .

Vineyard/Winery . . . .

Region . . . .

Name of wine tasted/purchased . . . .

. . . .

Vintage . . . .

Grape variety . . . .

Notes . . . .

. . . .

Date . . . .

Vineyard/Winery . . . .

Region . . . .

Name of wine tasted/purchased . . . .

. . . .

Vintage . . . .

Grape variety . . . .

Notes . . . .

. . . .

Date . . . .

Vineyard/Winery . . . .

Region . . . .

Name of wine tasted/purchased . . . .

. . . .

Vintage . . . .

Grape variety . . . .

Notes . . . .

. . . .

Date . . . .

Vineyard/Winery . . . .

Region . . . .

Name of wine tasted/purchased . . . .

. . . .

Vintage . . . .

Grape variety . . . .

Notes . . . .

. . . .

Date . . . .

Vineyard/Winery . . . .

Region . . . .

Name of wine tasted/purchased . . . .

. . . .

Vintage . . . .

Grape variety . . . .

Notes . . . .

. . . .